THE POWER OF UNWAVERING FOCUS

THE POWER

of

UNWAVERING FOCUS

Dandapani

PORTFOLIO · PENGUIN

Portfolio / Penguin
An imprint of Penguin Random House LLC
penguinrandomhouse.com

Most Portfolio books are available at a discount when purchased in quantity for sales promotions or corporate use. Special editions, which include personalized covers, excerpts, and corporate imprints, can be created when purchased in large quantities. For more information, please call (212) 572-2232 or e-mail specialmarkets@penguinrandomhouse.com. Your local bookstore can also assist with discounted bulk purchases using the Penguin Random House corporate Business-to-Business program. For assistance in locating a participating retailer, e-mail B2B@penguinrandomhouse.com.

Library of Congress Cataloging-in-Publication Data
Names: Satgunasingam, Dandapani, author.
Title: The power of unwavering focus / Dandapani Satgunasingam.
Description: First Edition. | New York: Portfolio / Penguin, [2022] | Includes index.
Identifiers: LCCN 2022007201 (print) | LCCN 2022007202 (ebook) |
ISBN 9780593420454 (hardcover) | ISBN 9780593420461 (ebook) |
ISBN 9780593544013 (international)
Subjects: LCSH: Attention. | Awareness. | Self-control.
Classification: LCC BF321 .S28 2022 (print) | LCC BF321 (ebook) |
DDC 153.7/33—dc23/eng/20220601
LC record available at https://lccn.loc.gov/2022007201
LC ebook record available at https://lccn.loc.gov/2022007202

Printed in the United States of America
1st Printing

Book design by Jennifer Daddio / Bookmark Design & Media Inc.

This book is dedicated to my guru,

SATGURU SIVAYA SUBRAMUNIYASWAMI,

affectionately known as Gurudeva.

*His unconditional love for me and personal commitment to my
unfoldment is at the heart of what has inspired me to write this book.
He has given me the greatest gift, the teachings and tools I need to know
myself and experience the divine within me, and the foundation of what
he taught me is contained within the pages of this book.*

CONTENTS

PART 4: A PANACEA FOR THE MIND

INTRODUCTION

The time that I spent living with my guru as an ordained Hindu monk in his cloistered monastery was the greatest blessing in my life. I learned so much and realized I have so much more to learn. He laid the foundation for my unfoldment, knowing that this would be a lifetime of work for me and that he would not be present that entire time to guide me in person. That was, sadly, more than true, for he passed away three years after I joined his monastic order.

Seven years after he died, having spent a decade living as a monk in his monastery, I chose not to renew my vows. I ventured into the world, making New York City my home and choosing to live as a Hindu priest. In Hinduism, priests are considered householders—they get married, work, and earn a living like most householders.

I left the monastery in the second half of 2008, during the height of the global financial crisis, with two sets of robes, a thousand dollars in cash, and a MacBook Pro. The cash and laptop were a generous love offering from the monastery to help me get started in the world. Though my physical possessions were few, I had been empowered by my guru with an array of teachings and tools that he had taught me to understand and apply in the monastery to help me with my spiritual unfoldment.

I knew that these teachings were all I needed to create the next phase of my life. I had seen them work in the monastery and knew that they would work in the world as well. These time-tested ancient teachings were anchored in universal truths. It truly did not matter where I was or what I was doing. They applied across the board to me and to anyone who grasped and understood them.

As a monk I often heard visitors to the monastery say, "It can't be hard to live a life of purpose and joy when you live in a serene monastery in Hawaii." I could not argue with that. Monastic life has intense challenges, but it was certainly easier to put the teachings into practice in an environment built to support that. But the experiences and results I had from implementing the teachings in my life left no shadow of doubt in my mind that they would work in the world outside the monastery as well.

I embraced a life of entrepreneurship, adopting the role of adviser to entrepreneurs, athletes, and individuals in all walks of life, helping them to understand and leverage their mind to live a life of purpose and joy. But it only made sense for me to be an adviser if I was able to successfully apply these teachings in my own life. My environment and lifestyle had undergone a very binary change. I had to come up with new ways of applying these teachings in my life as a husband, a father, an entrepreneur, and more—and continually refine how they were implemented as I grew and my clients changed.

Well over a decade now after having left the monastery, I can confidently confirm to you that, yes, these teachings work as well outside the monastery walls as they do within them. I have watched with great joy a child of seven years apply them in her life to rid herself of anxiety. I've seen highly successful entrepreneurs and athletes use them to increase their performance and better their lives. Countless testimonials from people around the world sharing how these teachings have transformed their lives further affirmed what I had initially intuited. These teachings work well, just as they always have.

This book shares with you the foundational training that I received from my guru—teachings, insights, and tools that I learned from him, and some that I have developed myself, refined over a decade for life in the world through practical application in my life and in training companies and thousands of individuals worldwide.

If I was dying and I could share only one thing with you, the contents of this book would be it. It is my greatest gift to you. I cannot emphasize enough how life-transforming these teachings and tools are. One must simply have a burning desire to implement them consistently in one's life for them to bear results.

This book is divided into four parts. Each part is made up of chapters and lessons.

Part 1 is dedicated to the question of *why* you should lead a focused life. This is critical. Without realizing the purpose for leading a focused life, one may not be motivated to make the teachings and tools in this book a part of one's life. (The words "concentration" and "focus" are synonymous, and I use them interchangeably throughout the book.) In part 2, we begin learning about our own mind, the most important tool (*or* technology) we possess—it creates our very reality—and yet the only one that comes without a user's manual. Understanding the mind is the foundation for building a focused life. Part 3 shares how we can learn to concentrate and to develop our willpower, the two indispensable ingredients for becoming the stewards of our own mind. Part 4 details practical applications of these teachings to overcome life's most common challenges—such as fear, worry, anxiety, and stress—and to transform your productivity and performance in the worlds of work, the arts, and sports. I also share how applying these teachings will improve your mental health and will help you to be present so that you truly experience your life.

My goal in this book is not to inundate you with tools. I am a firm believer that we do not need many tools in life. Rather, a few tools that are aligned and serve in fulfilling our purpose in life are sufficient. These tools are to be understood well and then consistently applied.

You will not find any magic, shortcuts, or hacks in this book—only a clearly defined, step-by-step, and goal-oriented approach to living a focused life, not as a mental exercise for its own sake, but for what it gives you. That's why I live a focused life.

The ability to concentrate has opened untold possibilities for me and given me a life that I could not have imagined for myself. I attempt to share with you, within these pages, a sliver of the rewards of a focused life.

Read these teachings carefully. Strive to grasp them. Be unrelenting in your efforts to implement them in your life. These teachings are life-transforming, but only if you put them into practice—and even more, only if you truly desire to transform your life. Without a strong and sincere desire for transformation on your part, all the contents of this book would matter very little.

Your biggest gift to me, should you ever wish to say thank you for these teachings, is to truly understand the contents of this book and master awareness in the mind. It is my wish, as you embark on the study of this book, that you will adopt the attitude that you are at the beginning of the path—you are eager, enthusiastic, open to learning, and know absolutely nothing.

PART 1

A LIFE OF
PURPOSE AND JOY

Chapter 1

FOUNDATIONS FOR A
CONCENTRATED
MIND

Living a Purpose-Focused Life

*There is nothing more important than knowing
who you are, the path that you are on, and its final end.*

~ GURUDEVA

It was a cold and windy winter evening in Munich as we hurriedly walked toward the restaurant we were heading to. As much as I love walking around in this old Bavarian city, my favorite place in Germany, I was eager to get out of the cold. It wasn't long before we arrived at our destination, and the warmth of this quaint restaurant with its well-worn hardwood floors was a welcome embrace. We made our way to a table in the corner, draped the chairs with our layers of winter wear, ordered some wine, and continued the conversation we had been having on the walk here.

I was spending the evening with one of my dear friends, Moritz, a German entrepreneur whom I have known for a few years. He reached over to his glass of wine, took a sip, placed it back on the table, and asked me, "If you say that knowing one's purpose in life is so important, critical, in fact, then why do you always talk about the mind and focus? Why do you not start with teaching people how to find one's purpose in life?"

The wood chair creaked as I leaned forward and responded, "We discover our purpose in life with our mind. To do so, we need to have sufficient understanding and mastery of our mind, plus the ability to focus it. Only then can we maintain a state of self-reflection consistently over time to come to a clear and definitive conclusion of our life's purpose. So, though it may appear that seeking one's life purpose is where we should start, it is, in fact, not the case."

I continued, "When I ask people what they want in life, most people respond with some version of 'to be happy.' You often hear parents saying to their kids, 'We just want you to be happy.' Happiness should never be pursued. Rather, one should pursue a lifestyle where the by-product of living that lifestyle is happiness. For example, I have a glass of wine with one of my dearest friends in my favorite city in Germany and I feel happy. So the key is then to have good wine with good friends in Germany."

Moritz laughed and responded with, "I'll toast to that!"

"Cheers!" I smiled as we clinked our wineglasses.

It was warm inside, but sitting next to the window I could feel the cold desperately trying to seep in through the glass. "It's a sequential process," I shared. "Having a good understanding of the inner workings of the mind and the ability to focus is the foundation of what is needed to discover our purpose in life. Our purpose defines our priorities, and our priorities define the lifestyle we should lead. The by-product of living a life that has been defined by our purpose is happiness."

Moritz responded, "Well, when you put it that way, it all makes sense why you would want to start with understanding the mind and learning to focus."

"When we can live a purpose-focused life we can live a rewarding life."

This book will give you the foundational teachings and tools necessary to understand and leverage the mind and the power of unwavering focus. Understanding these two things—your mind and how to focus it—will allow you to begin the process of discovering your life's purpose, and subsequently defining your priorities and focusing on them, thus enabling you to live a life of purpose and joy. In the upcoming chapters, we will learn, among other things, how to use these learnings to live in the present as well as to heal many of the ailments that plague our mind, such as worry, fear, anxiety, and stress.

I'll share with you a step-by-step process of understanding how the mind works so that you can learn to control and direct it. You will also learn how to focus. In addition, I will share with you a range of simple, practical, but highly effective tools to help you become good at controlling the mind and focusing. You will learn ways to implement these tools easily and consistently in your daily life to sustain your progress toward the goals you want to achieve. Don't expect to master any of these tools by the end of the book; rather, expect to get a good and solid understanding of how these tools work, and practical techniques for applying them in every aspect of your life. It's your consistency in applying these tools in the coming weeks and months that will determine how much you actually benefit from them. Eventually, if you are consistent enough in your application, you will find that your mental patterns, your habit patterns, start to change, and you will create a different lifestyle for yourself.

The ability to focus is one of humanity's greatest assets. It is at the core of all human success and endeavor, because the ability to concentrate is what helps a person manifest their goals in life. Most people want to experience some version of happiness, contentment, enlightenment, or other such uplifting feelings, but they do not know how to attain such states because they are never taught that the key to creating the life they want is concentration. Additionally, most people are never taught how to harness and direct the powers of concentration as a tool for manifestation.

Now, the question will be asked, "Do I need to live a focused life?"

My answer is "No." You absolutely do not *need* to live a focused life. Living a focused life is a choice, and we all have the choice of whether we want to or not. It's your life, and you should decide how you want to live it. That said, living a focused life supports you in having a more rewarding life.

There is a reason you are reading this book, and I hope it's because something inside you is telling you that leading a focused life or a purpose-focused life will improve the quality of your life and bring greater meaning to it.

What's the difference between a focused life and a purpose-focused life? A focused life is one in which you are able to give whoever and whatever you are engaged with your undivided attention. You are fully present in all your experiences and thus creating a truly rewarding life, though your experiences are not driven by a greater overarching purpose. A purpose-focused life, on the other hand, is one in which your life's purpose defines your priorities, and your priorities drive what you focus on. Your life is lived very intentionally. You make wise choices each day based on your life's purpose: who you spend time with, what you spend your time on, what music you listen to, what books you read, what shows you watch, what foods you eat, and more. You give who and what you are engaged with your undivided attention, but the who and what are intentionally chosen.

Ultimately, the goal of this book is to help you live a focused life or a purpose-focused life and reap its boundless benefits.

LESSON 1.2

Taking Charge

We have the choice of what we focus on in life. This choice is not always easy. Sometimes, if not often, it is extremely difficult, but we do have the choice.

When I was a monk living in my guru's monastery, I met a man from the island country of Mauritius who always smiled. He was, for lack of a better word, interning at the monastery for a few months, and during this time I got to know him. One day I asked him, "Why are you always smiling?"

He looked at me and said, "My father died when I was very young. My widowed mother had to raise me and my siblings all by herself, and we were quite poor. Every morning my mother would wake us up, get us to stand in a line, and then make us all laugh for five minutes. That was how we started our day."

I cannot even begin to tell you how that story has impacted my life. This lady, faced with the loss of her husband and forced now to provide for her children and herself, made the choice of how she would

9

start her day. She chose what she wanted her kids to focus on. She chose what to impress on their malleable subconscious first thing in the morning. Little did she know that her actions would ripple halfway across the world to Hawaii in the living example of her son and then be told in a book one day.

Nelson Mandela spent twenty-seven years in prison only to be released, topple South Africa's racist system of apartheid, and become president. This is a great lesson of a person who chose what he would focus on in his mind while in prison.

These are two examples of people who took charge of their mind and made the conscious choice of what to focus on in life. We cannot leave it up to our environment to determine what we focus on. The outcome would be disastrous. We must take charge of what it is we wish to focus on in life. We also cannot leave it to our mind, because the mind has no ability to discriminate between what is good for you and what is not good for you.

If my mind knew what was good for me, I would be perfect. Every time I picked up a bowl of French fries, my mind would say, "Have three fries and then have this bowl of salad, it's healthier." But my mind doesn't say that. My mind says, "Yes, go for it. Have that bowl of fries, and put on extra ketchup, because it's really, really good." And then, "Have some of these onion rings, too."

The mind has no idea what is good for you and what is not good for you until you have trained it to discriminate between the two. Once you have trained and programmed the mind to be able to determine wisely what is physically, mentally, emotionally, and spiritually uplifting to you, then it can help you make better choices in life.

There was a time when people were sold the concept that smoking was good for you. They believed it, told their minds that smoking was good for them, and smoked themselves to death. Now, if the mind knew that smoking was bad for them, it would have said, "You idiot!

Smoking kills. Stop doing it. You're gonna kill us both." But it didn't say that because unless you give the mind the right information, it has no ability to guide you in the right direction.

That said, there is a part of the mind that does know what is good for you. It's called the superconscious mind.

The Three States of Mind

To better understand the mind, you can view it in three states. This book does not dive deep into understanding the various states of mind, but I want to give you a brief, simplified insight, as it will support many of the points I bring up throughout the book.

You can view these three states of the mind as the conscious, the subconscious, and the superconscious mind. To better understand this, imagine the mind as a three-story building, with the superconscious mind on the top floor, the subconscious in the middle, and the conscious mind on the ground floor. Let's look at the characteristics of each of these states of mind.

The conscious mind is the external mind, oriented to the world around us, and is tied to our five senses. It is the instinctive part of us, and I often refer to it as the instinctive mind. It governs, for example, our hunger and thirst, the basic faculties of perception and movement, procreation, impulsive thought processes, and more.

The subconscious mind is our intellectual mind. It is the seat of reason and logical thinking. You could also say that the subconscious mind is our "hard drive." It records all the conscious mind's experiences, whether those experiences are remembered or not. Additionally, it stores impressions and habit patterns, and also governs involuntary physiological processes.

The superconscious mind, as Gurudeva describes it, is "the mind of light, the all-knowing intelligence of the soul." At its deepest level, the superconscious can be described as spiritual consciousness or non-dual consciousness. The superconscious is the source of creativity, intuition, profound spiritual experiences, and more.

Viewing the three states of mind as a three-story building, we can make the following conclusions. To impress something upon the subconscious mind, we would need to go through the conscious mind (we would have to go through the first floor to get to the second floor). Intuition, which comes from the superconscious mind, must pass through the subconscious mind to get to the conscious mind for us to perceive it. A cluttered subconscious would make it difficult for intuition to get through.

Of these three states of mind, only the superconscious knows what is good for you. It is, after all, the all-knowing intelligence of the soul. This is a problem because people mostly function in the conscious and subconscious mind, with an occasional flash of intuitive wisdom coming through from the superconscious mind.

The subconscious mind basically doesn't know what is good for you unless you have trained it to know. To train it, you must first have a good understanding and control of the mind in general. Then you have to gather the right information, digest it, form clear conclusions, and input these conclusions into the subconscious in an organized way, so the subconscious can use these conclusions to guide you. This is when the subconscious becomes an incredible asset. A clarified subconscious working in harmony with the superconscious is an unfathomable power you are entitled to.

In today's world, the tsunami of information that barrages us daily devastates the very landscape of our subconscious mind. The subconscious dies a slow death of information indigestion, leading to the inability to make decisions (even simple ones), confusion, overthinking, anxiety, stress, and more. We consume information faster than a starving man would food, but do not give any time to the processing of that information and the critical stage of forming clear conclusions.

This act debilitates the subconscious. More and more people are simply unable to make decisions or even to know what they want in life.

At any point in time during the day, your awareness is functioning in one of these states of mind (and we will learn about awareness in chapter 3). How you act and react to experiences in life is based on which of these states of mind your awareness is in. Ultimately, you should be in charge of where in your mind your awareness goes.

In taking charge of your life, you should also not leave the outcome of your life to your environment or, God forbid, "the Universe"! To all the people who say, "The Universe is going to guide me," I can assure you that Jupiter, Pluto, and Uranus are not sitting around figuring out how to solve the complexities of your life. Your mind is a tool. You are in charge of it. Understand how it works and focus it to create the life you want.

The earlier in life you learn these teachings, the more time you will have to apply them in life and reap their benefits. Even if you have a decade left to live, you can still leverage these teachings to live the most amazing decade of your life. This is one of the greatest gifts you can give yourself. It's also a great gift that you can give other people. As you uplift yourself and become a better version of you, you uplift everyone who is connected to you.

I remember a few months after joining the monastery I felt quite sad, as I hadn't spoken to my family in a long time. I was missing them. Part of living as an ordained Hindu monk in a cloistered monastery in my tradition was that we were no longer in touch with the people we previously knew. One day I went to see Gurudeva in his office to share with him what I was feeling.

I said to him, "Gurudeva, I'm feeling really sad. I miss my family. I miss my friends, my relatives. And sometimes I can't help feeling that being in the monastery might be slightly selfish, that I'm not really helping them."

He listened patiently with undivided attention, as he always did, and then he did something really interesting. He reached over to a box on his desk and pulled out a tissue. He spread it flat on the table and said, "You are here in the middle. Your father is in this corner, your mother is in this corner, your brother is in that corner, and your other brother is in this corner."

Then he put his fingers in the middle of the tissue and started to pull it up toward the ceiling and said, "You are in the middle, and as you uplift yourself, look at what you are doing to everybody else: You are uplifting everyone else as well." As he continued to lift the middle of the tissue, all four sides got lifted up off the desk.

He went on to say, "You are energetically connected to all those who are in your life. As you uplift yourself, you uplift all of them as well, so investing your time in developing yourself is not selfish."

It was a simple yet deeply profound lesson for me. It left an indelible impression in my mind that the work I do to be a better version of myself not only impacts my life but all those around me.

The fact that you have a life is the only reason you need to take charge of it and live the best life you can. The insights, tools, and practices in this book are the fundamental teachings you need to do so.

Desire, Life's Supreme Force

Without an inextinguishable desire, nothing is achieved.

Napoleon Hill, the twentieth-century mystic, said in his book *Think and Grow Rich*, "Behind this demand for new and better things, there is one quality one must possess to win, and that is *definiteness of purpose*, the knowledge of what one wants, and a burning *desire* to possess it."

Knowing what you want and the desire to possess it. If you are clear that you want to live a focused life, then the subsequent question is: How badly do you desire it? Most don't desire it badly enough, and the lack of intensity of this desire is what ultimately causes them to not be able to live a focused life. This applies to anything we pursue.

The Wright brothers desired to fly. Edison desired to light up the night by his own means. Hillary and Norgay desired to summit Everest. Rosa Parks desired equal rights. Gandhi desired independence through nonviolence. The list goes on beyond the archives of history of the men and women who channeled the power of desire to manifest that which they sought. The power of an inextinguishable desire can mow down all opposition and surmount any obstacle. It is the silencer of the flatulent voices of critics and disbelievers. It is the veil that shrouds the eyes of all obstacles. The supreme force behind success.

I first met my guru when I was around nine years old. My second meeting with him was when I was twenty-one years old. The very first thing that I ever said to him, in my second meeting, was my desire for my life's purpose, Self-Realization. Having stated that, I immediately asked him if he would train me and help me achieve this.

He looked me in the eyes and asked, "What are you willing to do for it?"

I responded, without any hesitation and with a conviction that had already been cemented in me for years, "I'm willing to give my life for it."

I saw no doubt in his face as he heard my words, nor did it matter to me what he thought of my statement. My desire and what I was willing to do for it was paramount. I was resolved in what I wanted. I needed a guide. Someone who had experienced the goal many times and knew definitively the path to it. It was his choice now to accept me or not as his student.

The subsequent years saw him test my desire and conviction. Challenge after challenge, test after test, I remained firmly resolved to join his monastic order and commit my life to his training and the pursuit of my purpose. Three years later, in my pursuit of Self-Realization, I left my family and the world I had known since I was born to commit my life to a Hindu monastic way of living in my guru's cloistered monastery.

This act of renunciation involved no longer communicating with my family, relatives, friends, and people I previously knew. Music, shows, foods, drinks, clothing, preferences . . . my life as I knew it was no longer to be. It mattered naught to me. My life's purpose eclipsed all other desires. My life was now to be a channeling of all other desires to the solitary desire of Self-Realization, the ultimate spiritual attainment within the Hindu philosophy that I subscribe to.

It all comes down to how badly you desire what it is you seek. The intensity of this desire will determine what you are willing to do for it and what you are willing to give up in the pursuit of it. In my case, I was willing to give my life for my life's ultimate desire.

Let me also be transparent in saying that the pursuit of such a solitary desire at the expense of all else in life should not imply that I never doubted or questioned my path. I don't want to paint a picture of a superhero or a stoic monk immune to the throes of life. We often wish to paint those we hold in high regard with broad strokes of perfectionism and messianic qualities. I can assure you we are all human, every last one of us. I broke, I cried, I failed, I faltered, became desperate, got confused, questioned myself, and more. But I never gave up the pursuit of my life's purpose. That desire is ever present and is what defines what I do in life and the focus of my energy.

Anyone who tells you he has never thought of quitting is selling you a tropical island in the Arctic.

In a conversation with Joe De Sena, the founder of Spartan Race— military-style obstacle races designed to test mental fortitude and physical strength—I asked him if he ever thought of quitting any of the long endurance races he participates in. The words were barely out of my mouth before he replied with "All the time. I want to quit every race I do." I couldn't help thinking to myself at that moment what an honest answer that was.

I can assure you that portraying a life devoid of uncertainty and imbued with perfectionism does not inspire hope but rather falsely paints a picture of a painless path to success—a picture that will leave all hopelessly disappointed by their inability to reach such heights. The glorified narrow pointed peaks of success that most people like to focus on are of but a fraction of the breadth and depth of the chasms that achievers spend most of their time crawling out of. This book tells the story and shares the learnings of an ordinary man's journey from a distracted child to an adult who can be focused in all of his life's engagements. There are no miracles, no walking on water or splitting of the seas. Just an inextinguishable desire for a clearly defined purpose on a journey that saw more downs than ups on the path to a focused life.

One must be pathologically oblivious to anything but the belief in the fulfillment of one's desire. It is such belief in a solitary desire that eventually extinguishes the flame of doubt and unfurls a path forward to the manifestation of that desire.

Ultimately, you must want it. You must truly want what you seek and believe wholeheartedly that you can and will get it. This desire must be accompanied by steadfast patience, and acceptance that the manifestation of your desire could take decades.

To quote Hill again, "There is nothing, right or wrong, which *belief*, plus *burning desire*, cannot make real. These qualities are free to everyone."

LESSON 1.4

Making the Case

Over the years I have met countless people who were keen on living a focused life. They have expressed this desire to me in all earnestness, but most of these people never ended up living a focused life. I knew their lack of success was because their desire for leading a focused life was not strong enough. Perhaps, when they shared their convictions with me, they were going through a challenging phase in life, and the pain of it caused them to seek an alternative way of living. But often, when the pain subsides, the desire to live a different way of life ebbs away with the pain, and people default back to who they are.

Besides the lack of desire, I often wondered what else was missing to account for their failure to pursue their conviction to success. It wasn't until a chilly fall evening in Seoul, South Korea, that I learned what I felt was a key missing component in the path to success. It was October 2017, and I was invited to speak at the 18th World Knowledge Forum. The three-day event had around 3,000 attendees and an impressive lineup of speakers that included former prime ministers and presidents of countries, Nobel Prize winners, many CEOs of global corporations, and so on.

On one of the evenings, I was invited to a private dinner with seventy or eighty dignitaries who were attending the event. The gathering took place in a gorgeous space that was built in the style of a *hanok*, a traditional Korean house, with curved tiled roofs set upon thick timber rafters and frames. Standing in the courtyard of this simple, immaculate, and elegant home, I could not help but feel transported to what eighteenth-century Korea must have felt like. As I was standing and speaking to a couple of people, a gentleman walked up to me and asked, "Hi, who are you and what are you here speaking about?" I introduced myself to him and shared a little about my talk. He then introduced himself as a former White House chief of staff.

In our conversation, he pointed out that the primary reason why people are not successful in conveying their message is that "they do not make their case."

I asked him to elaborate on that, and he went on to point to a speech given earlier in the day by Ban Ki-moon (the former Secretary-General of the United Nations) about environmental issues in the world. He shared that one thing Ban Ki-moon could have done to drive his point home more strongly was to make the case. He went on to say, "For example, how do we make the case to a single mother of three living in Pennsylvania who has two jobs that she needs to care for the environment, when all she can think of is caring for her kids and making ends meet? When you make the case, you can get people to buy in. You need to connect the dots for them. When you can make the case to the single mother of three in Pennsylvania, then she will buy into doing her part for the environment. But you have to make the case."

The phrase "make the case" was a big revelation to me, and probably one of my most significant learnings that year. I have traveled the world to teach people about focus, but in this conversation with the former White House staffer, I realized that I had not really made the case for *why* we need to focus. It made me also realize that most people likely never made the case to themselves about why they need to live a focused life. In other words, they have not sold it to themselves and hence have not bought into the concept. Because of this, they lack one of the key ingredients for sustaining the pursuit of living a focused life.

Unless we make the case to ourselves for why we need to live a focused life, we will not do so. Similarly, in teaching or encouraging others to learn to focus, we have to make the case to them as well. After this conversation in Seoul, I started to make the case each time I spoke about focus, and I saw immediately that my message had a more significant impact on my audience.

So, as you learn to focus and feel inspired to share and teach your children, friends, family, employees, or colleagues the art of focus, just make sure you "make the case." Don't just tell your children to focus, because if you do, this will be just one more thing you are telling them to do without giving them a reason. You need to make the case to them, and unless you do, there will be very little impetus for them to focus. You need to get them to buy in on why it is important to learn to focus.

In the next chapter, we will dive into making the case for living a focused life. This is critical, for when you can make the case to yourself to live a focused life, then you will make the teachings and tools in this book a part of your life. We will also explore a few attitudes to adopt that are essential to support living a focused life.

Chapter 2

SETTING UP FOR SUCCESS

Life Is Meant to Be Lived Joyously

(The First Impetus for Leading a Focused Life)

Supposing you want to live a life of focus, do you know why you want to do so? I have made the case to myself, and hence I have, over the last four decades, pursued and strived to live a purpose-focused life. In making the case to myself, I have come to the realization that there are three general impetuses for why anyone should lead a focused life: happiness, manifesting our goals, and death. Let's look at the first impetus, happiness.

My guru once said, "Life is meant to be lived joyously." This quote deeply impressed me. When I heard it I asked myself, "Yes, why shouldn't life be lived joyously?" I grew up very spiritually inclined, and I encountered prevailing views that a spiritual life was a life of austerities, deprivation, solemnity, rules, moral conduct, restrictions, and more. Joy and happiness were not things I heard spoken of often. My guru was the first one to make it clear to me that a spiritual life can be and should be a joyous life—that life truly is meant to be lived joyously. Seriously, how many people want to lead a miserable life? Many people live in self-created misery, but most of them would, I assume, choose a joyous life if they could or if they knew how to.

When one has absolute clarity around one's purpose in life, the subsequent priorities that this clarity defines, and the ability to live focused on these priorities, the resulting effect is a joyous life. If I have the choice between living a joyous life or a miserable one, I will choose a joyous life. If you're with me on this, read on.

When my guru was dying and knew that he had only days left on this earthly plane, he said to some of the monks that had gathered around him, "What an amazing life. I would not have traded it for anything in the world." What profound words to hear from a dying man. What a gift, to be able to review your life at the point of death and declare it amazing.

How many people can truly say that? Most can't. Most can't because they didn't live a life of purpose. They were not clear what their purpose in life was, and as a result they were not clear about their priorities (who and what is important) and thus didn't know what to focus on. One source of joy and happiness is giving your undivided attention to all the people and things that truly matter to you, including the experiences in life that you have so thoughtfully chosen to have. When you focus on people and things that are not important to you, the resulting outcome is never the same as that of focusing on the people and things that matter to you. You will never experience the level of joy and happiness that you would from focusing on the latter.

If you go through your life, year after year, knowing clearly who and what you want to engage with and focus on, you will have rich and high-quality experiences in your life. The by-product of these experiences is happiness. Why would you not want this?

One of the greatest blessings of knowing who and what to focus on in life is knowing who and what not to focus on.

When you spend time with people you love and you can focus on them when you are with them, the by-product of that is the feeling of happiness. When you spend time doing something you love and can focus on doing that thing, the by-product of that is feeling happiness. Construct a lifestyle, based on your purpose and priorities, whose by-product is happiness. That said, it is impossible to live a lifestyle that only results in happiness, because out of necessity, we often have to do things that we don't particularly enjoy, and that is OK. This is the reality of life, but we can certainly work toward constructing a life in which the overall result is happiness.

In doing the things that make you happy, how do you truly get the most out of them? The answer is to be completely present in all your engagements so that you can fully experience them. How can you be completely present? By developing unwavering focus. A lot of people talk about being present and living in the moment, but hardly anyone shows you how to do it. When my guru taught me about awareness and the mind, and how to hold awareness on what or whom I am engaged with, I finally learned how to actually be present. In being completely present in the experiences I was having, I realized I got the most out of them, which resulted in me being happy.

I like being happy and I know the more focused I am, the more I am able to be present in the experiences that I am having, and the more I get out of them. The result is a greater sense of happiness. This is a huge impetus for me to work on leading a highly focused life.

Now let's look at the second impetus for living a focused life.

LESSON 2.2

Manifesting the Life You Want

(The Second Impetus for Leading a Focused Life)

We all have goals and dreams in life, and the challenge has always been to manifest them. Many factors are involved in bringing a vision to reality, but there are some fundamental character traits that are definitely needed to do so. The ability to focus is one of them.

The second impetus for leading a focused life is that unwavering focus gives you the ability to manifest your goals. And for this reason, learning how to focus well is eminently worth striving for.

Life is a manifestation of where you invest your energy.

~DANDAPANI

The best way to understand this statement is to look at energy the same way you look at water. If I took a watering can and I watered a garden bed, would the weeds or the flowers grow? The answer is both, because water has no ability to differentiate between weeds and flowers. Whatever gets watered in the garden will start to grow.

Energy works in exactly the same way: whatever I invest my energy in will start to grow. If I invest my energy in something positive, it will grow and become more positive. If I invest my energy in something negative, it will grow and become more negative. Energy has no ability to discriminate between what is positive and what is negative. Whatever I invest energy in will start to grow and manifest in my life. To manifest something or someone in my life, I invest energy in it.

Right this moment you are the sum total of where you have been investing your energy your entire life. Your physical, mental, and emotional makeup and more are a by-product of your conscious or unconscious investment of energy. If I choose to follow a well-thought-through diet and an exercise routine for myself, I will be investing energy in creating a healthier physical body. If I choose to affirm only positive statements to my subconscious, filter out negativity, and meditate, I will be investing energy in creating a healthier mind for myself.

Most people are not conscious of where they are investing their energy each day, primarily because they lack clarity around their purpose in life and thus lack clarity on their priorities in life. Consequently, there is no clear point of focus directing where their energy should go. As a result, not much of what they desire manifests in their life. Once we are clear on our purpose and priorities in life, the ability to focus then becomes a critical skill to learn.

Later in our study of the mind and awareness, you will learn that by focusing where your awareness goes, you can focus where your energy is flowing, and thus determine what is manifesting in your life— another massively important reason to learn to focus.

Death, the Greatest Impetus

(The Third Impetus for Leading a Focused Life)

There is no greater impetus for leading a focused life than the indisputable fact that death is patiently waiting to greet us all one day.

Death is a topic most people don't like to talk about. It makes many extremely uncomfortable and others fearful, and stirs strong emotions in some. We've been evolving on this planet for a very long time, and though each of us has a myriad of unique experiences, we all share two intense common experiences: birth and death, the former not remembered by most, and the latter feared by most.

This will be an uncomfortable topic for quite a few of you. When I embarked on the mission to write this book, I told myself I would do so in the spirit of selfless service. I pledged to ask myself each day if what I was writing was truly in service to the reader. I also promised myself that I would not hold back in sharing what I felt was important, even if what I wrote would make some readers uncomfortable. If I stuck to the intent of serving the reader, I knew I would be creating the biggest impact possible.

I'll quote the Dalai Lama, who so wisely summarizes the intent of this lesson in a single phrase: "Analysis of death is not for the sake of becoming fearful but to appreciate this precious lifetime." By embracing the fact that we will die one day, we come to realize the preciousness of life. Death is not to be feared, but rather embraced as a natural part of our existence on this earthly plane.

We have all directly experienced or indirectly known of someone we care about dying. Losing someone we love is a devastating experience. I know. I lost my guru and my life was never the same again. Most people don't like to talk about death, as it evokes feelings of sadness, loss, fear, and more. And because of this hesitation to talk or think about it, it is not something that people understand well. Most of us grow up not being taught about death at home or school. Most parents feel their lack of knowledge around the topic makes them too uninformed to speak about it to their children, and they often feel that death is a topic that may frighten their children.

That said, people's understanding of death is often based on the religious upbringing they have had, and every religion or philosophy has a different perspective on what happens after the point of death. But no one really knows for sure, because no one has ever died, gone to heaven, taken a selfie, come back, and posted it on Instagram with the caption, "Here's me in heaven!" followed by #PearlyGates. We all have our beliefs, and we may hold firmly to them, but no one knows for sure. And even if you've had a near-death experience, it's kind of hard to prove it to people.

My guru's death was the most devastating experience in my life. It brought me to the stark realization that the people we love die. As my guru would often say, "Once you realize something, you can't unrealize it." To understand something intellectually is one thing. To realize something is a completely different experience.

The *Oxford Dictionary of English* defines realization as "an act of becoming fully aware of something as a fact." A person can have an experience of something but may not realize it. Here's an example. Julie's father dies and the experience devastates Julie. She is in mourning for many months, and even years later deeply misses her father. The death of her father has impacted her emotionally, but not necessarily brought upon her the realization that life is finite. She goes about her life as normal, bearing the burden of sadness, but the death of her father has not changed the way she lives her life. So we can conclude that she intellectually understands that everyone dies but has not realized the reality of death.

Realizing something causes a complete shift in perspective that then results in a permanent change in behavior—the way we act and react to life's experiences.

You can truly tell how much an experience has impacted a person based on their behavior after the experience. For some there is no change. For others, there is a temporary change that ebbs with the waning pain. For a few, life is never the same again, as the realization gained from the experience catapults them into a new way of living.

The death of my guru brought about a profound realization within me that the people we love die, that all of us die, that indeed our time on this planet is finite. The common phrase repeated by most people is that "life is short." I vehemently disagree.

Life Is NOT Short

Standing behind someone in line for a latte for a minute while they fumble through their purse for the correct change can feel like a long time. Hearing an announcement from the pilot that we will be stuck on the tarmac for another thirty minutes often, if not always, results in a coordinated orchestra of groans and moans. When your toddler is screaming his head off at the start of a transatlantic flight, you have the profound spiritual experience of what eternity is. Being stuck in traffic for three hours feels like forever. How, then, is one year not a long time? The statement "Life is short" is anything but true. Let us stop repeating this statement mindlessly because everyone else is doing so.

When we realize that our life is not short, but rather that our life is finite, we also come to the realization that life is in fact quite long. Replace the phrase "Life is short" with "Life is finite." Let's try to reflect on what we are saying before we say it. There is a clear, definitive end to life. We just don't know when that end is.

Many people live their lives like they are going to live forever. And many also think that their loved ones will live forever. Frankly, most people just avoid thinking about the fact that they and their loved ones will die someday.

Most parents don't look at their five-year-old daughter and think to themselves that she will die one day. Generally, parents look at their child and envision a great future for them, one in which she will grow up to be a teenager, go to university, have a career, get married, have children, grow old, have grandchildren, and, many, many decades from now, die, though the last piece may not even be in the vision. Sadly, this is not always the case, because one is never too young to die. Infants die all the time, young children die all the time, as do teenagers, young adults, middle-aged and older people. We all die at some point.

Death should and must drive us in making it a priority to know our purpose in life. We learn to focus so we can discover our purpose. Our purpose defines our priorities and our priorities guide us in what to focus on. The by-product of this is that we live a fulfilled life. So many exit this earthly life unfulfilled.

The nineteenth-century American abolitionist and author Harriet Beecher Stowe so expressively said of an unfulfilled life, "The bitterest tears shed over graves are for words left unsaid and deeds left undone."

How Does Death Help Us Prioritize What We Focus On in Life?

Since we really don't understand death, and it is not a pleasant topic, nor an experience most of us want to have anytime soon or want our loved ones to have, we avoid talking about it. Avoiding the topic and pushing it out of our minds gives us the false sense that we will live forever and have an infinite amount of life, so to speak. This is where the problem begins.

When we feel like we and our loved ones will live forever, by avoiding the topic of death in any way or form, then we naturally take everyone and everything that is not important to us and place them on top of our priority list, and move everything and everyone that is important to the bottom of our list. Our focus now is directed toward the top of the list—to those that matter less to us. We do this because the people we love, and that love us back, have a greater tolerance level and breaking point with us. We can push the boundaries of that love a lot before the cracks start to show or before it breaks.

For example, a person can keep coming home late from work every day for weeks and miss family dinners, but it's going to take a lot more than that before their spouse leaves them. Some parents physically hit their child, and a week later the child will say to them, "I love you, Daddy!" Because they have a higher breaking point, there is little impetus to focus on them, as you know they will tolerate your lack of prioritization and focus on them. After all, in your mind they will be around forever, so why focus on them now? You can pay attention to them later: when work settles down, when you have more time, after the football game . . .

In contrast, people like your clients or coworkers, and others that you are not indeed very close to, will not hang around too long if you ignore them. Stop returning your client's calls, and they will move on to someone else. Skip too many nights out with your boss, and you may not get that promotion you have been hoping for. These people have a much lower tolerance for your inattention, or a lower breaking point, and if you push those boundaries too much, they will be out of your life very quickly. And because of this, they often become the top priorities in your life.

All of this holds true if you avoid realizing death, the fact that life is finite and we all die.

But once you realize that life is finite, your priorities change. Often in my in-person workshops I create a hypothetical situation by saying, "If someone were to walk into this room and say that everyone in this room had three hours to live, how many of you would stay for the rest of my workshop?" Sadly, no one in all the workshops I've conducted around the world has ever said, "I would." The answer is always, "I'd leave right now and go home to see my spouse and kids."

I then ask, "If your favorite store was having its biggest annual sale, would you stop by on the way home to buy something?" The answer is always "No." I continue my inquiry and ask, "If someone you did not like was calling you, would you pick up the phone and talk to them?" Again the answer is no. I persist and ask, "Would you stop by a café and stand in line for twenty minutes to buy one last cup of latte?" Again, a straight clear no.

When you shrink time, you increase the clarity of focus.

None of the participants ever spent any time thinking about what they would do if they had three hours to live. They instantaneously knew who and what they wanted to focus on. When you shrink the time you think you have in this life, you increase the clarity of focus, allowing you to know who and what is important in your life and what order of priority they all fall into. All of a sudden, you know precisely who and what to focus on.

When I asked my audience, "If you had fifty years to live, who would leave this workshop?" No one raised their hands. I continued and asked, "If you had twenty years to live, who would leave this workshop?" A couple of people raised their hands. I asked again, shrinking the time frame even shorter, "If you had five years to live, who would leave this workshop?" A lot more hands went up. Finally, I asked, "If you had three hours to live, who would leave this workshop?" Every hand in the room went up.

As their time shrank, they inevitably became clearer on who and what is important to them. This simple mental act of shrinking time allowed them to very quickly bring to the surface of their mind who the most important people and things in their lives are. Their priorities in life became evident swiftly. You have to squeeze the orange to get the juice. Death drives one to the realization of one's priorities in life. Priorities drive focus.

Once you realize that life is finite, and have the clarity of who and what is important in your life, then you know precisely where to direct your focus. This realization shifts your perspective and causes you to live a different way—a way that focuses on your true priorities and as a result creates a happy and fulfilled life. Death can provide tremendous clarity on life and is, ultimately, the greatest impetus for leading a focused life.

Death brings everything into perspective. Family, friends, work, life itself, all fall into a natural order of priority when death beckons. Your awareness, and so your energy, is directed in a concentrated manner like never before. Not a moment is wasted. Life is lived to its fullest.

Someone once asked me, "Dandapani, how often do you think about dying?"

I said, "To be honest with you, I hardly ever think about dying. But what I do think about almost every day is that my time on earth is finite, and because it's finite, I remind myself to focus on my priorities in life."

An Amazing Life

Another thing death does is make you think about how you want to live your life. In the final days of your life, how will you look back on your life and what will you say? Often people focus on what others will say about their life, but it really doesn't matter what others think. There will always be those who praise you and others who criticize you. What truly matters is what you say about your life.

Will you be able to look back and say that you lived an amazing life? Or a rewarding life, or a fulfilled life? I want to live an amazing life. This amazing life I want to live is not for others to see and admire. It is for me. It is driven by the fact that I have one life and it is the most precious gift I've been given.

Regardless of the philosophy, religion, or belief that you subscribe to, you have to realize that you only have one life as you. I believe in reincarnation, but even so, I know I have one life as Dandapani, and I want this life to be an amazing one. Knowing that my life is finite is the greatest impetus for me to live a focused life. As Gurudeva would often say, "Life is meant to be lived joyously!" You have one life as you. Make it count. Live it in a way so that on your deathbed you can look back on your life and say to yourself, "What an amazing life I lived!"

LESSON 2.4

The Law of Practice

The tools that I will share in this book have an amazing capacity to create change in a person's life. They are time-tested tools that have been practiced by Hindu monks of my guru's lineage for millennia. If applied correctly, they work and are life-transforming. But it all comes down to you and the consistency with which you choose to apply them in your life. To truly reap the benefits of these tools, practice them. My promise to you is that the more consistent you are in applying these tools in your everyday life, the greater the change you will experience. The tools will not fail you, but don't fail yourself by not putting them into practice.

My guru used to tell me that you could hang these tools up on the wall and they would make beautiful displays. They are lovely to look at and to talk about, especially if you are an intellectual type. You can sit down and talk to friends about them over dinner, and sound very wise and knowledgeable. You can impress everyone with what you have read or heard and quote memorized wisdom to them. There are a lot of people in this world who collect tools. They read one self-help book after another and they feel the more knowledge they acquire, the more they are growing and improving as a person. They become a library of self-help tools.

All of the self-help tools in the world do not do a thing for you unless you apply them—and apply them correctly and consistently in your life. The same goes for the tools that I am sharing. All of the tools in this book don't do a thing for you unless you put them into consistent practice in the way that you are instructed to.

The Law of Practice

As I shared with you in a previous lesson, the intellectual mind has no ability to discriminate between what is good for you and what is not good for you, unless you have given it the ability to do so. This applies to everything you practice on a daily basis as well, whether you are conscious of these practices or not.

The proof of this statement is that so many of us have practices or habits that result in negative outcomes. Often, we are unaware of these until we are made conscious of them by others or through our own self-reflection. Until that happens, the mind lives those habits in self-destructive ignorance. If the mind knew better, it would not indulge in those practices. The all-knowing superconscious mind can tell you what is good and not good for you, but unless you're able to tap into this state of mind, you won't benefit from its wisdom.

If you practice negative acts, acts that are not conducive to your growth, you become really good at these negative acts. If you practice positive acts, acts that are conducive to your growth, you become really good at these positive acts.

What I call "The Law of Practice" states that whatever it is you practice is that which you become good at.

I was once invited to a private dinner in New York City that was attended by some well-known individuals. After dinner, one of the attendees, a famous author, came up to me and said, "Hi, I'm . . ."

I responded with, "I'm Dandapani."

He immediately replied, "Oh, I'm not going to remember that. I'm terrible with names."

And I thought to myself, "I'm sure you are, because that is what you must tell yourself all the time." If you constantly practice telling yourself that you are terrible with names, then that is what you are going to be good at. We become good at what we practice even if what we are practicing is not good for us.

When it comes to practice, two things are essential: practicing the right way and consistency. The more you practice something, the better you get at it. If you practice a bad technique, you eventually get better at that bad technique. My guru shared a story once that illustrates the importance of practicing the right thing. When he was a teenager, he was the principal dancer for the San Francisco Ballet, and he shared how he was not allowed to practice on his own lest he develop a movement that was not supportive of his development in dance.

Once you learn to practice something the right way, then consistency is key. If I wanted to be an average piano player, I might only sit down once or twice a week at the piano for a few minutes at a time to practice a song. But if I really wanted to be one of the top pianists in the world, then, I assume, I might need to practice five to eight hours a day, every day, month after month, to get really good. After six months, I'd be better at playing the piano. After a year, I might be pretty good. And after two or three years, I'll probably be a very good pianist. The consistency in practicing the piano the right way is what will help me get the results I want.

The same applies to the tools that I share in this book. Both— practicing the right way and consistency—are critical. I recall a client sharing with me once that the tool I taught him was not working well for him. I asked him if he was practicing it consistently. He said yes. Then I asked him, "Are you applying all three parts of the tool when you practice it?"

He said, "No, I've only been doing one of the three parts that you taught me."

Well, don't expect to successfully bake a cake if you don't use all the ingredients. This is where obedience comes in. If you've been instructed on how to use a tool and you don't follow those instructions to the letter, then how do you expect to get the results you desire? If you are not obedient in your external life, don't expect to be obedient in your internal life.

There were times in the monastery when I was crippled by inner challenges I was facing. Overwhelmed by them, I would seek out my guru and share my mental ailments with him. He would always patiently and compassionately listen to me with undivided attention. When I finished unloading my burden on him, he would often ask me, "Are you applying the tools that I gave you?" My answer was often "No." After answering his question, I would get up and leave. What more was there to talk about? He had prescribed me the medicine for my ailment and the methods by which I should consume it, but I did not adhere to his instructions. The ball is in my court and the burden of responsibility lies solely on me. If I refuse to accept this responsibility, then I must bear the consequences, painful as they may be.

If you apply the tools consistently in your life, you will become really good at using them because this is what you are practicing. If you don't, then you will not be good at them, and you will not receive the benefits that one gets from consistently practicing the tools.

People are excited to learn new tools and techniques, but once the excitement wears off, they find it easier to seek the next tool than to consistently apply the tool that they have learned. As a society we are groomed to move on to the next thing. Here's the latest iPhone, a TV that displays in 8K, the latest fashion trend, the new model of a particular car, and more. Society loves all that is shiny, but as soon as the shine wears off, not a moment is wasted as it makes its way to the next thing.

To make progress with the tools in this book, or in anything that you are trying to learn or change, adopt the attitude you would take if you were learning a fine art, as in the example of the piano. You would not expect to master it in a few weeks or months. Concentration is a fine art as well. It takes having a solid understanding of the mind first, then learning and practicing concentration. Like any art form, the first step is learning it, and the second step is practicing it.

Don't expect to read this book, get to the end, and find yourself a master of the concepts. This work is going to take time, and you may want to revisit various chapters, lessons, and concepts again and again. Think of this as your life's work and be kind, gentle, loving, and patient with yourself as you change and grow. If you consistently apply these tools in your life, you will find changes starting to take place in the coming weeks and months. As my guru always lovingly reminded me, "The rewards are far greater than the efforts put into it."

You will never regret challenging yourself to grow. It is well worth your time. This work is the greatest gift that you can give yourself in your journey toward becoming a better, more focused, and more realized version of yourself.

I'm not one to quote movie lines, but there is one bit of dialogue from a TV show that is worth quoting here. In the Netflix TV series *Marco Polo*, the character Hundred Eyes, a blind monk, asks Marco Polo how, if he returns to the West, he will explain "this strange word, kung fu." Hundred Eyes goes on to answer the question himself: "Kung fu: it means supreme skill from hard work. A great poet has reached kung fu. A painter . . . can be said to have kung fu. Even the cook. The one who sweeps steps. Or a masterful servant can have kung fu. Practice. Preparation. Endless repetition. Until your mind is weary, and your bones ache. Until you are too tired to sweat. Too wasted to breathe. That is the way. The only way one acquires kung fu."

Sounds like it is right out of Hollywood, and it is. All this is to say that focus is a skill. Mastery of focus can be achieved by anyone who is willing to put in the preparation, hard work, practice, and endless repetition. And you will learn in this book how to bring the practice of focus into everything you do, from painting to cooking to sweeping the steps.

Endless repetition is where many, if not most, fail. Another question that I get asked so very often is, "What's next?" I've been focused on repeating the very same practice my guru gave me almost three decades ago.

You don't need to learn many tools. The secret lies in learning a few essential tools and mastering them. Go narrow and deep as opposed to shallow and wide. The more you experience a tool, the more it unveils to you. In a world where the majority asks, "What's next?" be the one who is focused on mastering the tool you've embraced.

This book is for people who want to leverage the power of unwavering focus to live a truly rewarding life.

Learning through Repetition

My guru believed that people need repetition to learn, and that was how I was taught by him in the monastery. Repetition is a technique that I will use a lot in this book, and in the lessons you will find within it. You will hear me repeating a lot of the concepts over and over because repetition is a very effective way to program the subconscious. This was how my guru trained me, and it is a very effective tool for getting concepts to stick in the mind as you learn.

Let me tell you a story to illustrate this.

One day in the monastery, I was walking from my office to the dining hall when my guru came up to me, told me something, and immediately after telling it to me, turned and walked away. I thought to myself, "He told me that yesterday and the day before that, and last week as well. Has he forgotten that he's told me this already?"

Being a newish monk at the time, I was confused about this, so I went to one of the senior monks and shared my experience with him. I asked, "Could it be that Gurudeva is getting old and he does not remember that he already shared that with me a few times?" The monk laughed and responded, "You and I very well know that that is not the case. You know how incredible his memory is. He repeats things over and over because he knows how long it takes to impress the subconscious. Through constant repetition, he can create a lasting pattern in your subconscious."

I'm going to take the same approach with you. I'm going to impress your subconscious with the fundamental concepts of understanding the mind and learning how to focus, and when you hear me repeat myself, please don't think, "Not this again! I know this already!" As soon as you think this, know that you really don't grasp the concept yet. The more my guru repeated himself to me, the more I learned. I knew he was repeating himself because I had not yet fully grasped the concept. With each repetition, I listened more intently, and it sank deeper into my consciousness and revealed a deeper insight into what he was saying. Even today, after decades of studying his teachings, I never say to myself, "I know this." Each time I hear the same message another layer of insights unveils itself to me.

As you go forward, read these lessons with an open and curious mind. Reflect deeply on these fundamental concepts, and in time your understanding of them will deepen, and you will see how profound these concepts really are. If you approach this book with the right attitude, you will experience that when you hear these ideas repeated, you will learn something that you may have previously missed or didn't yet fully comprehend. These ideas may seem simple at first, but like any deep truth, they can take years to fully understand and ultimately experience and realize. The more you use them and reflect on them, the better you will understand them, and the more they will help you.

LESSON 2.5

Intention and Obedience

It's important that we establish a few guidelines and parameters to avoid failure and assure your success.

The very first question to ask yourself prior to reading the rest of this book is, "Why have I purchased this book?" Write down your answer succinctly and with great clarity. It is paramount that you define your intention for buying this book. What you write down now becomes your purpose for reading this book, which will completely determine what you get out of it. It will be the sole driving factor of how much you benefit from it. There are a handful of books that have changed my life. I have read and reread them multiple times; highlighted lines, marked them up, and dog-eared the pages. They have become a beacon in guiding me because I was clear about what I wanted to get out of them.

I learned early on in my life to be able to identify people who have sacrificed a great amount in their life in the pursuit of their purpose. When blessed to be in their presence, I took it as a great personal responsibility to extract the core of what they have learned. I approached them with humility and my complete presence, which was brought about by my ability to focus. In that moment of conversation with these individuals, they could feel my complete presence, my undivided attention, and my sincerity and humility to learn. What ensued was more than often life-changing to me. By approaching them with preparedness and a clear intention, I was able to move their awareness to an area of the mind that inspired their intuition to flow. I was then the truly blessed recipient of all that came through.

This is not going to happen if you consume this book while doing something else. Or if you speed-read through it as another book that you can say you have read and found to be insightful. If you are listening to an audio version of this book, then just do that. Just listen without doing anything else. Renounce the need to multitask. Renounce all the reasoning you have about why you can multitask and listen to this book at the same time. Sit down, listen, and give me your undivided attention. I've committed to this journey, and I hope you will, too. Transformation will take place when we meet in the middle, but I need you to meet me there.

I've invested so much of my life to put this book together and share the most precious thing I've learned from my guru over almost three decades of learning, contemplation, endless practice, and dedication. For you to fully benefit from the contents of this book, it is paramount that you approach it with the right mindset.

The contents of this book have changed my life and continue to change my life. I acquired this content because I approached my guru in the right way. I need you to understand this, otherwise the outcome of your reading this book will be futile. Failure to focus will be inevitable, and you will not reap its priceless benefits.

Obedience

As a monastic, one of the vows I took was the vow of obedience. Now, people have a really hard time with obedience. The common outcry is, "Don't tell me what to do!" Obedience doesn't mean subjugating yourself to someone else blindly. My guru would often divide obedience into two forms: blind obedience and intelligent obedience. Blind obedience is following someone or something without ever questioning, reasoning, or clarifying their motives. Intelligent obedience to someone you trust is a surrender to the experiential wisdom born of their years of successfully navigating and learning from the subject they have dedicated themselves to. In the case of intelligent obedience, one is encouraged always to ask for clarification should the need arise. This was what Gurudeva worked to cultivate in his monastics.

The patient awaiting a heart transplant trusts the surgeon and his team. Intelligent obedience. Millions of travelers, every day, trust a pilot to safely fly a 900,000-pound winged metal canister across an ocean and land it safely. Intelligent obedience.

Napoleon Hill's book *Think and Grow Rich* was the result of over twenty years of study of some of the most financially successful people of his time. When a person goes to that length and depth of work and summarizes some of the greatest learnings on the power of the mind, one must listen to him.

When I lived with my guru, I saw many people approach him to ask for advice. A fair number of them did so out of curiosity to know what his opinion was. Most had their answer or had already decided on what they wanted to do prior to meeting him. You should never approach a person like that and not take their advice.

For decades I've sought out people who have become highly successful or the best in their field. If I were ever to ask them for advice, which I often did, I would then apply whatever insights they shared with me in my life.

Many years ago, in Toronto, after presenting at an event, I found myself standing backstage with Marc Ecko, an American fashion designer and entrepreneur. He had just spoken as well, and in my conversation with him I took the opportunity to ask for his insight on entrepreneurship. At that time, I was just beginning my journey in this field and was keen to learn as much as I could from the right people. I asked him, "If you had one piece of advice to give a former monk on entrepreneurship, what would it be?"

He looked at me and said, "Stay narrow and deep." He paused and then repeated, "Stay narrow and deep. As you progress and become successful, you will be faced with the temptation to do many things and grab at many opportunities. This is how many fail. Stay narrow and deep."

His advice has been a tremendous help to me over the years. Though focus is what I teach and strive to live, his words did prove true in my life. As the years went on, I was offered many opportunities, and a few of them I was beyond tempted to grab. I would then remind myself of staying focused on my purpose and would silently repeat to myself, "Stay narrow and deep."

When I was a monk, I met a highly talented and successful photographer. Sadly, I don't recall her name today, but in our meeting I asked her, "If you had one piece of advice on photography for a monk, what would it be?"

She replied, "Look at a subject from many angles and photograph it from those angles. You'll be amazed by what you discover." I've obediently followed her counsel for two decades, and it's changed the way I photograph and the photos I've been able to produce.

Obedience simply means you will strive to follow their advice to the letter. If there is any part of their instruction that you do not understand, you should ask for clarification. Obedience does not mean you won't fail at doing what they instruct or that you will actually be able to follow their counsel to the letter. You may fail many times in executing it until you eventually become really good at living that advice.

It's amusing to me how some people ask for advice, then take that advice and modify it into a version that suits their wants. Why ask for advice in the first place if you are not going to follow it? Imagine wanting to learn ballet, signing up for ballet classes with a professional, well-respected teacher of this art, listening to her instructions, then saying to yourself, "I'm just going to do it my way." This type of rebellious nature is a clear sign that the instinctive mind has not been well harnessed.

If you trust me as your guide to teach you how to focus, having done your due diligence in looking for a guide on focus, then follow my counsel.

When you hire a guide to take you on a boat ride through the Florida Everglades, you trust that the guide will take you on an exploratory journey to experience the Everglades, and not take you to a remote section and feed you to the alligators. You trust the guide. I need you to trust me as you embark on this journey with me in this book. There are no alligators waiting for you, but I cannot do my work if I can't get you to commit in the way I need you to.

Your intention for reading this book and your obedience to its contents will determine how much you get from it.

The Power of Small

The journey toward leading a focused life can appear to be an overwhelming endeavor at the outset. The feeling of being overwhelmed is also often the by-product of not being able to see the path to the goal. This lack of clarity fuels the feeling of being overwhelmed and the subsequent feeling of anxiety, which eventually leads to abandoning the quest. A journey to climb to the top of a mountain can be overwhelming as well, but if you have a guide who can navigate for you each step of the way, then it inspires confidence and makes it all more achievable.

How will we approach this study of focus? The answer is: patiently, methodically, and in small bite-size pieces.

Swallowing a 10-inch pizza is a very different experience from taking a bite out of it and savoring all its yumminess. Taking a bite and chewing is no longer as appealing, and I mean this as a metaphor for how many people approach much of life. We want it all and we want it now. We are an impatient lot, and we have grown increasingly impatient as time goes on. We are impatient with the world around us, with ourselves, and with our ability to manifest and accomplish things.

Technology has fueled our impatience. It has done so by delivering what we want to our fingertips in a matter of seconds or milliseconds. Anything taking an extra few seconds to download as it is beamed to our phone from thousands of miles away is enough to send our eyes rolling to the back of our heads. This technological instant gratification is training us to bring this expectation to other aspects of our life. As patterns of delusional expectations are repeatedly formed and reinforced in our minds, we become prone to more experiences of disappointment in our lives. Disappointment, frustration, and depression are among the children born of a mind that is unable to discriminate between the instant gratification that technology provides and the nonurgent way that life delivers its outcomes.

It took a person about thirty-six years of strict discipline and training while living as a celibate monk in my guru's cloistered Hindu monastery before they were given the title *Acharya*, spiritual teacher. Today, yoga teachers are churned out at machine-gun speed after a mere 200-hour training program. Then there is the weekend program to lose weight, the 5 hacks for becoming a millionaire, the 9-day silent retreat for self-discovery, mastering the piano in 30 days, and more to drench us in an endless monsoon of quick-reward taradiddles.

The impatient beast is mercilessly fed daily by all those seeking to gain from its impetuous nature, and the outcome of it choking and suffocating on its own haste for quick gratification is becoming more evident in the rise of degraded societal behavior.

I cannot even begin to tell you how many times I get asked the question, "How long will it take me to get focused?" My answer to that question is often, "A very, very long time if you approach it that way."

This book is the antithesis of that. There are no hacks, no quick tips or shortcuts, but rather a time-tested approach that relies on consistency and patience as the crutches for success.

In your pursuit to live a focused life, be willing to take time. I love this quote from Bill Gates: "We always overestimate the change that will occur in the next two years and underestimate the change that will occur in the next ten." Now, I am not saying that it will take you ten years to learn how to live a focused life. The point I am trying to make is that we should patiently and realistically allocate sufficient time in the pursuit of creating sustainable changes in our life—changes that require a rewiring of our mind, so to speak, and of how we live our life.

Once we accept that the journey to living a focused life will take time, the next thing we need to embrace and accept is how we approach this journey. This is critical. The journey itself is long, and when we view it that way it can be and often is overwhelming. I can sincerely empathize with you on this. But when we view it as small steps, the feeling is very different.

It's important for you to understand that the journey to the summit of a focused life is a long one. And as for any long journey, you need to prepare mentally, emotionally, and physically for it. Don't expect to summit Everest in a day. But the critical thing I want you to keep in mind here is our approach toward this long journey.

Ask me to walk from New York City to Los Angeles and I will feel daunted by the request, but ask me to take just one step in that direction and I will feel incontrovertibly confident in my ability to do so. My job is to define the goal and outline the path to it in small steps. Your job is to focus on just taking the next step.

In that conversation with Joe De Sena that I shared with you earlier, I asked him a follow-up question about quitting. "What do you do when in the middle of those long endurance races you think of quitting?"

Joe replied, "I tell myself that all I have to do is make it to that tree. That I know I can do. When I get to that tree, then I tell myself I need to make it to that rock. And eventually I am at the finish line."

A quote from Gurudeva encapsulates the power of small steps: "A temple made of bricks is built one brick at a time." One brick, one brick, one brick . . . and many years later you have a giant spiritual citadel that stands for more than a thousand years. King Suryavarman II built Angkor Wat over a period of thirty years, creating the world's largest temple complex, covering an area measuring 162.6 hectares, and it is still standing almost 900 years later.

Nature is willing to take the time and work in small steps as well. The Colorado River patiently carved out the Grand Canyon over an estimated six million years, leaving us with one of nature's great wonders. Much of this sculpting continues to happen each day, but in small ways that we are oblivious to. But credit must go to Mother Nature for her consistency and dedication to the task.

The power of small, consistent steps is underestimated by so many people. Small things lead to big things. Small things are doable. Small steps are achievable. Small steps create no pressure. Small goals create no pressure. Being faithful to small consistent steps is an expression of understanding, love, and compassion toward the needs of our mind and body.

Anita Roddick, the British entrepreneur, human rights activist, and environmental campaigner, so cleverly observed, "If you think you're too small to have an impact, try going to bed with a mosquito in the room." So true. I have slapped my face so many times in the darkness of the night, wholeheartedly believing that the insolent winged beast performing a facial blood draw on me would be no match for the swiftness of my hand. I was wrong.

We always *start* with the big picture. What do we want? What is the destination? As Hill says, "Definiteness of purpose, the knowledge of what one wants." This needs to be articulated clearly: the ability to look into the future and see clearly a detailed picture of one's goal. In the case of this book, it is unwavering focus.

Once we know this, we come back to the present and start outlining the path to that goal. As you begin to embark on the path to that goal, think in terms of small steps. Doable steps. I always keep the big picture in the back of my mind but focus on the small steps needed to get there. I know I just need to take one step in the direction I want to go in. Once I've taken that step, then I just need to take another step in the same direction. And so on.

If my goal is to walk from New York to Los Angeles, then my first step is to head west. I take one step in that direction. Having done that, I then take another step. We must be disciplined in doing so and avoid the temptation to accelerate and shortcut the process. Many torment their mind and body each day with an incessant need to accelerate change and shorten the time to reward. Your body needs time to grow from a child to an adult, and similarly, it needs time to remold its inner nature. Our mind needs to learn and practice focus. So do our nervous system, our muscles, our body. This takes time. Be gentle and patient with yourself.

As we make our way to the top of the mountain, we will enjoy many scenic views. Great views are not solely reserved for the summit; rather, they are available to all those willing to embark on the climb. In your pursuit of living a focused life you will start to experience its benefits early on. Unlike climbing a mountain, there is no summit to be reached here, as we can always work to be better at being focused. And the better we get at it, the more we realize we can be better at it.

Investing in learning to focus now will pay unfathomable dividends in your future.

PART 2

THE INEFFABLE
MIND

Chapter 3

UNDERSTANDING

THE MIND

The World's Most Powerful Tool

O f all the things I had the great blessing of learning from my guru, there is one that I consider far greater than all the rest and that I feel needs to be conveyed to every man, woman, and child around the world, and that is the understanding of how the mind works.

We all have a mind, and many of us are blessed with a fully functioning mind. We are born with it. We live with it. We can't detach it from ourselves. Like our body, it is our companion every second of our earthly expedition. Throughout our entire life, we function in the mind, whether in our waking or sleeping state. It's the one thing we spend twenty-four hours a day with, though this fact may not be something most people are conscious of. We don't even spend that much time with the people or things we love. In spite of its loyal companionship our entire life, the mind sadly remains a stranger to most people—a companion most are unaware of or choose not to get to know. Like a royal butler who is there to serve, but not to be acquainted with.

The mind has manifested the nonnatural world around us. It has reshaped, often for the worse, much of the natural world around us. It created computers and smartphones; put a rover on Mars and shuttles in space; discovered cures for diseases; harnessed the power of the sun; allowed us to travel to distant lands in a matter of hours; and many other such inventions. And we are only just beginning to tap into its unfathomable powers.

The mind is the most powerful tool in the world, accoutred with functionality beyond our comprehension. And you own it. It has been given to you at no cost, except that if you fail to understand and govern it, you may suffer the consequences of an unharnessed mind, and in the worst case, it could result in the end of this earthly journey.

Yet for all its powers and functions, known and unknown, there is no manual for the mind. Not even a "Quick Start" guide to it like you would find in the packages of most electronic devices you buy.

Almost everything else comes with a manual. You buy a blender, and you get a thirty-page manual in twelve languages on how to use it, printed in a font size that would put the eyes of a hawk to the test. Even food comes with directions! Take a box of rice, for example. There are instructions on how to cook the rice printed right on the box. Takeaway coffee cups warn you of their hot contents. Frozen dinners have step-by-step instructions on how to resurrect your deceased meal.

But, alas, the mind did not come with any manual. In addition to this, most, if not all, of us, have never had any education whatsoever on the mind—on understanding it, on how it works, on how to harness it, and more. It's no wonder that so many people struggle with their mind and that there is an abundance of mental health issues. We've been given the most powerful tool in the world yet never taught how to use it. With all the issues and conversations surrounding mental health all around the world, why have we not come to the conclusion, many decades ago, that education about and of the mind is a necessary, if not mandatory, requirement for every child in school? Some education on it would be better than none.

Why does understanding the mind matter so much? Because it is the tool that we use to design and manifest our known reality every day of our lives. The heaven or hell that we create in our internal or external lives finds its origins in the mind. If we can understand how the mind works, we can harness and direct it to create the life that we want. But it all comes down to understanding what we're working with, and it is very difficult to work with something when you don't understand it. The inability of many people to create the life that they want lies not in the fact that they do not have the ability to do so, but rather in the fact that they do not understand the tool that they are working with, which is the mind.

My friend once emailed me a photo he had taken of a MINI Cooper parked by the side of a road. In that email, he wrote, "Hey, I took this photo of a MINI and touched it up in Photoshop. What do you think?" It was an OK photo, but it didn't stand out to me as anything impressive. I wrote back, saying, "It's nice but it's nothing special. Am I not seeing something?" He is a decent photographer, and this photo was subpar for his photography skills. A day later I got this reply to my email: "They don't make four-door MINIs!" (They didn't, back then.) He had taken a photo of a two-door MINI Cooper and in Photoshop stretched it out, added two additional doors, and touched it up to the point that I could not tell it was Photoshopped.

The purpose of this story is to convey the point that if we understand how our mind works, we can leverage that understanding to use it to shape our lives in the way we want to. Because so many of us have very little understanding of the inner workings of our mind, we don't have the ability to do very much with it. Though I have used Photoshop for many years, I would still classify myself as a beginner; I do not have the understanding of all of its features and the skills to use them to do what my friend did. His years of dedication to learning this tool have led him to have an excellent command of it, so that he can create what he wants with it. Likewise, the better we understand our mind, the more we can leverage its abilities to create the life we want.

When I joined my guru's monastery, one of the things he asked me early on was, "Do you know how the mind works?"

I answered, "No, I do not. Nobody has ever taught me anything about it."

He replied, "Then that's where we are going to start. We are going to start by getting a clear intellectual understanding of how the mind works."

He had a gift, born of his deep realizations of the mind, for simplifying the understanding of the mind in a way that allowed one to gain a solid foundational understanding in a short time. I would frequently and consistently ask questions to gain further clarity on the subject and extract from him the essence of the mind, so that I could distill it down to a few cardinal axioms that I could focus on experiencing.

Once my understanding of the mind had been established to some degree, then my goal was to begin the process of experiencing what I had learned intellectually. You can read all you want about standing on a peak overlooking the Himalayas, but unless you experience it you will never know what that is like.

This is where many fail. I had a person excitedly share with me once, after having just completed a weekend course, how she could not wait to take the contents of what she had just learned and share it in her own workshop with others. This kind of learning and sharing is quickly becoming a common trend. I would in fact shy away from calling it "learning." It would more appropriately be called "gathering information."

There are those who simply pursue an intellectual learning of the mind—scouring books and screens for any insights they can amass, piecing it all together in what can be described as nothing more than a tossed salad. Enough to impress the unfortunate passenger sitting next to them on a flight, but not enough to result in sustainable change in their life. The mere acquisition of knowledge does not translate to learning. This must be understood. Do not deceive yourself that the more information you acquire, the more you are growing as a person. I highly discourage the pursuit of the mere acquisition of knowledge.

Intellectual learning is where one must begin, but this must be followed by, and confirmed with, experiential learning. And often it must take many repeated experiences of the subject to have a deeper experiential understanding and learning of it.

In the subsequent chapters and lessons in this book, I will share with you an intellectual understanding of the various subjects that I will present. This will be followed by providing you with a framework to then experience what you have intellectually understood. Your ability to match your experience with what you have learned will inform you of how well you have grasped the contents of this book. Creating sustainable change from it shows that you have realized the contents of this book. That is where I intend to help you get to.

LESSON 3.2

The Mind's Great Secret

A very basic understanding of the mind is more than sufficient to create the most monumental shift in your life and empower you with the ability to understand, harness, and focus the most powerful tool in the world, your mind, so that you can take charge of your life.

I want to assure you and put your mind at ease that you have the ability to understand well what I will share with you in this lesson. No painfully acquired university degree or highly developed intellect is needed for this. Understanding the mind is not a complex task, though there are those who make it complex. It need not be so.

My guru's ability to articulate the inner workings of the mind in clear and simple words that everyone can understand conveyed to me the depth of his understanding and experience of the mind. It also conveyed to me his intention, which was to help others. Within this desire was his desire to help people get to a place of understanding of what he was teaching so that it could positively impact their lives.

What I am sharing with you in this book is my personal experience of the mind. My understanding of the mind did not come from reading hundreds of books and summarizing their content, nor from doing research and lab tests, getting results back, and drawing correlations and charts. Not at all. It was first born as an intellectual understanding as my guru unfurled the inner workings of the mind to me. The countless subsequent conversations I had with him further deepened my understanding of the mind. As I better understood the mind, he guided me to simultaneously experience everything that I was learning, and I've been at it for over two and a half decades. The conclusions on the inner workings of the mind that I share with you in this book were born out of the repeated experiences I've had of the mind.

I want to share with you this quote from a dear friend and mentor of mine, Michael Lutzenkirchen: "While I appear as a teacher to you, I'm a student of the subject. And I hope it always stays that way."

This statement best describes where I am in my journey of understanding the mind. I am a student of the subject. Not a master. Not an expert. For the more I experience and learn about the mind, the more I realize how much I do not know. What you are getting from me in this book are my experiential learnings of the mind at the time of publication—or, in reality, when my publisher told me I could no longer edit this book!

You should always adopt the attitude that you are at the beginning of the path—you are eager, enthusiastic, and open to learning, and you know absolutely nothing.

What I am about to share with you forms the basis, the foundational teachings, of everything that you will learn in this book. It is the single most important thing I wish for you to take away from this read. Please make a great effort to understand this section carefully, so that you get a solid understanding of it. I highly recommend reading the upcoming part of this lesson multiple times. Your ability to intellectually grasp what I am about to share and then experience it will change your life in ways you cannot even begin to fathom. My life has never been the same again ever since I grasped this lesson.

Awareness and the Mind

The most powerful tool in the world, for all its seeming complexities and unfathomable powers, can be simplified down to two components— *awareness* and *the mind*.

You've heard these words, "awareness" and "mind," before and have probably used them many times in conversation. Because they may mean different things to each of you, I'd like to begin our study by first defining these words. Doing so will allow us to create a *shared vocabulary*, in turn a shared understanding of the meaning of these words, and also a shared understanding of how these words should be applied in the context of our study together. Recalibrating your understanding of these words and the use of them will allow you to better understand what I am sharing. Others may use these words differently, but it is very important in order for us to work successfully together that we have a shared vocabulary.

Let's start by defining the mind. *I define the mind as a vast space with many different areas within it.*

For example, one area of the mind is happiness, another area of the mind is jealousy, yet another area is anger. One area of the mind is the repository for memories, another the source of intuition and creativity, yet another the essence of all you need to know about food. There are areas of the mind where you can learn about dance, photography, computer programming, gardening, and more. The mind is a vast space with many different areas within it. That is how I would like you to look at the mind.

Now let's define awareness. *I define awareness as a glowing ball of light. An untethered glowing orb, so to speak, that can float around.*

You may have other ideas about how to define these words, but as

I expressed, for the purpose of creating a shared vocabulary, this is how they are being defined. Please refrain from making them any more complex than this by intellectually ramifying the definitions you have just read. For the sake of learning, we want to keep it incredibly simple. Trust the process. It's important for you to hold on to these definitions clearly as you proceed with your study. One suggestion is that you write down on a piece of paper these two definitions and post them somewhere that will allow you to see them daily. Commit them to memory. I cannot emphasize enough how important it is for you to understand them the way I have defined them for you in order to truly grasp the essence of the inner workings of the mind.

Having defined awareness and the mind, let's explore their characteristics and how they interact and work together.

Awareness and the mind are two distinctly different and separate things. Awareness moves, the mind does not.

Your awareness, untethered, can move to any area of the mind. If awareness, this glowing ball of light, moves to a particular area of the mind, then it lights up that specific area of the mind. It is a glowing ball of light, after all, and wherever it goes in the mind, that area of the mind gets lit up.

When it lights up a particular area of the mind, you become conscious of that area of the mind. As long as awareness remains in this area of the mind, this area will continue to remain lit up and you will be conscious of it.

As an example, say awareness moves to the area of the mind that is called happiness. When this glowing ball of light goes to the area of the mind that is happiness, it is going to light up that area of the mind. And when it lights up that area of the mind, you become conscious of being happy. You experience being happy. You are in the happy area of the mind.

Here's an important thing to note. Are you happy? No! You are not happy. You are in an area of the mind called happiness. Because your awareness is in the happy area of the mind, you are conscious of being happy.

You are pure awareness functioning in an area of the mind called happiness.

If awareness moves from the area of the mind called happiness and goes to an area of the mind called sadness, it will light up this area of the mind. Now you will become conscious of being sad.

Are you sad? No! You are pure awareness residing temporarily in an area of the mind called sadness and having a sad experience. As long as your awareness is in this area of the mind, you will experience being sad. Thankfully, you can move awareness from the sad area of the mind to any other area of the mind you wish to go to.

And you can do this by using your willpower and powers of concentration. We will learn about this in the upcoming chapters.

The conclusion is, you are not the mind. Rather, you are pure awareness traveling through various areas of the mind. Awareness moves, the mind does not. Wherever you go, wherever awareness goes in the mind, that particular area of the mind lights up. When that particular area lights up, you become conscious of that area of the mind, and you experience that area of the mind.

Take a moment to truly grasp this concept, as it will form the foundation of everything we will study together. At this point I'm sharing with you the theory of how awareness and the mind work. In subsequent lessons I will share examples of how awareness and the mind function in daily life.

Another conclusion that we can surmise from all this is that when you are in the angry area of the mind, you are no longer conscious of being in the sad area of the mind, nor are you conscious of being in the happy area of the mind, or the fear area of the mind, or any other area of the mind. You are only conscious of being in the angry area of the mind until awareness moves out of that area and moves to another area of the mind, and you then become conscious of this new area.

Imagine yourself exploring a large, dark cave while holding a lantern in your hand. The cave is your mind and the lantern is your awareness, that glowing ball of light. As you walk to one corner of the cave, the lantern lights up that corner, and you are able to see everything here and experience this corner of the cave. Now, if you were to leave this corner and walk to the other side of the dark cave, the corner that you were in would no longer be lit up, and you would not be able to see anything there or experience it. Wherever in the cave you walk with your lantern is what you will see and experience. Awareness and the mind work exactly the same way, except that you are the lantern, young Grasshopper.

The area of the mind where awareness parks itself determines what you are conscious of in your mind at that very moment.

Let's summarize this lesson in point form so that it is crystal clear to us:

1. The first step in understanding the mind is to understand that awareness and the mind are two distinctly different things.
2. You are not the mind. You are pure awareness traveling through different areas of the mind.
3. Awareness moves, the mind does not.
4. Whatever area of the mind awareness goes to is the area of the mind that you become conscious of.
5. By using your willpower and powers of concentration, you can move your awareness, this glowing ball of light, to any area of the mind you want to go to.

This simple, profound, and timeless insight into the inner workings of the mind was shared with me by my guru. It has been at the heart of the spiritual teachings of my guru's lineage for well over two millennia and is one of the central pillars of Hindu metaphysics. This insight single-handedly changed everything in my life. The knowledge that I am pure awareness traveling through various areas of the mind made me realize that I have the power to choose, at any given moment, which area of the mind I wish to be in. If I can choose which area of the mind I wish to be in, then I am also choosing what my experience is.

This revelation, articulated so clearly and simply, empowered me with the fact that my experience in this life is completely in my control. This was liberating to me. The realization of this insight began to unravel infinite possibilities and uses of this knowledge.

I hope that you are starting to understand why what I have shared in this lesson is so important. Your first step is to intellectually understand how awareness and the mind work as I have shared it. Your next step is to experience it within your mind. The realization of this profound insight will come after you have many repeated experiences of being able to control where your awareness goes in your mind.

Tipping the Scale of Experiences

One experience is not always enough to make a profound change within someone. Often, we need multiple similar experiences to create the change that we want.

Imagine a scale that is tilted to one side. The pan on the right is carrying the weight of the experiences you have had that shape your current perspective on the mind. As you have new experiences of the mind by your understanding of how awareness and the mind work, you add weight to the pan on the left. The more experiences you have of knowing that you can control where awareness goes in your mind, the more weight is added to this pan. At some point, you have enough accumulated experiences to tip the scale to the left. At this moment change is created, and you take on a new way of viewing your mind. The realization that you can control where awareness goes in your mind sets in. And as my guru shared with me, "Once you realize something, you can't unrealize it."

The insights acquired from accumulated repeated experiences of controlling awareness in the mind now drive how you use your mind on a daily basis.

In the next two lessons I'll share various analogies to describe awareness and the mind so that you can better understand it. Grasping this concept is so critical for success that it is due its appropriate time and attention.

The Mind as a Mansion

In better understanding awareness and the mind, let's view the mind as a mansion.

Imagine a grand mansion set on an estate at the end of a long, meandering paved driveway with sprawling gardens around it. Large front double doors open into a marble-floored foyer graced with a sweeping staircase at the front, a grand chandelier overhead, and flanked with hallways and towering wood-paneled walls. You are now about to explore its catacomb of hallways, stairwells, floors, and rooms.

This mansion is your mind. Now imagine awareness as you.

Just like any house you live in, you can go to any room within it that you want to go to. Each room in this mansion represents a different area of the mind. One room is joy, another room is happiness, another anger, another jealousy, and so on. Imagine yourself, pure awareness, walking through this mansion.

You walk up the sweeping staircase, arrive at a grand landing, and take the passage to the left. You open the first door that you see, step into the room, and close the door behind you.

You realize that you have stepped into a room that represents an area of the mind called happiness. You become conscious of being happy. You are not conscious of what is in the next room, or the room down the hall, or the room upstairs, or the room downstairs. You, awareness, is absorbed in being in this room called happiness and experiencing being happy. Are you happy? No, you are not. You are pure awareness residing temporarily in the happy area of the mind.

Now you step out of the room, close the door behind you, and walk down to the end of the hallway. You choose to open another door, walk into the room, and close the door behind you. You discover that you are now in the angry room—an area of the mind called anger—and therefore you experience being angry. Are you angry? No, you are not. You are in an area of the mind called anger, but *you* are not anger. You are pure awareness residing temporarily in the anger area of the mind.

While you are in the anger area of the mind, or the angry room in the case of the mansion, you do not experience happiness. You do not experience what is in the room you were in previously. Why? Because you are no longer in that room. You are in a different room right now, and therefore will experience what this room has to offer, and this room holds the feeling of anger. You also realize while you are here that you were just in happiness and that you consciously moved to anger.

You leave the angry room and continue with your exploration of this mansion. Each room offers a different experience, and while you are in a particular room you are not conscious of the other rooms you were previously in.

This is just like awareness and the mind. When you look at the mind as a mansion with many different rooms, where each room is a different area of the mind, you realize that you can choose which room in the mansion of the mind to visit, or even to live in. The choice is yours. The longer you stay in one area of the mind, the more comfortable it becomes to you. There is nothing wrong with choosing to stay in one area of the mind, or in one particular room, as long as that area is uplifting and is serving you well.

Have you ever known someone to live in a house so long that they become overly attached to it? Maybe they live in a small two-bedroom house with six children, but they are so attached to the house that they won't move, even when they have the money for a larger home and it is clear that the house is no longer serving them well. This is just an example to illustrate that people can get very attached to different "houses," or areas of the mind. I know people who have become so attached to the fear area of the mind that they live there permanently. They have moved into this room, thrown away their passport since they have no intention to leave, applied for residency, and been approved to be a permanent resident in the Country of Fear. As a result, they live in a perpetual state of fear.

How does a man like Mandela, who was imprisoned for twenty-seven years, maintain a positive state of mind? Was it because he was able to keep his awareness anchored, with his willpower and powers of concentration, in an area of the mind that was the source of his vision of freedom for his people? Perhaps so, because if he was not able to control his awareness, the terrible conditions he was subjected to would have taken his awareness to truly miserable areas of the mind, and the vision he had of ending apartheid most likely would never have come to fruition.

He was not in denial of his physical environment. However, he was keenly aware that though he could not control his physical environment, he *could* choose where he wished to reside in his mind. The jail cell could imprison his body but not his awareness. His glowing ball of light was free to live in the room of freedom in his mind, and thrive and plan the freedom of millions.

When you hear someone say, "My mind wanders all over the

place," you know now that this is an incorrect statement. It is incorrect because your mind does not wander. What wanders? Awareness! Awareness is moving from one area of the mind to another. In the case of this analogy, the mansion is not moving. The mansion stays rooted to its foundation. It is you, pure awareness, that is moving from one room to another within this mansion and having a different experience as you travel from one room to another.

Now, you may not live in a mansion, but many of you experience something similar in your home. Let's assume that in your home you do have a kitchen, a bathroom, perhaps multiple bedrooms, and a living room. Each room is designed for a different purpose and experience. If you go to the kitchen, it may be for the purpose of preparing a meal, getting a drink, or opening the refrigerator for the umpteenth time that day to see if miraculously its contents have changed. The kitchen represents the food area of the mind. You don't go to the kitchen because you need to take a nap or do not feel clean. There are other rooms for these things. Each room in your house serves a function and provides you with a different experience. The mind is no different.

The analogy of the mind as a mansion is another way to convey the concept that there is a clear separation between awareness and the mind. You are not the mind; rather, you are pure awareness moving through different areas of the mind and, most important, you can choose what areas of the mind (which rooms in the mansion) you wish to spend time in.

When I share this, people lament, "Oh, but this is so difficult." Everything is difficult if you have never learned how to do it and you never practice doing it. Making pizza from scratch is difficult if you don't know how to do it, have never been taught how to do it, have never done it before, and have never practiced doing it. Why would learning to control awareness in the mind be any different?

The rewards born of learning to control awareness in the mind far exceed the effort that goes into doing so.

LESSON 3.4

Awareness as a Traveler

In this lesson, to help deepen and solidify our understanding of awareness and the mind, let's look at awareness as a traveler and the mind as the world. This is an analogy my guru would often use to bring clarity to this topic.

Imagine yourself, pure awareness, boarding a plane at JFK airport in New York, flying across the United States, and landing in San Francisco. An hour later you find yourself in downtown San Francisco experiencing this city and all that it has to offer. Although you are in a place called San Francisco, having San Francisco experiences, you are *not* San Francisco. You are pure awareness, having San Francisco experiences. And it is quite evident that you are certainly not in New York anymore.

A few days later, you leave San Francisco and board a plane to New Delhi. Hours later, consumed by jet lag, you stumble out of the airport, only to find yourself surrounded by a horde of people. The sights, sounds, and smells intrude on your senses uninvited, forcing a stark awakening that you are no longer in San Francisco.

You are now in New Delhi, having New Delhi experiences. Are *you* New Delhi? No, you are in a place called New Delhi, but you are not New Delhi. You are pure awareness. The experiences you have in this city are vastly different than those you had in San Francisco. When you are in New Delhi, you no longer experience San Francisco because you are no longer there. When you are in New Delhi, you experience what this city has to offer.

Let's surmise a few things from this.

1. The same way a traveler can go to different cities around the world and have a variety of experiences, your awareness can travel within the mind and have many types of experiences.

2. As a traveler traveling the world experiencing various cities, at any given point in time, you can only experience one city at a time. The same is true for awareness in the mind. It can only experience one area of the mind at a time.

3. Whatever area of the mind awareness visits, it is not that area. It is simply experiencing the area that it is visiting. It always is pure awareness. Similarly, you are never the city you visit.

You are always experiencing some area of the mind, but do not think for a moment that the area of the mind that you are experiencing is you. *You are pure awareness* experiencing whatever area of the mind you have traveled to.

When you feel angry, no longer think or say, "I am angry." This is an incorrect statement. Rather say to yourself, "I am in the angry area of the mind and experiencing being angry. I am not angry, I am pure awareness having an angry experience."

Similarly, when you feel happy you can say, "I've traveled to the happy area of the mind and I am having a happy experience. I am not happy, I am pure awareness having a happy experience."

By doing so, you will realize that you are not the mind: rather, you are pure awareness traveling within the mind. You are a free citizen of the mind and are free to travel to any area of the mind you wish to go to. This is your right. Claim it. Use this given freedom wisely, bearing in mind that our travels within the mind are not without their consequences.

The Prepared Traveler

Here's an important observation from this analogy for you to note. As a traveler, you chose which city you wanted to go to. You made the choice, then proceeded to travel there. This ability to make a conscious decision about where you want to travel to is available to your awareness as well. You can choose which area of the mind you wish to go to. Most people surrender this decision-making process to their environment. And *I define the environment in this case as the people and things around you.* They allow their environment to dictate where their awareness goes in their mind, and, as a result, to dictate the type of experiences they will have.

When you choose which city you wish to travel to, you can prepare for the journey. If I choose to go to Anchorage, Alaska, it may be wise for me to pack some warm clothing. I definitely will not need warm clothing if I am headed to Madurai, India, in April during its scorching summer.

If I am going to talk to my daughter about something that is bothering her emotionally, then I may choose to move my awareness to the empathy area of the mind. When my awareness is there, I can better express empathy to her. Doing so allows me to prepare for the conversation. I'm now equipped to express the emotions that are most helpful to her at this moment. If we do not have sufficient control over our awareness, in such a case our awareness could go to the problem-solving area of the mind, and instead of expressing empathy to her I would be giving her solutions—perhaps not the most helpful and timely thing for her to hear at that moment.

Being able to control where your awareness goes in your mind al-lows you to be prepared for an experience the same way that a traveler who knows her destination can prepare accordingly for it.

Chapter 4

WHERE AWARENESS GOES,
ENERGY FLOWS

The Importance of Terminology

A s we proceed with our study together, I want to strongly empha-size the importance of using the correct terminology. I would like you to use the words "awareness" and "mind" precisely as I have defined them in this book.

This is important because we want to train our subconscious to understand the specific meaning of these words. A "word" is defined as "a single distinct meaningful element of speech or writing." Based on this definition and for the sake of clarity, it is really important to have one meaning for a word and not multiple meanings. When we have multiple different definitions of a word, it confuses the subconscious mind.

Here's an example to illustrate what I mean. If we give the command "sit" to a dog, it understands, based on the training we have given it, that it has to lower its hind legs and essentially sit. Now, if we start using the word "sit" to indicate that we want it to run, that will confuse the dog. Every time we say "sit," it will not know whether to sit or to run. But if we reserve one word for one action, then there is no confusion at all as to what we mean by it.

Our mind is no different. A lot of people will make statements such as, "Walking my dog each evening is my meditation." I've heard others say, "Cooking is my meditation." Then there are others who sit down cross-legged, eyes closed, spine erect, while consciously regulating their breath, and call this their meditation. Which is it? How can these vastly different acts that range from picking up poop, preparing a meal, and being conscious of breathing all be called meditation?

When we assign such varying definitions to one word, the meaning gets muddied, and it confuses our subconscious mind. Once it is in its confused state, the subconscious is no longer able to effectively help us.

When the subconscious understands the meaning of a word and what it specifically represents, it can better leverage this understanding to guide us.

For the purpose of us working together, it is important that I recalibrate your subconscious to the definition of awareness and the mind that I use. This will eliminate any confusion in your subconscious as to what these words mean and how to use them appropriately. The subconscious is built on information that is put into it. This information can be acquired through reading, experiencing, seeing, repetition of action, and more. In order not to confuse or overburden the subconscious, the acquired information must be defined and organized. Doing so gives the subconscious the ability to use this information to serve us in a way that behooves us.

We want to train the subconscious by giving it clear definitions and concepts so that it can have a clear intellectual understanding of how everything works. Once the subconscious is trained in this way, then it can in turn help guide us in getting a deeper understanding of concepts such as awareness and the mind.

For those of you who may want a little deeper insight into this, here is a side note for you. When the subconscious is trained in this way, it becomes easier for the superconscious mind to work through the subconscious mind, because the superconscious mind works best with an organized, structured, disciplined, and clarified subconscious. A big part of the training I had with my guru was to reprogram my subconscious so that I could better access my superconscious mind. Hence, routines and rituals were a big part of monastic training, in part to help structure the subconscious.

Now, back to using the correct terminology. As you start to use the correct terminology in the way you've been instructed to, you reinforce what you have learned and train your subconscious in clearly understanding these new concepts. New patterns will form in your subconscious, which in turn will then start to guide you.

Here's an example. Instead of saying "My mind wanders all the time," the correct statement would be "My awareness wanders all the time."

We know this because the mind does not wander, but rather, awareness moves within the mind. By using the correct terminology, we train the subconscious to understand how awareness and the mind work. In doing so, we are also teaching the subconscious to understand the characteristics of each of them, the laws that govern them, and more.

If we are not disciplined in using the correct terminology but instead use these words interchangeably, saying at times, "My mind just wandered away," and at other times, "Sorry, could you repeat what you just said? My awareness just wandered away," then we confuse the subconscious mind. We would be doing to the subconscious mind what we did to the dog in the example I gave earlier, where we used the word "sit" to represent "sit" and "run."

It's highly critical as part of our study that you begin using the correct terminology. Going forward, be very conscious of how you use these words in your daily speech.

Awareness in Daily Life

Now that I have given you a theoretical insight into how awareness and the mind work, let me give you a few real-life scenarios that depict how they work in an everyday setting.

Let's take a night out at the movies as an example. It's a quiet Saturday afternoon, and you're lounging around your home not doing anything particularly important when your friend calls you up and says, "Hey, let's go watch the latest Bond movie. Let's see what James is up to this time."

You excitedly reply, "Let's do it."

Within an hour you find yourself sitting in a seat next to your friend, chatting while the ads play before the movie starts. You're there early to get a good seat, secure enough popcorn to feed a whole village in a developing nation just for yourself, and add a drink large enough to make your bladder feel defeated at the mere sight of it.

You and your friend are analyzing last night's political debate. Awareness is anchored in this area of the mind. Partway through your conversation the lights begin to dim and the crowd starts to go silent. You both end your conversation and shift your awareness to the screen.

If the movie you are about to watch was created by an outstanding director, the story will be able to move your awareness from one area of the mind to another.

The opening scene of a James Bond movie is always riveting: conjured up from the depths of the director's wildest imagination, it has the ability to snatch your awareness away from the area of the mind that it was in and anchor it in the area of the mind that is exciting. Bond makes a miraculous escape as you hold your breath, completely fixated on the screen.

The scene ends, and the movie's opening credits begin. Enticing music accompanying an artfully crafted title sequence with silhouettes of dancing women has the potent power to take the awareness of every boy who dreamed of being a spy to a sensual area of the mind. From here, awareness could be taken to the technology area of the mind as Bond assesses Q's latest array of innovations. Then, as M divulges to Bond intel on the bad guy's maniacal plans to rule the world, your awareness is redirected to the fear area of the mind.

And so it continues. Awareness is catapulted from one area of the mind to another, driven by the carefully crafted emotional scenes of the movie, until the end is reached. The power of emotion has the magnetic force to latch on to your awareness and move it to areas of the mind associated with that emotion. As the lights in the theater come up and your emotions begin to subside, you turn to your friend excitedly and exclaim, "That was so awesome! I freaking love Bond!"

The better the movie, the less conscious you will be of watching it. In a deeply enthralling movie, your awareness would be so absorbed in what you were watching that you could be oblivious of passing time and all that is around you. As your subconscious mechanically guides your hand to repeatedly stuff popcorn in your mouth, your awareness is on a ride in your mind that was meticulously designed by the film's director, experiencing one area after another. And with each area of the mind that you visit, you experience the emotions associated with that area.

Now, this is obviously what you paid for. You signed up to be entertained—to be taken to all these various areas of the mind and experience them. You gave the director and the story *permission* to take your awareness on a journey in the mind in order to have all of these different experiences.

The important thing to realize is that the exact same thing happens to most people all day long. Most people unknowingly give their environment, the people and things around them, permission to move their awareness from one area of the mind to another all day, every day.

For most people, the people and things in their lives become the director of their daily experiences. Their environment dictates where their awareness goes, causing them to have a myriad of experiences throughout the day. Not all of these experiences are sanctioned by the experiencer. Some of these experiences are uplifting, others not. Some are emotionally disturbing and others joyful. It's as unpredictable as where a falling leaf might land on the ground.

Unlike a movie, in which you are quite conscious of the genre of emotions you are about to experience, these unreviewed and not preapproved emotions can cause an upheaval in your state of mind and result in an unpredictable day.

When we allow our environment to dictate where our awareness goes, we essentially become a slave to everyone and everything around us. Our awareness becomes an actor in an unscripted show. The unpredictability of the unwritten script leaves our mind and nervous system at the mercy of our environment—things could go well or be horribly painful.

Let me give you an example. Priya is an entrepreneur, married with two kids. When she wakes up in the morning her awareness is mostly absorbed in her family, whom she loves very much. Though there is some amount of chaos in the morning as she finagles with the whims of her kids to get them ready and out the door for school, her awareness is mostly in the happy area of the mind. After dropping her kids off, she heads to her office.

As she drives down the freeway, a car swerves in front of her, almost causing a collision. Priya is very conscious of how close she just came to being in a pretty bad accident, and this upsets her considerably. When the car cut her off, her awareness was flung to the fear area of the mind momentarily before ricocheting off to the angry area of the mind. The happy area of the mind that she was in a few moments ago is now a distant memory at best. Seething with anger, she mentally curses the driver as she continues on her drive to work.

She pulls into the parking lot in front of her office, still emotionally agitated by the incident on the freeway. She realizes that she can't begin her day this way and desperately tries to move her awareness to a more uplifting area of the mind, knowing that her state of mind has a massive impact on her team. She walks through her beautifully designed office, greeting some of her team members, as she makes her way to her private room on the second floor.

Barely has she sat at her desk when a team member walks in wearing a shamefaced look on his face and confesses, "Priya, I'm so sorry. I forgot to order the part that we needed for our project on time. So now it will come in tomorrow, and we are not going to finish our project today as you had planned. I just felt you needed to know right away."

Upon hearing this, Priya reacts, and her awareness is dragged to a frustrated area of her mind. Her head collapses into her hands. Almost immediately, she looks up in exasperation and says, "How could you have forgotten to order it? We discussed this last week, and I told you we needed it today."

After a brief conversation aimed at finding a solution to this problem, her employee leaves the room, and Priya leans back in her chair, exhaling slowly. Her day is only just beginning. A minute later her phone rings and she picks it up. It's a potential client whom they've been trying to bid for a job with for the last seven months. The voice on the other end of the line says, "We love the proposal that you put together for us. We are happy with everything and think it's great. We want to hire your company for the job!"

She's elated. They've worked tirelessly to secure this client, and it has paid off. At this news, her awareness is propelled into the excited area of the mind. After hanging up, she opens her laptop and decides to check her email. She sees fifty-three new messages in her inbox, including notifications of four meetings she needs to attend before lunch. Her awareness begins a slow but inevitable slide to the overwhelmed area of the mind. The elation of the moment starts to dissipate. Her awareness had barely any time to stay in the excited area of the mind before it was summoned to the next location.

This is only the first couple of hours of Priya's day. Her awareness has bounced around the mind like a ball in a pinball machine. The rest of her day is no different.

Because Priya allows the people and things around her to dictate where her awareness goes for the greater part of her day, it causes her to experience a rapid fire of changing emotions. This is not only mentally and emotionally exhausting for her, but it also creates a tremendous strain on her nervous system, which has to experience a variety of emotions in such a short period.

As a result, Priya becomes a slave to everyone and everything around her. Her environment dictates most of what her awareness experiences throughout the day. Unknowingly, she has given her environment permission to take her awareness from one area of the mind to another, and consequently, she is uplifted or brought down by the areas of the mind she visits.

Unfortunately, this is how the majority of people live and go about their daily lives. They hand over control of their awareness to everyone and everything around them. What they experience throughout the day is mainly dictated by what their environment has chosen for them to experience. A cat video on a social feed could bring a massive smile to their face. A text message could send them into a frenzied mental argument for three hours. Watching the news sends a depressive wave over them and causes them to question the direction the world is going in. And so it goes throughout the day—their awareness is nothing more than a puppet dancing to the whims and megrims of the people and things around them.

The inability to sufficiently control where your awareness goes in the mind results in you living as a slave to your environment.

But we do not need to live this way. Instead, we can free ourselves from such a tumultuous state of mind by realizing that we can take control of our awareness and choose exactly where we want it to go in our mind. When we decide to do this, we gain freedom, because when we direct our awareness to where we want it to go, we are choosing what we experience. Once we take control of our awareness, nobody can decide how we feel unless we give them permission to do so.

LESSON 4.3

Awareness the Dog

We can compare awareness being tugged every which way by its environment to a dog on a walk. Imagine awareness as a dog, and let's view this dog in three categories: trained, untrained and leashed, and untrained and unleashed.

We've all most likely seen a dog that is untrained and unleashed. It is the one running wild in a park, evoking a small degree of fear in you as it hurtles in your direction with a crazed look in its glazed eyes and tongue flapping in the wind. Its unshackled energy drives the erratic course on which it bounds. It doesn't take much for something to get this dog's attention and engagement—be it a whiff of a cat, another canine, or a freaked-out pigeon. There is little to no control over this four-legged beast. It does not heed the calls of its owner. Getting it to return is a virtually impossible task until it's ready to eat and rest.

There are people whose awareness is not dissimilar to that of this untrained and unleashed dog. Their glowing ball of light, unrestrained by their willpower, indiscriminately engages with anything and everything around them. Any of these engagements could cause a reaction and send awareness hurtling off into some area of the mind, triggering an outburst of corresponding emotions. And when the external world is not present to engage with this untrained awareness, it bounds around within the mind like an untrained dog off its leash. It, awareness, simply won't stop moving in the mind, and this is demonstrated by incessant thoughts, mental conversations and arguments, indecision, and more. Fatigue inevitably sets in; the body falls asleep, but awareness is still bounding around the mind, causing restlessness, odd dreams, and a body that wakes up hours later unrested. This tireless dog then begins another mercurial day.

Let's look at the untrained and leashed dog now. This is a dog that is bound by a leash but still has the behavioral patterns of the dog I just described. It wants to run all over the place, but the leash that it is attached to keeps it bound in a fixed proximity to its owner.

Having lived in New York City for over a decade, I've seen many dogs take their owners for a walk. These dogs are always leading the way, yanking their owners all over the place as the smells of the city overwhelm their nostrils and evoke a feeling of sidewalk exploratory adventure. The tug of war between human and hound is the natural state.

This is similar to people who have some control over their awareness. They may not always be conscious of where their awareness is at any given point in time, but when they are, they often have sufficient willpower to rein it back. It's those times when you realize that your dog has its nose in something you don't want it to be in, and you rein the leash back in. The dog may have some unidentifiable stuff on its nose that you may need to wipe off, but you've prevented a disaster by responding in time. Similarly, these people may find their awareness engaged in a situation that is progressively getting worse, but they have sufficient control to withdraw their awareness from it before it escalates into something regrettable.

Finally, we have the trained dog. And for this I'll share with you an experience I had in the Virgin Islands once. On a holiday there I got to know a person who worked for the FBI and was part of their K-9 unit. Consequently, he was assigned a German shepherd. This person shared with me that whenever he walks his dog it stays by his side. This trained and unleashed dog even knows the exact distance from its owner it needs to be.

The man demonstrated to me one day the dog's level of self-control. He placed a big bowl of food in front of his dog and instructed it to sit and wait, for what must have seemed like hours to this dog, as saliva cascaded from its mouth. This entire time the dog made no attempt to eat the food, though he did glance beseechingly at his owner a few times. Almost a minute went by before he gave the command to the dog to eat, at which moment his dog pounced on the bowl and devoured its contents.

There are a few people who have trained their awareness to be like this dog. Obedient. Sitting at attention awaiting instruction, having renounced the need to engage indiscriminately with its environment. Willpower is its reins and wisdom is its guide. Freedom and peace are born from the ability to choose what and whom to engage with, and when. For these rare individuals, their mind, the epicenter of control over their life's experiences, is a sanctuary to be safeguarded. These souls know that an unbridled awareness inevitably leads to a beleaguered state of mind.

Now, I know I have been writing in a way that makes it sound like our awareness is something that is separate from us. I do this intentionally so that I can communicate concepts clearly to you. Please know that you are pure awareness. When awareness is aware of itself, which we will learn about, awareness can direct itself.

To let your awareness be like an untrained dog is an exhausting way to live, and it wastes so much of your incredibly precious, finite time and energy on this planet. Ultimately, we want to train awareness to be like this K-9 dog: obedient, and awaiting your instruction before it goes and gets itself entangled in someone or something.

The benefit of having control over your awareness is that you will have so much more control over your life, over how you interact with your environment, react and respond to experiences, make decisions, and more, all of which will lead to better outcomes in life.

LESSON 4.4

The Story of Energy

In the first half of the twentieth century, my guru coined the phrase, "Where awareness goes, energy flows." It was born out of his many profound realizations of the inner workings of the mind—realizations that led to his own Self-Realization and the transformation of countless lives over many decades. This phrase perfectly encapsulates the relationship between awareness and energy.

Since then, sadly, many have modified the words of this phrase and claimed it as their own. Plagiarism is anything but flattery. When you can feel secure in your own realizations, acknowledging others for theirs comes naturally and is done with honor.

For all the attention that I've given awareness in this book, energy deserves no less. After all, energy is everything. One of the critical things in learning about the mind is to understand the role that energy plays in it.

Let's begin our foray into energy by sticking to tradition and defining it first. It is a word so commonly used, but I must wonder how many people can accurately define it. Scientists define energy as the ability or capacity to do work. Dictionaries add additional definitions, one of which is "the physical or mental strength that allows you to do things."

Science further expounds on energy by sharing these properties:

- Energy cannot be created or destroyed;
- Energy can be transferred from one thing to another;
- Energy can be transformed from one form to another.

I see energy, at its core, as a pure intelligent force permeating all existence. It is in you, in me, in the trees that sway in the wind, in the water that flows and evaporates, in the clouds that shade us, in the stars that glitter in the night sky, and in all that is seen and unseen. Though it changes, it is the one constant in life. It makes up all of life. It is the very essence of us.

The Serbian-American scientist Nikola Tesla added a great additional insight into energy. He said, "If you want to find the secrets of the universe, think in terms of energy, frequency and vibration." This statement so succinctly captures the fundamental principles of the Hindu philosophy that I practice.

I'll elaborate on Tesla's quote just a little and say that everything is made up of energy and that energy is vibrating at a certain frequency. Some of us feel energy, and depending on the frequency it is vibrating at, it may align with us or not. At that point, we may be heard to make statements such as "This has good energy," or "I feel a lot of bad energy in this place."

Ultimately, there is no such thing as good or bad energy. There is just energy, vibrating at frequencies that are aligned with us or not. Heavy metal music vibrates at a certain frequency that is uplifting to some and draining to others.

In a previous lesson, I suggested that one way to look at energy is to look at it the same way we look at water. I pointed out that whatever we water in the garden will start to grow, be it weeds or flowers. Energy works the same way, meaning that whatever we invest energy in, be it something positive or negative, it will start to grow and manifest in our life. It's important to be reminded and to note that energy has no ability to discriminate between what is positive and what is negative. Our life is a manifestation of where we invest our energy.

Keeping this in mind, as well as Gurudeva's phrase "Where awareness goes, energy flows," we can form the conclusion that where our awareness goes is where our energy flows, and where our energy flows is what manifests in our lives. This is a critical principle to grasp. It forms the foundation of how things manifest in our lives, how patterns are formed and strengthened in our mind, and more.

Where awareness goes, energy flows. Commit this to memory.

Let's look at how the mind, awareness, and energy work together.

If awareness, this glowing ball of light, travels to a particular area of the mind, then that is where energy is flowing, because as Gurudeva says, "Where awareness goes, energy flows." If awareness goes to the happy area of the mind, then that is where your energy is flowing, and when energy is flowing to the happy area of the mind, it strengthens that area of the mind.

The more frequently I send my ball of light to the happy area of the mind, the more energy flows to this area of the mind, and the more energy I deposit in this area of the mind.

The Mind as the Garden

Imagine the mind as a beautiful vast garden with many garden beds within it. Old reclaimed hardwood shapes the beds that are filled with black, healthy soil. Picture one garden bed planted with tomatoes, another with kale, another with green beans, and so on. There are at least forty garden beds in this vast garden, each bed is planted with a vegetable or an herb, and all are equally spaced from one another with gravel paths separating them.

Imagine that every day for a month you only watered the garden bed that had tomatoes planted in it. The tomato plants would grow tall and beautiful, but all the other plants—the green beans, kale, pumpkins—would start to wither, become flaccid, and die. Only the garden bed that is watered would thrive.

Now see your mind as a big garden with lots of garden beds in it, but in this visualization, each garden bed represents a different area of the mind. One garden bed could be compassion, another happiness, another jealousy, with the one next to it anger (anger and jealousy are neighbors, you know), another joy, and so forth.

When your awareness goes to the angry garden bed, that is where your energy is flowing. This means that you are watering this garden bed and everything in it will start to grow. As energy flows here, the angry garden bed, this area of the mind, starts to strengthen. The more energy you deposit here, the stronger this area of the mind becomes.

If awareness goes to the happy garden bed, the happy area of the mind, then that is where your energy is flowing. This garden bed, this area of the mind, begins to thrive and strengthens as it is infused with more energy than the rest.

If your awareness is constantly going to one particular garden bed, or area of the mind, then that is where your energy is flowing, and this is the area of the mind that you are "watering," so to speak. The more you water this area of the mind with your energy, the stronger it becomes. There are consequences to a particular area of the mind getting strengthened, and we will look at that soon.

So how do you control where your energy flows and which area of your mind is being strengthened? The answer should be quite evident now!

Control where your awareness goes, and you will control where your energy flows. Control where your energy is flowing, and you will control the area of the mind that is being strengthened and, essentially, what is manifesting in your life.

You must strive to grasp this fundamental principle of how the mind, awareness, and energy relate to one another. First understand it intellectually; then strive to experience it within you.

You can probably already identify areas of the mind, garden beds, that you have been watering over the years. Some of these garden beds are areas of your mind that express the best of you and others are perhaps the gnarly, thorny weeds that we all need to manage and eradicate.

LESSON 4.5

Emotion's Magnetic Power

In the previous lesson, I shared with you that as awareness repeatedly goes to a particular area of the mind, the more energy flows there, and that area becomes strengthened. What does it mean when I say an area of the mind gets strengthened? To answer this question, we need to understand the relationship between energy, emotion, and awareness.

Strong areas of the mind are built by consistent investment of energy. Now, "strong areas" does not necessarily mean they are positive areas of the mind. There are many who have created very strong negative areas of the mind through their consistency in repeatedly moving awareness to that area, thus moving energy there as well.

We've looked at some of the fundamental laws associated with energy, and now I want to share with you a characteristic of energy that is important: energy is magnetic. As energy builds in an area of the mind, that area strengthens and becomes more magnetic. The more magnetic it becomes, the more power it has to draw awareness to it.

When energy flows to a particular area of the mind, it takes on the characteristic of that area of the mind. For example, if energy flows to the angry area of the mind, this energy now becomes angry emotions. Similarly, if energy flows to the happy area of the mind, it becomes happy emotions.

The Icing on the Cake

I define emotion as energy expressing itself. There is energy inside you, and when that energy comes out of you, it can do so in the form of emotion, such as happiness, anger, sadness, joy, and so forth. Just so we're clear about this, emotion is not the only way energy can come out of you.

When your awareness goes to the happy area of the mind, energy flows there. When energy flows through the happy area of the mind, its frequency changes from what it was to the frequency that is associated with happiness. This energy, now vibrating at the frequency of happiness, comes out of you and expresses itself as happy emotions.

Have you ever put icing on a cake before? You take your favorite icing and stuff it into the decorating syringe-tube. You screw onto one end the frosting tip that has your chosen pattern, and then you start pushing the icing through the syringe. The icing comes out of the syringe in the shape of the pattern of the frosting tip that you have affixed to the syringe.

In this analogy, the mind is the syringe. The icing within it is energy. The various patterned frosting tips are the different areas of the mind.

The icing in the tube is the icing in the tube. It's just icing. The pattern of the frosting tip is what causes the icing to appear differently as it comes out. Similarly, energy is energy. As energy flows through an area of the mind and comes out the other side, so to speak, it takes on the vibration of the area of the mind that it just flowed through.

Energy flowing through the frosting tip of the mind that is shaped like happiness will cause energy to be expressed as happy emotions. Energy flowing through the frosting tip of the mind that is shaped like anger will cause energy to be expressed as angry emotions.

At the heart of it, it's just energy, now vibrating at a different frequency. That's why I love Tesla's saying so much, as it encapsulates so succinctly and beautifully the essence of energy: to "think in terms of energy, frequency and vibration." Understanding this, and awareness and the mind, is so powerful.

Emotion is energy and energy is magnetic. The more the emotion, the more the energy, and the more its magnetic power over awareness.

Some people have areas of the mind that they have been depositing energy into for decades. These areas are so filled with energy that awareness can barely escape its gravitational (magnetic) field. They live in these areas of the mind almost permanently. These areas could be positive or negative, and you've probably met someone who is always negative or sad or depressed. Over the years he has invested so much energy into these areas that they have become so magnetic they have the ability to hold awareness in their proximity throughout the day. When you meet such a person, you may remark to yourself or someone else, "My god, he is such a depressing sod!" Because his awareness lives in a negative area all the time, his response is always one of a negative nature.

These areas of the mind, so filled with energy, become permanent homes for their awareness. But these are not the only places that draw awareness to them.

Many people have unresolved emotional experiences in their subconscious mind—experiences that took place at some point in their life but were never brought to a resolution. These experiences are embedded with emotion and act like strong magnets pulling one's awareness repeatedly to them, causing people to relive their past over and over again. The stronger or more intense the emotions that are tied to the experience, the greater its magnetic pull over awareness. This is another form of accumulated energy within the mind that influences where awareness goes. Unresolved emotional experiences in the subconscious mind are crippling mental leviathans of unfathomable proportions.

For example, you have a heated argument with someone close to you and you choose to let it remain unresolved. You have now created an experience that resides in your subconscious mind and has emotion embedded in it. Since this heated argument created lots of emotion, the magnetic force of this experience in your subconscious is very strong. Throughout the day, you find your awareness being pulled back to this experience in your subconscious mind. Each time your awareness engages with this unresolved emotional experience, you relive the issue and have a mental argument about it.

Until the emotion that is embedded in the experience can be effectively transferred from the experience, it will continue to have the magnetic power to draw awareness to it. But once the emotion has been transferred out of the experience, then this experience that is residing in the subconscious mind no longer has the magnetic power to draw awareness toward it. At this point, this experience no longer has any emotional influence over you.

If you were to observe your mind, you would see that any experience you have in your subconscious that has lots of emotion attached to it, be it uplifting or not, has a greater ability to pull your awareness toward it.

Let's take negative experiences, for example. Some of these experiences could have been created in recent years and others decades ago, and although they were formed decades ago, they still contain emotions, as you have not resolved them, and therefore they still have power over your awareness. To resolve an unresolved emotional experience means to bring that problem to the light of understanding, where the emotions within it no longer affect us, thus allowing us to view the experience objectively and learn from it. This can be accomplished through various forms of therapy and spiritual practices. It's very challenging to learn from an experience if we are emotionally reacting to it.

The Veiled Truth

Where awareness goes, energy flows. What is this phrase saying? Where your awareness goes, that is where your energy is flowing. Quite obvious, isn't it? There is a deeper message here. Can you intuit what that is?

If where awareness goes, energy flows, then can it not be concluded that awareness and energy are the same thing? They are.

Awareness is concentrated energy. As you focus your awareness, you focus your energy. As energy gets ramified, so does awareness.

That is why when you regulate your breath and withdraw energy into one place, you feel more centered. As you withdraw energy, you withdraw awareness. As you center your energy, you center your awareness.

The Power to Manifest

If you want to manifest something in your life, put energy into it. Remember, your life is a manifestation of where you invest your energy. The people around you, the things around you, the opportunities around you—they are all a manifestation of where you have been investing your energy and a testament to the areas of the mind your awareness has been spending time in. Whatever you invest your energy in will start to manifest in your life.

By controlling where your awareness goes, you will control where your energy is flowing, and therefore you will control what manifests in your life. This is the reason why I constantly talk about the importance of understanding awareness and the mind, and the importance of controlling where your awareness goes in your mind.

Failure to manifest is largely due to one's inability to harness and focus awareness, hence one's inability to harness and focus energy. And if you can't sufficiently invest energy in something, don't expect it to come to fruition. Needless to say, other things are needed as well in the process of manifesting what you want in your life, but the ability to harness and focus awareness and energy is an essential ingredient.

So many people are unconscious of where their awareness goes throughout the day. Every minute in the day is an opportunity for awareness to go to an unwholesome area of the mind, deposit energy there, and start to manifest that in your life. Likewise, it is also an opportunity to consciously and wisely choose for awareness to go to an uplifting area of the mind and deposit energy there.

Where awareness goes in your mind is a choice you have. No one can take this away from you. You truly are the steward of your awareness.

Mastery of awareness in the mind is imperative. Everything manifests in the mind before it manifests on the physical plane. And it begins with where awareness is consistently going in your mind.

Similarly, if you want to remove something from your life, take energy out of it, and it will naturally start to fall away. How do you take energy out of it? By moving your awareness away from it. Because once you move your awareness away from it, your energy starts to flow away from it, and it no longer grows. That is how awareness and energy work.

Please read everything I just shared here on awareness and energy a few times, reflect on it, and make every effort to grasp it.

The Mycelium of the Mind

The intrepid travelers among us love exploring the world—seeing new places, experiencing different cultures and traditions, food, art, music, and more. Despite our love of exploring, there are a few places that we love returning to. Whenever we go to these places, we feel like we've returned home. The old familiarity of them—knowing where to go for our favorite meal or coffee, streets to stroll on, familiar faces to greet that we've gotten to know over the years—brings us a sense of comfort.

This experience is mirrored in the mind. Some of us love exploring the mind, and this shows up in the form of curiosity, interest in learning, and fascination with new things, for example. These are among the motives that cause our awareness to explore various areas of the mind.

Then there are areas of the mind that we visit regularly. These are familiar places. Some of them are uplifting places, and others are not. They have become habitual haunts because we have frequented them often over a long period of time. We know these places well. We know what to expect when we go there. Familiarity breeds security—we feel safe with what we know, even if what we know may not be good for us.

Some of these places we visit consciously and are very cognizant that we are there. And some of these places we visit unknowingly. We are taken there by old habit patterns that are ingrained in our subconscious mind, or by the influence of the people and things around us. For example, a person may have a parent who always undermines them, year after year, and this recurring erosion of their self-esteem takes them frequently to a depressive area of the mind.

These areas of the mind that are like home to us have roads that lead to them, pathways that have been carved by awareness traveling back and forth to them for years.

Imagine an explorer in the jungles of Costa Rica. After a few days of making his way through the dense rainforest, he comes across a magnificent thirty-foot-high waterfall. He's keen to share his discovery with others. He knows that to bring others here he needs to create a path to the waterfall. He traces his way back to where he began, leaving markers along the way to map a path to what he has discovered. A month later he brings a group with him. The jungle has voraciously grown back, his markers are less visible, and so as they hike to the waterfall, they clear some of the growth to make the path more navigable and evident.

Five years later, thousands of people have visited the waterfall. What do you think that path looks like now? Is it exactly like what the group experienced the very first time the explorer brought someone to see the waterfall? Of course not. Now there is a clear five-foot-wide trail leading to the waterfall. The journey there is an unhindered one, allowing quick and easy access for anyone wishing to see the waterfall.

Awareness and the mind work the same way. You can look at awareness as the explorer and the mind as the jungle. As your awareness goes back and forth to a particular area of the mind, it creates a path in your mind, the same way a path was created to the waterfall. The more awareness travels up and down this path, the more defined the path becomes. Eventually, a groove starts to form. The consistency and frequency of awareness traveling this path is what shapes the path. The deeper the groove, this mental rut, the easier it is for awareness to stay on track to get to the area of the mind that it frequents. A new trail need not be created each time, and all awareness has to do is travel down this well-formed trench to its destination.

Have you ever come across a person who is so quick to get angry? Even the smallest thing will trigger him and cause him to react with anger. This person, you could say, has paved a groove, a deep mental rut, to the angry area of the mind. Awareness can get from wherever it was in the mind to the angry area of the mind in no time, because there is a well-defined, unhindered path to it.

Awareness travels there with so much ease and with no resistance whatsoever. When awareness reaches the angry area of the mind, so does energy. And here this energy is transformed in its vibration to the frequency of anger, and thus expresses itself as angry emotions. A person who can so easily and quickly get angry is a person who has paved a highway to the angry area of the mind.

Then there are those who have paved a deep groove to uplifting areas of the mind. The gentleman from Mauritius whom I wrote about earlier in the book, whose awareness was always swift to travel to the happy area of the mind, tells me that he has paved a deep groove that leads to this area. The mere sight of a familiar face was enough to send his awareness hurtling to the happy area of the mind, causing his energy to now vibrate at the frequency of happiness, and thus to express itself as happy emotions and an infectious smile.

The mind is filled with paths, paths that we created consciously or unconsciously. Not unlike mycelium, the underground network of fungal threads that links together a forest, there is an endless network of paths in the mind that we created in this life and even in past lives. If you were to carefully observe yourself, you would notice some deeply ingrained grooves in the mind that were not created in this life. Deep reflection would reveal that you did not have sufficient experiences in this life to produce such pathways within the mind. I share this with you for the purpose of helping you understand that not all pathways within the mind may have been created in this life.

So much of where awareness goes in the mind each day is dictated by the paths that exist in the mind. The lack of conscious mastery of where awareness goes in the mind surrenders the fate of awareness, its destination and experience, to these established tracks in the mind.

Now let's tie this learning in with the previous two lessons on energy and emotion. We can surmise from these learnings that as awareness travels repeatedly to an area of the mind, a few things happen for certain:

1. Energy accumulates at the location that awareness goes to;
2. This area, strengthened by the accumulation of energy, is highly magnetic;
3. A well-defined path to this area is created.

It is easy for awareness to succumb to the combination of a well-defined path and an area of the mind that is so magnetically charged. These are the areas of the mind that you find your awareness easily slipping into. The magnetic force of such an area exerts a consistent pull on awareness, and if the conscious grip on awareness loosens, then awareness will travel down the well-paved path to the area that is pulling it.

A person who wakes up in the morning and chooses to spend an hour immersed in a traditional time-tested meditation practice as one of the first acts of the day is certainly paving a path to higher states of mind. She can guide her awareness from the conscious mind nimbly through the subconscious and into the superconscious area of the mind. The consistency with which she performs this practice, and the adherence to clearly defined rituals, all lend strength to the establishment of a path within her mind and the depositing of energy at its final destination. Before long, a deep groove and a highly magnetized area of the mind are created.

This highly magnetized area with a well-defined path to it is accessible to awareness at all times. Its pull on awareness is constant. If this person were to have a challenging experience during the day, it would be quite easy for her awareness to travel down this path to this uplifting area of the mind. The resulting effect would be that she would get to view the experience from a higher state of consciousness, thus allowing her to make wiser decisions on how to respond to the challenge.

I know a few entrepreneurs who have cultivated a path to a higher state of mind that allows them to always have wiser insights into challenges they or their companies face. Upon facing a problem, it is quite easy for their awareness to travel down a well-trodden path that they have spent years creating to a higher state of mind. Upon arrival at this destination, they now have an elevated perspective on the issue, allowing them to see solutions that others can't. This highly magnetized area becomes the default go-to area for their awareness. A person can have multiple such areas in the mind.

On the other hand, some people revel in being terrified by having their awareness taken to the fear area of the mind while watching horror movies every weekend. As this process is repeated, a deep groove leading to the fear area of the mind is created, and vast amounts of energy are deposited here, making this area of the mind highly magnetized. The default perspective and reaction during the day will then tend to be fear, because this is the path of least resistance in the mind, and awareness will travel this road to fear if you do not have enough conscious mastery over it.

My guru was the one who first introduced to me the concept of paths within the mind. He had laid out paths to various areas of the mind, in particular the superconscious state, which helped his monastics experience very precise areas of the mind. The more we traveled to these clearly defined destinations, the more defined the paths to them became, which made it easier for us to get there each time.

We, as humans, have been prolific in carving out paths on earth. Each one of these paths was defined by a clear destination. No government would invest time, energy, and millions of dollars in building a highway to nowhere. There is a path to the top of Everest, highways that take you from New York to Los Angeles, hiking trails through national parks that lead to waterfalls or stunning vistas, and even a lighted path out of a darkened theater when a movie is playing.

We can create and build new paths within the mind. *The path is critical, the destination even more so, because it is the destination that defines the path.* So define the destination first, then build the path to it. Once the destination is known, conscious mastery of awareness in the mind is necessary, and only then can the process of building paths begin. It is, however, critical for you to know that any repeated action, conscious or unconscious, will begin the process of creating a path within the mind.

To summarize, a highly magnetized area of the mind and a well-paved path to it, born of awareness's frequent visits, is the destination of choice for awareness. This is another reason why we must strive to understand how awareness and the mind work, and then strive to gain mastery of awareness in the mind.

Chapter 5

MASTERING AWARENESS

LESSON 5.1

Defining the Purpose and Goal

What are the purpose and the goal of learning how awareness and the mind work? The goal is to gain a conscious mastery of awareness in the mind—to consciously choose where in the mind you want to move awareness to at any given moment. The purpose is manyfold: improving your ability to concentrate, overcoming fear and worry, eliminating anxiety and stress, being more observant, experiencing higher states of mind, and more.

It's important to understand what conscious mastery of awareness in the mind means. It means having the ability to choose, at any given moment in time, where your awareness resides in the mind. This also means having the ability to overcome any internal or external forces that may be attempting to move awareness to an area of the mind that is not of your choosing.

Let's look at a real-world example. The story I am about to share with you is something that I have witnessed many times in New York City. When I lived there, I would quite often take the subway to get

THE POWER OF UNWAVERING FOCUS • DANDAPANI

around the city. On one such subway ride, I was sitting and reading an article on my phone when I noticed a couple, who were standing not far from me, getting into an argument.

The subway car was not too crowded, which in NYC means all the seats were taken and there were only a few people standing. The couple began exchanging emotional words while holding on to the metal stanchion—the petri dish for a slew of visiting international bacteria—which appeared to be the only unshakable thing in their relationship.

As the train hurtled its way to the next stop, their voices rose, allowing those nearby to hear what was being said.

"I can't believe you did that. That is so inappropriate," she exclaimed.

"I can do whatever the hell I want. I don't need your goddamn permission!" he retorted.

His response was fuel for her already intensifying emotions. They started to become more upset and angrier with each other. Their awareness was totally absorbed in the argument, and they were oblivious to the fact that their raised voices were now easily heard by many in the car. As the argument escalated, I started to see the ripple effects of it on the other passengers.

"What a great opportunity for a study of awareness and the mind," I thought as I put my phone down to watch the next episode of "Life in the Subway" unfold. This was going to be more edifying than the article I was reading.

Their raised voices began to get the attention of the people around them. Those closest to the couple started to react first as their awareness was drawn to the argument. You could see, by each person's reaction to the situation, how much control they had over their awareness. And you could also see by their reaction where in their mind their awareness was going.

A lady standing next to the couple sighs as she rolls her eyes, then reaches down, picks up her grocery bag, and huffs off to the other end of the car. Her awareness has gone to the frustrated area of the mind.

A young man, bobbing his head to deafening music emitted by his headphones, breaks into a smile. His awareness has moved to the amused area of the mind. He's keen to see how all of this unfolds. He has no intention of stepping away. This is going to be good.

A man seated across from me exclaims out loud, "Oh, for fuck's sake, enough already!" as he jumps up from his seat, scours the car with his eyes, and makes his way to the connecting door so he can migrate to the next car. He's done listening to this. The couple's argument has upset him so much that he has a physical reaction and needs to remove himself from their proximity.

An elderly lady sitting next to me, wearing a look of great disappointment, turns to me, saying, "There is absolutely no reason to speak to anyone this way, especially your partner. He has no respect for her. What a terrible person." She has allowed her awareness to leave what she was doing and get absorbed in the experience she is witnessing, and the result is that she is now functioning in the same area of the mind that they are in. She's emotionally disturbed and upset by what she has allowed her awareness to get absorbed in.

It isn't long before most people in the subway car are reacting to the couple. Some riders can be seen mumbling something to themselves, expressing their opinion on the argument that they have now made their own. Most of them seem disturbed by this argument in one way or another. Like the elderly lady, they've allowed their awareness to go to the area of the mind that the couple are in—the precincts of annoyance and anger—and therefore have become upset.

This is a completely exhausting way to live. When you have little control over your awareness, your state of mind is at the mercy of everyone and everything around you. You can go from feeling happy to angry in a matter of seconds.

There may be a wiser individual in the subway car, a more mature soul who has greater control over her awareness—enough control so that she can simply observe the couple arguing a few feet away, but not allow her awareness to get emotionally entangled in the area of the mind the couple is in. She holds her awareness steady where it is currently in her mind and watches from there the couple arguing. This is observation, and we will study more about this later.

Who would have thought that the subway was a great classroom for the study of the mind?

When you allow your awareness to get entangled in an experience that is occurring outside of you, you allow yourself to rejoice or suffer from its emotional repercussions. That is why having a conscious mastery over awareness in the mind is so critical: it gives you the freedom, the decision-making power, to decide if you would like to engage in something or not. By having this choice, you are inevitably choosing how you will react as well.

If there is something fun going on, I may choose to let my awareness get engaged in it and therefore have a happy reaction. If there is something unpleasant going on, I can choose not to let my awareness get involved, and therefore not have an emotionally disturbing reaction. This can only start to happen as you gain sufficient mastery over awareness in the mind.

The world is an amusement park for awareness, though not all rides leave you feeling happy. For those who have little control over their awareness in the mind, this amusement park provides a roller coaster of endless highs and lows. The extreme polarity of emotions that one can go through on a daily basis as a result of not managing awareness is exhausting and debilitating to the nervous system, and energetically draining.

The harnessing and focusing of awareness in the mind are of utmost importance in the journey of staying aligned with one's purpose in life.

Moving Awareness in the Mind

Now that I've expatiated on the theory of awareness and the mind and shared real-world examples of it at work, let's experience a practical application of this theory. I believe that it is really important to put theories to the test and into practice and see for yourself if they work.

In order to perform this exercise, I'll need you to be seated on a chair or on the floor. If you choose to sit on a chair, select a chair that has a firm surface; if you have chosen the floor, you can sit directly on the floor or place a small firm cushion and sit on that. Make sure you're comfortable, so that any discomfort is not distracting you from the exercise we are about to perform.

Now that you're seated comfortably, let's switch our focus to your posture. Please sit with your spine straight and your head nicely balanced on top of your spine. Make sure your head is not tilting to either side or to the front or the back. Relax your mouth by letting your jaw relax and allowing your lower teeth to separate from the upper teeth. Lips together, teeth apart.

Take a slow deep breath in. And slowly exhale. Do so at your own pace.

Once you have exhaled fully, I want you to take another slow deep breath in and then slowly exhale again. Do this three more times, totaling five deep breaths. Typically, I would have you close your eyes and guide you through this exercise, but since you have to read this, let's take the following approach.

Please read this next paragraph, then close your eyes and practice what I've shared for a minute or two.

Close your eyes. Become conscious of the room that you are sitting in. Do so first with your physical body. Feel the chair or floor that you are sitting on. Feel your feet or legs on the ground. Become conscious of your skin. Do you feel cold or hot or is the temperature of the room just right? Expand your consciousness beyond your body. Are there any noises in the room? Are there any other noises coming from outside the room? Can you smell anything in the room?

Spend a minute or two just being conscious of everything in the room with your eyes closed. Once you've done that, slowly open your eyes and read the next set of instructions.

Please read the next two paragraphs, then close your eyes and practice what I've shared for three minutes.

I want you to recall the most recent wedding that you attended and attempt to do so in as much detail as possible. Here are some questions to guide you. Whose wedding was it? Did you go by yourself? Did you go with your spouse or with your whole family? Do you recall what you wore? Were you happy for the couple getting married? Do you remember what the bride wore? Did she make a good choice with the dress?

How was the food? Did they serve alcohol, and if so, did you drink a lot? Was there good music and dancing? Did you participate on the dance floor? Did you have a good time at the wedding? Try to think of as much detail as you can about this wedding. The questions I have asked here are merely a guide for this exercise. Now close your eyes and do so for the next three minutes. If at any point during the exercise you find your awareness drifting away, then gently and lovingly bring it back to the recollection of the memory of this wedding.

Now that you are done with recalling the memory of the wedding, please read the next two paragraphs, then close your eyes and practice what I've shared for three minutes.

I want you to recall the most recent vacation that you went on. If you have recently vacationed overseas, choose that one for this exercise instead of a vacation that you took domestically. What kind of vacation was it? A yoga retreat? Surf trip? Skiing holiday? Camping or road trip? Where did you go? What was the weather like where you went? Hot? Cold? Humid? Rainy? Dry?

What was the food like? Was it spicy? Was it bland? Did you get sick eating the food? If you stayed in a few different places, was there one that stood out more to you than the others? Did you shop a lot? What was the thing you bought that you loved the most? Did you do a lot of activities? Try to think of as much detail as you can about this vacation. Now close your eyes and do so for the next three minutes. If at any point during the exercise you find your awareness drifting away, then gently and lovingly bring it back to the recollection of the memory of this vacation.

Once you're done with recalling the memory of the vacation, for the final step of this exercise, I want you to please read this next paragraph, then close your eyes and practice what I've shared for a minute or two.

Become conscious of your posture. Is your spine still straight? Is your head still nicely balanced on top of your spine? Are you still physically comfortable? Become conscious of the temperature of the room. Is it warm, cold, or just right? Expand your consciousness beyond your physical body and begin to be conscious of the room around you. Are there any noises in or outside of the room? Now close your eyes and hold your awareness in this room and be as conscious as possible of your surroundings for the next minute or two.

As you open your eyes and bring your focus back to this book, allow yourself a few moments to adjust to your surroundings.

Let's review the exercise you just did with regard to awareness and the mind. You began the exercise by first becoming conscious of the room that you were sitting in. As you did so, you became more keenly cognizant of your surroundings. During this point of the exercise, your awareness was in the conscious mind—engaged in your surroundings.

From here, your awareness embarked on a journey from your conscious mind to your subconscious mind, where the memory of the wedding resided. When your awareness arrived at its destination, the memory of the wedding, you started to become more conscious of that experience. The better your ability to hold your awareness in this area of the mind, the more you recall details of this nuptial day. Experiences, embedded with emotion, started to surface. Some made you smile, perhaps laugh, and even shed a tear of happiness again. As awareness lingered here you began reliving that whole wedding experience.

Before I requested that you go to this specific memory in your subconscious, you were most likely not even thinking of this wedding. And while your awareness was immersed in that wedding experience, a memory in your subconscious, you were no longer conscious of the room you were sitting in. You were no longer conscious of the temperature of the room, your posture, and more. You were no longer conscious of these things because your awareness was no longer in the room.

Wherever your awareness is in the mind, that is what you become conscious of.

Your awareness then traveled from the area of the subconscious that holds the memory of the wedding to an area of the subconscious that houses the memory of the vacation. When your awareness arrived at this new location within the subconscious, you became acutely conscious of that holiday you were on.

Detailed accounts of that respite from your quotidian life unveiled themselves to your consciousness as you held your awareness in the kernel of the memory of that experience. Consequently, a medley of emotions sprang to the surface as awareness bounced from one specific memory to another within the bubble of this overall experience called the vacation. You start to relive that vacation.

As awareness is firmly anchored here, you are no longer conscious of the room you are sitting in or of the wedding. The sweet reminiscence of the vacation ends. You pry your eyelids open and turn your gaze to the book, wondering, "What next?" I instruct you then to move your awareness back to the room, and as you do so, you start to become conscious of all the things associated with it.

Suddenly you are conscious that your spine is no longer straight and your head is tilted to one side. You immediately correct your posture and begin to become conscious of all the other things I listed. While your awareness adjusts back to this area of the mind, you are no longer conscious of the wedding or the vacation. No memories from those two events are present in your mind as your awareness is firmly anchored in what you are absorbed in now, which is taking note of your surroundings.

Finally, you open your eyes and adjust yourself to your surroundings.

By following my instructions, you moved your awareness from the room to the wedding area of the mind, to the vacation area of the mind, and back to the room again. You used your willpower to move your awareness and then you used your powers of concentration to keep your awareness in each of those areas for an extended period of time.

Let's conclude a few things from this. I wanted you to perform this exercise to experience and prove to yourself a few of the fundamental principles of awareness and the mind that I shared with you in previous lessons. I'll list them for the sake of clarity.

1. *Awareness moves, your mind does not.*
   The fact that you can take your awareness to a few different areas of the mind shows that your awareness moves within the mind and the mind itself does not move.

2. *Awareness and the mind are two distinctly different things.*
   The ability to move awareness within the mind shows that the mind and awareness are not the same thing. They do not move together. One travels within the other; hence there is a clear separation between awareness and the mind.

3. *You are not the mind.*
   You are not your mind. You are pure awareness moving through various areas of the mind. And whatever area of the mind you go to, that is what you experience. Wherever your awareness is in the mind, that is what you become conscious of.

Bringing Awareness to Attention

Now that you have an understanding that awareness and the mind are two distinctly different things and that you are pure awareness moving through different areas of the mind, the next step is to control where awareness goes.

The first step in controlling where awareness goes is to bring awareness to attention.

One definition found in a dictionary defines attention as the act of directing the mind to listen, see, or understand; to notice. We can apply this definition to awareness. Bringing awareness to attention can then be said to be the act of making awareness notice itself, or as my guru would say, "awareness being aware of itself."

Allow me to give you an example to elucidate this. Imagine your friend sitting on your couch watching a movie. She is snuggled in a corner of the sofa, wrapped in a cozy blanket that is peppered with cookie crumbs, and her awareness is totally absorbed in the movie, completely oblivious of everything that is going on around her.

To get her attention, you need to bring her awareness to attention. To do this, you would need to detach her awareness from what it is aware of, in this case the movie, and shift her awareness to you.

There are many ways to do this. You could turn off the TV, throw a cushion at her head, or call her name. You decide to call her name, and you say out loud, "Amira!" Her awareness detaches from the movie at the sound of her name and she turns to face you. You have now captured the attention of her awareness. You have brought her awareness to attention.

Once you have brought her awareness to attention, you can choose to move it to wherever you want it to go (if she gives you permission). To carry on with this example, now that you have her attention, you could direct her awareness to her wineglass by saying, "Your glass is empty. Would you like a refill?" Amira glances down at her glass, then looks back up at you and says, "That would be great." Then she redirects her awareness back to the movie in full faith that you will replenish her wineglass.

To get Amira to be conscious of you, you first needed to bring her awareness to attention. Once you had accomplished this, then you could redirect it to where you wanted it to go. Many of you parents probably experience this on a daily basis with your children. Now you have the vocabulary to describe the process. Remember the lesson titled "The Importance of Terminology"? As you repeat the act of bringing your child's awareness to attention for the umpteenth time in the day, mentally describe to yourself, using the correct terminology, what it is you are doing. This process of correctly naming what you are doing trains your subconscious in understanding how awareness and the mind work.

My daughter, at three years old, loves standing about two feet in front of the television. To get her to move back, my first step is to pry her awareness away from what she is watching. Calling her name often does the trick. Her awareness is yanked away from the screen and her head spins around to look at me. My next step is to redirect her awareness to where I want it to go.

"Can you please move back to the couch?" I despairingly plead again, while considering somewhere deep in the crevices of my mind how I could build a moat around the television.

Upon hearing my request, her gaze shifts to the couch, and almost instantaneously she bolts over to it. She jumps on the couch, and her awareness is sucked back into the screen with a gravitational force strong enough to capture any planet.

The examples I just gave are of bringing someone's awareness to attention. You can also do this with yourself. You can bring your own awareness to attention.

When your awareness starts to drift away from what it is focused on, call it to attention or bring it to attention. Once you have brought it to attention, you can then use your willpower to bring it back to the object of concentration. We are going to learn about developing willpower later in the book.

So how does one bring one's own awareness to attention? To call your awareness to attention, your awareness needs to be aware of itself. And this is what our next lesson is all about.

LESSON 5.4

Detaching Awareness

The act of bringing awareness to attention involves detaching awareness from what it is aware of. Let's examine this closely, as this is a critical piece in this process that we have not dived into yet.

In an earlier lesson I gave the example of watching a movie, and how the director can take your awareness from one area of the mind to another. Have you ever noticed that in a really good movie, your awareness can get so absorbed in it that you are no longer conscious of anything else around you? You are so completely absorbed in it that you are reacting to all the scenes in the movie as the director wants you to.

At this moment, awareness is completely absorbed in what it is aware of. *Awareness and what it is aware of are one.*

The important thing to note in what we are examining here is that awareness can be in one of two states. Firstly, awareness can be aware of what it is observing. Secondly, awareness can be absorbed in what it is observing.

Let's use the example of the subway ride in New York City to describe the first state. A couple was arguing in the subway car, and my awareness was brought to attention as a result of it. At that moment I had the choice to simply be observant of the argument or to allow my awareness to get absorbed in it. I chose to hold my awareness with me rather than allow it to travel to the couple and get emotionally engaged in their quarrel.

In this case, awareness was being aware of what it was observing. This is the ideal scenario: awareness is aware of what it is that it is observing, and then has the ability to choose if it wishes to get absorbed in it or not.

Let's use another example in the book to examine the second state. In the case of watching the movie in the theater, awareness can be observant of the fact that there is a movie playing on the screen, and then it can decide to get absorbed in it or not. In this case, it would make sense for awareness to get absorbed in the movie, because that is what you paid for—to have a certain type of experience based on the theme of the movie. Here, awareness is absorbed in what it is observing.

We can conclude that awareness can be aware of what it is observing, or it can be absorbed in what it is observing. The prerogative is always available to you, and it is yours and yours only, though this may not always be an easy choice. This is very important, so I'd like you to take a moment to reflect on it.

Let's go back to the second state, where awareness is absorbed in what it is observing. The process of bringing awareness to attention is the process of separating awareness from that which it is aware of or absorbed in. This is one of the first steps in learning to focus.

In the example of the movie, the process is to pry awareness out of the movie that it is absorbed in so that awareness and the movie are no longer one. To do this, you need to (1) bring awareness to attention and then (2) pull awareness from the movie screen back to you.

Here's an exercise that you can do the next time you're watching a movie. When you are seated in the theater watching the movie, look down at your feet.

Wiggle your toes and watch yourself do it for a few seconds. Doing this brings your awareness to your toes. This is one way to pry your awareness away from being absorbed in the movie. Now direct your awareness from your toes to the movie screen again, but this time do not let your awareness be absorbed in the movie. Just observe the movie from where you are sitting in the theater and see it as nothing more than light on a big white screen. One way to do this is to look behind you, see the light coming from the projector, and follow that beam of light to the screen. And tell yourself that it is just light on a screen.

If you can do this, you have successfully separated awareness from that which it is aware of. You have learned the art of observation, which is keeping awareness with you and not allowing it to be absorbed in what it is observing.

As soon as you let awareness leave you and return to the screen, it will get absorbed in the movie again, and you will start reacting to whatever is going on in the movie. When this happens, you and what you are watching are one. If there is a funny scene in the movie you may laugh, and if there is a sad scene you may cry. Awareness is back to riding the movie train, going from one area of the mind to another under the direction of the movie director.

If you call awareness to attention again and separate awareness from that which it is aware of (pull awareness out of the movie), you become the observer. Now awareness is observing what is on the screen as opposed to being absorbed in the movie on the screen.

What a wonderful game to play. To let awareness be absorbed in the movie, experience the emotions of the scene, and then to consciously withdraw awareness and now become emotionally detached as an observer.

The more you practice this, the more you realize that you can control where your awareness goes, and that you can pull your awareness out of any experience it is absorbed in. Here we are using the analogy of the movie theater, but this applies in everyday life as well. If you are speaking with someone and you find that his awareness is going to a really negative area of the mind—and taking yours there as well—you can bring your awareness to attention, separate it from his, and withdraw it back to an area of the mind that you wish to be in. Otherwise your awareness would follow his awareness to the negative area of the mind and experience that negativity. But knowing how to separate awareness from what it is aware of and to bring awareness to attention puts the power of choice in your hands.

Imagine you're back in the movie theater. Look around you at everyone there and see how their awareness and the movie are one. They are so absorbed in the movie that they are not conscious of anything else. They are reacting to every scene on the screen because they have allowed their awareness and the movie to become one. When this happens, the director of the movie has control over their awareness and can take them on the journey of the movie and make them experience everything the movie has to offer, which is of course what they paid for.

In the example of the subway ride in New York City that I was on, we can conclude that the passengers who emotionally reacted to the couple arguing were individuals who did not have enough control over their awareness. The raised voices of the couple caused their awareness to detach itself from whatever it was absorbed in and brought their awareness to attention. Now their awareness was aware of the couple arguing, and in this moment they had the choice to move awareness back to what it was previously absorbed in or to allow the couple to draw their awareness into the argument. Most did not have sufficient control over their awareness in the mind, and allowed their awareness to be drawn into the same area of the mind the couple was in.

The ideal case here would be that the raised voices of the couple would cause your awareness to detach itself from what it was absorbed in, and then you would be observant enough to make the choice of whether you wanted to get mentally entangled in the argument or not.

We've looked at two examples here. In one, an external force caused awareness to be separated from that which it was aware of. In the other, it was you who, through your powers of observation, separated awareness from that which it was aware of.

Learning to separate awareness from that which it is aware of is an art, and one that you should strive to master.

The Practice of Separating Awareness

Take the same exercise I just suggested doing at the movie theater and apply it at home. This weekend, put on a movie that you love. While watching the movie, I want you to practice separating awareness from that which it is aware of. Here's how you can practice. During the movie I want you to move your awareness from the movie to your feet. Wiggle your toes and watch yourself do it. Doing so moves your awareness from the movie to your toes. Wiggle your toes for about seven seconds.

Now direct your awareness from your toes to the television screen again, but this time do not let your awareness be absorbed in the movie. Just observe the movie from where you are sitting on the couch and see it as nothing more than light on a screen.

Then bring awareness back to your toes and wiggle them for a few seconds. Awareness is back at your feet. Now move awareness back to the movie, and this time let it get absorbed again in the movie. Surrender awareness to the movie so you can truly enjoy it for the next few minutes.

Now call awareness to attention. That means to separate awareness from that which it is aware of—the movie. Bring awareness out of the movie and back to you.

Repeat the process. The more you practice this, the better you get at it. Play this game with your awareness and you will very quickly experience for yourself the art of separating awareness from that which it is aware of. If you can separate awareness by pulling it out of what it is aware of, you can actually sit back and observe what you are being aware of. You cannot observe something if your awareness is absorbed in it.

Observation is awareness being conscious of what it is being aware of. If you have ever wondered how to be observant, or what observation is, now you know. Observation is the ability to separate awareness from that which it is aware of and be aware of the experience without being absorbed in it. You can't learn about observation if you don't first learn about awareness and the mind.

Awareness Being Aware of Itself

In order for awareness to separate itself from what it is being aware of, awareness first needs to be aware of itself.

The ability to do this comes from the ability to be observant. Observation is a by-product of prolonged states of concentration. We will dive into observation and concentration in the chapters ahead. Only when my awareness has developed sufficient powers of observation can it then become aware of itself. Once it's aware of itself, it can bring itself to attention, or, to put it another way, bring itself to notice itself. Now that it has noticed itself, it can redirect itself to where it wants to go.

The better you learn to focus, the more observant you become. The more observant you become, the better awareness gets at being aware of itself. As you get better at this, you get better at separating awareness from that which it is aware of or absorbed in.

A person who cannot focus very well does not have well-developed powers of observation. If his awareness drifts away from what it was focused on, it may take a while before his awareness becomes aware of itself (he becomes self-aware) and realizes that he is distracted. For example, a person working on his laptop at work remembers that his favorite team played earlier in the day. So he switches from his accounting spreadsheet to his internet browser to look up the score. He finds out that his team had an emphatic win, and he's now eager to see the highlights. He searches on YouTube and finds the highlights. When he's done watching them, he clicks on a suggested thumbnail video and watches that. Thirty minutes later he becomes observant of the fact that he has been watching one video after another. Upon his awareness becoming aware of itself—or, said another way, upon his realizing this—he pries his awareness from YouTube and diverts it back to his spreadsheet.

His lack of ability to focus makes him not very observant, resulting in a much longer time before his awareness becomes aware of itself. During this period, much time and energy is lost. Productivity plummets, and ad revenue increases for YouTubers. There are many people who stand to benefit from people's inability to focus.

As you learn to focus and become good at it, your awareness will get better at being aware of itself.

LESSON 5.5

The Steward of Awareness

During the recent lessons we have explored two scenarios demonstrating how awareness moves within the mind.

The first scenario is when someone or something moves your awareness from one area of the mind to another. The examples I gave are of watching a movie, Priya the entrepreneur, and the couple having an argument on the train. In each of these scenarios, multiple external forces dictated the journey of awareness in the mind.

The second scenario is when you choose to move your awareness from one area of the mind to another. This was demonstrated in the exercise where you moved your awareness from the room to the wedding, to the vacation, and back to the room. Though I laid out the path for you to follow, you consciously took your awareness from one area of the mind to another.

We can *simplify* and say that there are two forces that control your awareness: you, and your environment. Remember, I define your environment as the people and things around you. At any given point in time, one of these forces is dictating where your awareness is going in your mind. The ideal is for you to be in charge of where your awareness goes.

When you dictate where your awareness goes in your mind, you are having conscious mastery of awareness in the mind.

The majority of people allow their environment to drive where their awareness goes in their mind. The people and things around them could take their awareness to uplifting areas of the mind or to not-uplifting areas of the mind. When you surrender the control of your awareness to your environment, you are surrendering your experience, and consequently your state of mind, to your environment.

These are not the only things that you are surrendering. You are also surrendering to your environment where you invest your energy. As your environment dictates where your awareness goes, it dictates where your energy is flowing, and consequently what is manifesting in your life.

Most people are unable to create what they want in life because they have very little control over where their awareness goes each day. As a result, their energy is flowing to places their environment dictates, and what is manifesting in their life is not what they had intended. Their awareness runs rampant throughout the day, driven so much in today's world by social media algorithms and technology. Their finite energy is dispersed across vast areas as opposed to being harnessed and focused on a few specific things. As a result, none of their goals manifests in their life. Frustration brews, eventually boiling over into discouragement. Persistent discouragement dampens the will, leading to the eventual evaporation of hope.

The conscious mastery of awareness in the mind is an education and a skill that must be taught to every individual. It is the fundamental building block needed to govern oneself effectively in order to live a truly rewarding life. If you were to teach your children one thing about the mind, teach them this. The understanding of how awareness and the mind works is more powerful than teaching them to meditate. Because unless they understand the inner workings of the mind, how can they effectively meditate?

Now that you know this, ask yourself, who or what controls where your awareness goes? You? Or the people and things around you? What percentage of the day does something or someone else control where your awareness goes, as opposed to you having control of your awareness?

You must make a choice. The choice is yours and yours alone. If you decide that you want to be in charge of your awareness, then firmly resolve right now that this is what you want: to be the master of your awareness and where it travels in your mind. Resolve today that you will work tirelessly to bring your awareness under the dominion of your will even if this endeavor takes years.

If this is what you want, then you can do this. You just need to make up your mind that from this day forth, you will use your willpower and powers of concentration to guide where your awareness goes in your mind. There will be days when you struggle to do so and there will be days when you fail. That is all part and parcel of the journey. True failure is not having tried. Never give up and don't lose hope!

Here's a wonderful quote from Gurudeva: "Those of you who are wrestling with the mind in your many endeavors to try to concentrate the mind, to try to meditate, to try to become quiet, to try to relax, keep trying. Every positive effort that you make is not in vain."

Affirm to yourself each morning as you wake up and each evening right before you go to bed, "I am the steward of my awareness!"

PART 3

WINGS OF THE MIND

Chapter 6

UNWAVERING FOCUS

LESSON 6.1

Please Don't Drug Me

I can only pray that I have done a good enough job of making the case to you why understanding how awareness and the mind work is of the utmost importance in life. Having this understanding of the inner workings of the mind paves the way for the next crucial step, which is to learn how to harness and direct awareness within the mind.

Concentration and willpower are the wings upon which awareness takes flight on its journey through the mind. And for those who have harnessed and developed these wings, there is no place in the mind that awareness cannot soar to.

Let's begin with learning how to concentrate. It is one of the greatest qualities that you can develop in life, one that will help you master where your awareness travels to in your mind. Some people are born with the ability to concentrate really well, others truly struggle with it, and in between lies a range of varying abilities to concentrate. This has, most likely, always been the case.

Unfortunately, concentration is not a skill that most of us were taught when growing up. That said, most of us have probably, at some point or another in our life, been told to concentrate.

Over the years, in my travels around the world speaking on the topic of focus, I have conducted an unorganized and undocumented simple survey of the education people have received on the topic of focus. I've asked two questions to most of my audience.

1. Have you ever been taught how to concentrate?
2. When you were in school, did you have daily formal hour-long classes on learning how to concentrate, the same way you had classes on math, science, history, and so on?

Thousands of people have heard me ask these questions, and no one has ever answered "Yes."

My follow-up question to this is, "Has anyone ever told you to concentrate?" The response to this question is always a resounding "Yes!" often followed by "All the time!"

Told Not Taught

I personally believe that there are two major reasons why most people can't concentrate. First, they have never been taught how to concentrate. How can you concentrate if you have never been instructed in how to do so? Second, they don't practice concentration. How can you expect to be good at something if you do not practice it? And you can't practice concentration if you have never been taught how to do it.

We tell people to concentrate, but we never teach them how.

As adults, you hear such requests in the workplace. Senior leaders or entrepreneurs can be heard saying things such as, "Hey, everyone, this project is due in ten days and I need everyone to be really focused!" Coaches of sports teams are guilty of this as well. "Guys, we have three minutes left on the clock and we are five points behind. I need all of you to focus when you go back out there."

Children are definitely not spared from being told to focus. It's so common to hear parents beseeching their kids, "Can you just focus for a second?" Throughout my childhood and into my teenage years, I was told to concentrate on one thing or another. I frequently heard adults say, "Dandapani, concentrate on your homework!" "Dandapani, concentrate on eating your food!" People told me to concentrate, but no one ever taught me how to concentrate. Isn't that strange? You tell a child to concentrate, but you don't show them how to do it.

In school, many of my classmates and I were repeatedly told to concentrate. To pay attention. To focus. We were easily distracted, and that distraction was often rewarded with an old-school ear twisting, knuckle whacking, or, if we were lucky—the good ole rattan cane. Now, that may seem somewhat barbaric to some of you, but I would take a good old caning over what is dished out today.

God forbid I had been born three decades later in the United States, I certainly would have been diagnosed with a mental malady, slapped with an acronym unworthy of affixing to my signature, and soddened with drugs. Perhaps the primitive proverb should be edited to read "Spare the rod, drug the child."

The caning left a temporary brand on my thigh, and that was the extent of its physical damage. Emotionally, it made me adopt a zero-tolerance policy toward violence against children. The chemical drugs that children today are prescribed in many parts of the world are significantly more mentally and physically devastating. Their effects have a longer tail, and much of it is unknown.

ADHD, which stands for attention deficit hyperactivity disorder, is considered one of the most common mental disorders affecting children and adults. The Centers for Disease Control and Prevention (CDC) in the United States shares that ADHD medicines can cause side effects such as poor appetite, stomachaches, irritability, sleep problems, and slowed growth. The National Health Service (NHS), the umbrella term for the publicly funded health care systems of the United Kingdom, shares on its website a list of the common side effects of its approved ADHD medication. Among the side effects are a small increase in blood pressure and heart rate, loss of appetite, trouble sleeping, headaches, mood swings, diarrhea, nausea and vomiting, agitation and aggression, and more. I could keep going, but it's eating into my limited word count for this book.

The CDC website states that health care providers in the United States use the guidelines in the American Psychiatric Association's *Diagnostic and Statistical Manual of Mental Disorders: DSM-5* (fifth edition) to help diagnose ADHD. *DSM-5* criteria for ADHD are to identify people that "show a persistent pattern of *inattention* and/or *hyperactivity*–impulsivity that interferes with functioning or development."

Yes, children can be hyperactive and impulsive. They have lots of energy, and that energy wants to flow somewhere. Not having structured channels and outlets for this energy causes children to be hyperactive and impulsive. What if we were to teach them to understand what energy is, to feel it, harness it, and channel it toward things they are passionate about? That could possibly help, could it not? The conscious use of energy leads to not mismanaging it.

Give athletes millions of dollars and no financial training, and a concerning percentage of them end up broke by the end of their career. The mismanagement of finances is no different from the mismanagement of energy. If you've never been taught to manage either of them, what consequences can one expect?

Now, if parents can't concentrate, then they can't be observant, and if they can't be observant, how can they observe what their child is passionate about and help the child channel their energy toward that? Oh, and parents would need to learn about energy as well, so that they could teach their child to properly harness and channel it.

Having not been taught about energy in any way, why would a child *not* be diagnosed as impulsive or hyperactive? The topic of energy and children is one to unburden on another time.

Then there is inattention as another primary ingredient of ADHD. Being easily distracted and having trouble holding attention on tasks or activities are among the symptoms of inattention listed in *DSM-5*.

A man shared with me that his child had been diagnosed with ADHD, and that this deeply concerned him.

"I'm sorry to hear this," I responded. "I'm not a medical expert, nor do I understand the details of what ADHD is, but can you share with me what the fundamental issue is?"

He replied with a saddened look on his face, "He's easily distracted, and he has lots of trouble paying attention at school and at home. He essentially can't focus. This is what the doctor concluded and hence diagnosed him with ADHD. Now he's on medication and I'm simply not happy about that. He's only six years old."

"This question may be out of left field, but has anyone ever taken the time to teach your child how to focus?"

"No," he replied with a somewhat quizzical look:

"Hmm. Interesting. Can your child play the piano?"

"No, he can't."

"What if we told him to play the piano and he failed to do so, and as a result we took him to the doctor, and had the doctor diagnose him for PPD (piano playing disorder) and drug him for it. That would be messed up, wouldn't it?"

"It certainly would be. I think I am starting to see where you are going with this."

"We don't drug someone for not being able to play the piano, do we? No, we don't. What do we do if they can't play the piano? We teach them how to play the piano. We train them. If we don't teach our children to focus and don't help them to practice being focused so that they can be good at it, how can we expect them to focus?"

There is nothing wrong with diagnosing a child, for example, with inattention. All that this diagnosis does is say that this person has trouble holding their attention on one thing for a period of time. The question is, if we choose to remedy this, how will we approach it? Drugs are one option. The other option is to choose first to teach them how to concentrate, then to help them practice concentration. Since inattention is the inability to hold awareness on one thing for a given period of time, can we not train them in how to do so? If after a few years of training in the art of concentration they still struggle to concentrate, then perhaps you may have a valid reason to label and drug them.

But it is unfair, unethical, in fact, to do that without having given them the education and training they need to focus—and, similarly, the education and training needed to manage, harness, and channel their energy.

We can't drug someone for not being able to do something they've never been taught to do!

I'm sure there are people (adults and children) who have some physiological conditions that make it hard for them to concentrate and perhaps these individuals may benefit from medication. In no way am I saying that we need to completely eradicate medication for inattention and hyperactivity. But I truly believe that most people can't concentrate because they have not been taught how to and they don't practice it. Even those with physiological barriers to concentration can be taught to become, with patience and perseverance, a bit more able to concentrate than they are now.

If I want to play the piano, the first thing I need to do is to learn how to play the piano. The ideal would be to have someone teach me. I could take weekly lessons for a year, and this should be sufficient for me to get going with some basic piano playing, at the very least. Taking lessons alone is insufficient. I need to practice what I am being taught. The natural next question is, "How much should I practice?"

The answer to that question comes in the form of a question, which is, "How good a piano player do I want to be?"

If I want to be good enough to play for family and friends, then perhaps practicing an hour a week would suffice. However, if I want to be one of the best piano players in the world and play in the most prestigious concerts globally, then one hour a week is not going to cut it. I may, I assume, need to practice five or more hours a day.

It's not any different for concentration. If I want to be able to lead a focused life, first I need to learn to focus, then I need to learn to practice it. How much do I practice? Well, how good do I want to be at it? Remember the Law of Practice? You become good at whatever it is you practice. If you really want to be good at concentration, then you need to practice it like you would practice to become one of the best pianists in the world.

It is beyond a shadow of a doubt that I would have been labeled with ADHD had I been born in another time and place. I had the symptoms they stated. Now I teach people around the world to focus—children and adults, individuals across a range of professions. Some of them are highly successful entrepreneurs and athletes who have notably upped their performance through a better understanding of their mind and an improved ability to focus.

In the first twenty-four years of my life I had no training in concentration whatsoever. Not until I met my guru did I find someone who lovingly invested his time and energy in training me in understanding the mind and the fine art of concentration. I share this only to tell you that you can learn to concentrate at any age. You are never too old to learn this fine art. I hope this is a ray of encouragement for you. All that is needed is your desire to live a focused life and your commitment to doing so. The tools and path to a focused life are outlined in this book.

LESSON 6.2

Defining Concentration

Concentration is the secret of strength in politics, in war, in
trade, in short in all management of human affairs.

~RALPH WALDO EMERSON

Sticking to the praxis of this book, I'll begin by defining what concentration is. Defining it will help us to have a shared vocabulary
surrounding the understanding and use of this word. And remember,
the words "concentration" and "focus" are synonymous and I'm using them interchangeably. The following definition applies to both of
these words.

I define concentration as the ability to keep awareness on one
thing until you consciously choose to move it to something else.

Let's analyze this, as there are a few parts to this definition that
must be clearly understood and some misconceptions that must be
dispelled.

If I can keep my awareness, that glowing ball of light within my
mind, on one thing or one person or in one area of the mind for a period of time until I choose to move it to the next object of focus—that
is my ability to concentrate. If I allow my awareness, my glowing ball

of light, to move from one thing to another in an uncontrolled way, then I am no longer concentrating.

Additionally, you can say that concentration is not only dependent on the duration that you can keep awareness in one area of the mind, but also on your ability to consciously choose to move awareness from one area to another. Allow me to unfold this in parts.

The longer I am able to hold my awareness on one thing without having it shift to anything else, the better I can concentrate. If I am speaking with Alice for thirty minutes, and during that entire conversation I can keep my awareness solely focused on her, then I am concentrating. It tells me that I have good levels of concentration that I am able to hold my awareness on her for that duration.

The other part of concentration is the ability to shift awareness consciously. For example, if I can hold my awareness on item A for a period of time, then I am concentrating. Now if I consciously shift my awareness to item B and hold it on item B, I am still concentrating. If I hold my awareness on item B for five seconds before consciously shifting it to item C and holding it on item C for a period of time, I am still concentrating.

It is really important to understand that it is not simply the duration of concentration that matters, but, more important, it is the conscious choice you make to move awareness from one thing to another that is key. When you can consciously move your awareness from A to B to C, then you are exhibiting a state of concentration. The amount of time you spend on each item is only one way to demonstrate how long you can concentrate.

Let me share with you a story to clarify this even further. Some years ago, I spoke to a group of nurses, and one of the nurses shared with me that it was impossible for her to concentrate at work due to the number of tasks she had to perform in a short period of time. She said to me, "In a space of five minutes I can easily do twenty different tasks, sometimes more. I feel like I am all over the place and doing anything but concentrating."

I asked her to describe the first minute of that five minutes. "Share with me what you would be doing in that first minute."

She looked at me and said, "Well, I work in the intensive care unit and have a lot of critical tasks to perform. If I am in a room with a patient, then I could be cleaning his arm with an alcohol swab to prepare him for an injection. That takes a few seconds. Then I prepare the syringe with the precise amount of medication before carefully injecting him. Then I will clean the area he was injected in and make sure that the syringe is disposed of properly. I may then check his pulse and other vital signs and record them."

"Let me stop you here," I said. "Each of the tasks that you described here tells me that it requires you to be fully concentrating when performing it. Would that be a correct assumption on my part?"

"Yes, that is correct."

"The reason you think you are not concentrating is because you are unclear about the definition of concentration. My sense is that you feel you need to be focused on one task for a long period of time and that would mean to you that you are concentrating. That is true, but that is not the only criteria for being focused."

I continued, "In each of the tasks that you performed you were concentrating fully. When you were done with one particular task, you consciously moved your awareness to the next task, and when you were on this new task, you were completely focused on that. The fact that you can consciously move your awareness from one thing to another and hold it there for as long as needed tells me you are a highly focused person. The fact that you hold your awareness on each task only for a few seconds is not critical. The more critical thing is that when you are doing that task you are completely focused on it, and then you make the conscious decision to shift to the next task."

She looked at me and said, "Hearing this has lifted such a weight off me. I've never looked at concentration in that way. I always felt I could not concentrate, but now I better understand what concentration is, and it makes perfect sense."

Even though this nurse performed multiple tasks in the space of a minute, she was completely focused on each task, and upon completion of one task she consciously moved her awareness to the next one. Both of these acts fall into the definition of having good concentration. Many people, like her, would assume that she was multitasking, but she was not. Rather, she was concentrating on one task at a time.

Somewhere else in the world, a veteran meditator is sitting in stillness for ten minutes. All the while, she is keeping her awareness completely absorbed in the power of her spine. Though it may look different on the surface, both the nurse and the meditator are concentrating. They are keeping their awareness anchored in the task they are performing for the respective duration. And when their tasks are completed, they will both consciously move their awareness to the next thing they must do.

Concentration is having mastery over your awareness.

To complete the definition, concentration is having mastery over your awareness, whereby you have the ability to keep your awareness on one thing until you consciously choose to move it to something else.

LESSON 6.3

Distraction—the Mental Plague

A t a time when many are experts at distraction, it may seem redundant to dedicate an entire lesson or more to the topic of distraction. But to deal with distraction, we must understand it and understand it well. When we can understand something, we can better navigate it.

Distraction, the antithesis of focus, is a silent mental plague sweeping across the world and inconspicuously seeping into the lives of many, young and old. Once in the human mind, its accrescent nature begins to metastasize at a prolific rate. The vicious wheel of distraction, as I call it, begins to turn and build upon itself. Before long it becomes the dominant nature of the mind, the sovereign ruler of one's life. Its reign is cancerous in every way. Its nature is destructive, and it is triumphant in its dismantling of the very fabric of relationships, visions, endeavors, and all that feeds the making of a rewarding life.

Sadly, the distracted mind is so distracted that it can't focus long enough to reflect and realize that it is distracted, and to do something about it.

The concomitants of a distracted mind are devastating, to say the least. Among the bastardized children born of this are fear, worry, anxiety, stress, a sense of purposelessness, indecision, mental and physical exhaustion, to name a few. These wretched children wreak endless havoc on the mind, wearing it down and crippling the will of the soul.

I truly believe that most people are unaware of the devastating consequences of a distracted mind. If they knew in depth what the outcomes were, they would, in self-preservation, pursue a cure. That antidote, the perfect vaccine for this ravaging disease, is focus.

Let us begin to understand distraction by defining it. I define distraction as my awareness being controlled by any external or internal source without conscious approval from me. Permit me to unfold this.

The example I used previously of watching a movie in the theater would not be considered a distraction. In this instance, we made a conscious choice to hand over control of our awareness to the director and allow him or her to move our awareness from one area of the mind to another. This does not fall under the umbrella of the definition.

Here's an example that would best exemplify what distraction means, and I will use a smartphone as our agent of distraction.

Giovanni is on his smartphone sending an urgent text message to his babysitter, asking her if she can stay later tonight because he needs to work late, and halfway through typing the message a call comes in. He answers the call and gets into a conversation with his coworker Emilia, who has called him to talk about a project they are both working on.

After Emilia has discussed with Giovanni what she has called him about, she tells him to check out an article on a website she frequents.

Giovanni goes to the website immediately after he ends the call with her. He's equally inspired by the article and decides to share it on his Facebook page. He copies the link, gets on Facebook, and updates his feed with a link to the article.

Since he is on Facebook, he decides to quickly scroll through his timeline and starts liking, commenting, and sharing other posts. As he scrolls through the timeline, notifications start to pop up at the bottom of his screen, letting him know that there is some activity on his timeline. Giovanni loves getting attention, so he thinks to himself, "Woohoo, somebody must have liked my post!" He clicks on the notifications to see what the interaction is and finds out that quite a few people have liked and commented on the article he posted, and so he engages with them and "likes" their comments and replies to some of them. At this point he has spent ten minutes on Facebook.

He thinks to himself, "This post is really popular. I should definitely tweet this." Giovanni switches apps from Facebook to Twitter and posts the link on his Twitter feed. After he has done so, he scrolls through his Twitter timeline favoriting, retweeting, and commenting on other tweets. Not much later he starts to see blue circles forming at the bottom of his Twitter account. He is getting excited that people are responding to his tweet! He clicks on the notification button to see what the recent activity is and then interacts with the responses that his post has generated.

He notices the time and realizes he'd better get back to work and get off social media. He switches apps, moves from Twitter to his email app, and starts responding to emails. After five minutes of attending to emails, Giovanni realizes that the babysitter never responded to the text he sent out more than twenty minutes ago. His awareness goes to the annoyed area of the mind and wonders why the babysitter hasn't responded to him, and he decides he must have a talk with her about responding faster to urgent requests. He switches apps again, moves from his email app to his text message app, and upon arriving sees the half-written message that he never sent. He blushes, knowing he got upset for no reason, quickly finishes his text, sends it, and then returns to the email app to attend to more emails. The rest of his evening continues in a similar fashion as he allows his environment to dictate what his awareness is engaged in.

Perhaps some of you can relate to Giovanni. So what happened here? Giovanni allowed his awareness to jump from one thing to another, dictated by his smartphone, its apps, and their notifications. The fact that an external force is dictating where his awareness is going without his conscious approval tells us that he is distracted.

Not only is his smartphone dictating where his awareness is going, but it is simultaneously dictating where his energy is flowing. In the case of distraction, when awareness goes all over the place, energy flows all over the place as well, and as a result nothing can get sufficient energy to start manifesting.

Mastering Distraction

Distraction, like concentration, requires practice to be good at. Those who have mastered distraction are unknowing stalwart practitioners of this modern burgeoning mindset. Recall the Law of Practice—we become good at whatever it is we practice. And this law applies whether you are consciously practicing something or not.

I gave the example earlier that if I wanted to be a great piano player I may, I assumed, need to practice five or more hours a day, and perhaps for five to six days a week. After six months I will definitely be a better pianist than when I started, but will I be playing at Carnegie Hall? Most likely not, even though that's a lot of practice. After a year of this, I'm going to be a much better pianist; I'm not convinced this is sufficient to get me to the highest level, but I can imagine I am getting very good at it.

Imagine if I practiced distraction six to eight hours a day for five to six days a week. After six months, how good will I be at distraction? Probably better than before I started my distraction practice. A year later, with the same time commitment, how good would I be? Conceivably very, very good at it.

The truth is that most people do not practice distraction for six to eight hours a day. There are 24 hours in a day, and let's assume that the average person sleeps a luxurious 8 hours every day. This gives him 16 hours of wake time, and out of these 16 hours, how many hours does he realistically practice distraction? Highly likely a lot more than 6 to 8 hours; 10 to 14 hours a day seems apt. And the chances of him practicing distraction only five to six days a week are highly unlikely. I'm going to assume that if you are distracted from Monday through Saturday, then the chances of Sunday being a day of focus are slim.

So with a possible 10 to 14 hours a day, seven days a week, for six months straight, I can safely conclude that you're going to be very good at distraction. A year or 18 months of this and you'll be well past grasshopper level and into the realms of the masters.

Most people are not conscious of the fact that the reason they are very good at being distracted is because they practice it so much. Besides the fact that they may not have been taught to concentrate, the reality is that they incessantly practice distraction throughout the day, and this is what makes them profoundly good at it.

The Cost of Distraction

We have all been endowed with two of life's greatest gifts—time and energy. Not all of us, however, realize how precious these gifts are, but those who do treat them with the greatest reverence. We only have a finite amount of time upon arrival on this planet. It's ever ebbing away. How we choose to use it depends solely on us. Similarly, we only have so much energy each day. How we choose to invest it is our choice.

Distraction is the thief of time and energy, robbing us of precious moments and connections in life without remorse. Distraction costs everyone time and energy, but not everyone feels the loss of them equally. The purposeless person has all the time and energy in the world to squander. The person with a purpose has finite time and energy, and for this person, distraction is too high a cost to bear.

For every minute awareness, hence energy, is taken away from what it should be focused on, that is a minute that is gone forever. My ability to focus allows me to be present in each of the moments of the experiences I share with my family and loved ones. Distraction would cost me those moments—moments, each unique in time and space, that I would never regain or be able to conjure up again. Moments I am not willing to sacrifice.

When the cost of distraction is too heavy to bear, the price of focus is worth paying.

So much precious time in life is wasted because people are perpetually distracted. So many precious moments with loved ones squandered because of people's inability to be focused in the present moment. The impact of distraction on an individual level is vast, though this impact may only be visible to those who can focus.

Because people can't focus, they grapple to be present in their life's experiences, which leads them to feel unfulfilled, even though they've had many experiences that could have been fulfilling had they been able to be present in each of them. Parents and children experience greater disconnects, with neither being able to stay focused long enough to have a meaningful interaction. Friends gather for a meal only to photograph their food and interact over their phones with those not present at the meal. Conversations are convoluted, having more twists and turns than a steep mountain road, never amounting to much, as staying with a topic to its natural conclusion is a near impossible task. So prevalent is distraction in every part of our society that its presence is sadly becoming an accepted norm.

LESSON 6.4

Integrating Focus into Life

I've laid the foundation for the understanding you need to begin to learn how to concentrate. Now begins our study of the art of concentration.

Let's briefly revisit the definition of concentration. I defined concentration as the ability to keep awareness on one thing until you consciously choose to move it to something else.

To become good at concentration, I integrate the definition of concentration into my everyday life. Throughout the day I practice keeping my awareness on one thing at a time until I consciously choose to move it to something else.

Let's look closely at this. Note that I started the above sentence with "Throughout the day." The words "throughout the day" are paramount to leading a focused life.

People often ask me, "If I meditate for five or ten minutes a day in the morning, will that help me concentrate?"

My response is often, "Firstly, meditation does not help you to concentrate. You need to be able to *concentrate to meditate*, but that is an entirely different topic. To answer the gist of your question, if you practice concentration for only five to ten minutes a day, it is going to take you a very long time to be good at concentrating."

Remember the example of playing the piano? If I were to practice the piano five to ten minutes a day, how long would it take me to be good at it? It would, most likely, take me a really, really long time. The same applies to concentration. Practicing concentration five to ten minutes a day is going to be inadequate to help you become good at concentration.

And I must ask this question: "What will you be doing the remaining twenty-three hours and fifty minutes of the day? If you will be practicing distraction for eight to ten hours a day during this period, the ten minutes of concentration in the morning is going to do very little to help you."

There are people who spend a brief period in the morning performing some form of exercise to help them feel more centered or focused, but the rest of their day is filled with habits and practices that counteract what they have done in the morning.

You need to approach your life the way a sprinter in the Olympics approaches his life. Let's use Usain Bolt as an example. I'll admit that I know very little about this man, but I do know that he is from Jamaica, that he's won eight gold medals in three consecutive Olympics, and that he holds the world record for the 100-meter sprint at 9.58 seconds.

I'm going to make a few assumptions about him, and you can correct me if I'm wrong. During the peak of his career, I assume he worked out consistently on the track and in the gym. I'm going to assume he ate healthy meals and adhered to a strict diet every day, drank lots of water, stretched regularly, got good amounts of rest and sleep, and more. Most of his day was likely filled with routines and practices that helped him to become the fastest man on earth.

In other words, you could say that the rituals and practices that he adhered to throughout the day helped him to clock 9.58 seconds on the 100-meter sprint. It was not 9.58 seconds spent each day to become the fastest man on earth. Similarly, you can't expect to practice concentration for ten minutes a day and hope to be very good at it. Like an Olympic sprinter, your whole day needs to be filled with routines and practices that support you being a highly focused person. Then and only then will you be good at concentration.

To summarize, to be good at concentration you need to integrate the practice of concentration—the practice of keeping awareness on one thing at a time until you consciously choose to move it to something else—into your whole day. When I say the whole day, I mean every aspect of the twenty-four hours in a day.

Making Focus a Part of My Day

The next natural question is, How, then, do I practice concentration throughout the day?

One of the best ways to integrate the practice of concentration into your life is to identify the nonnegotiable recurring events in an average day and integrate the practice of concentration into these events.

Let's look closely at the statement "nonnegotiable recurring events in an average day," break it down, and understand what it means.

I define "an average day" as a day on which I pretty much have a fixed routine. For me, and for most people I know, these days tend to be weekdays. This is a regular day in my life where I have a routine made up of recurring events that primarily relate to family, work, and myself. This is not a vacation day when I may have something out of the ordinary planned.

When I say "nonnegotiable recurring events," I'm referring to the events that occur each day that I deem necessary and nonnegotiable parts of my day. Examples in my life include going to the bathroom, eating, drinking, taking a shower, brushing my teeth, and so forth. Now, brushing my teeth and taking a shower are technically not non-negotiable, but what I'm getting at here is what I deem nonnegotiable.

I've had some people say to me that they've listed running in the morning or meditating as their nonnegotiable recurring event. I would not consider these nonnegotiable, because you can go a few days without running or meditating, but you can't go a few days without talking to your kids, eating and drinking, or going to the bathroom. It's best to make your nonnegotiable events things you really need to do.

Now that I have defined clearly what I mean by "nonnegotiable recurring events in an average day," let us look at some examples of how to integrate the practice of concentration into them.

In evaluating my average day, I ask myself, "What is one of the nonnegotiable recurring events in my average day?" Every day, I speak with my spouse. That is a nonnegotiable recurring event. On an average day, I may speak with her for a cumulative total of two to three hours. Let's average it at two and half hours for ease of conversation. The time spent speaking with her is spread throughout the day across various activities. Some of it takes place in the morning at breakfast, some during the day when we are working together on our project here in Costa Rica, some over meals and such. As I consider this a nonnegotiable recurring event in my average day, I can use it as a perfect opportunity to integrate the practice of concentration into it.

I integrate the practice of concentration into this event by keeping my awareness on her every time we are in conversation. I give her my undivided attention. If my awareness drifts away, I gently and lovingly bring it back to her. I hold it on her with my powers of concentration, which I am developing as I do so. If my awareness starts to drift away again, I use my willpower and I bring it back to her. I'm relentless with this practice.

Eventually, my awareness learns to stay concentrated on her alone. I've trained it to be focused. I use this daily time with my spouse as an opportunity to practice concentration. And because I spend around two and a half hours a day speaking with her on an average day, then that is two and a half hours I am practicing concentration each day. After six months of doing this, I find myself better at concentrating. Similarly, if I practiced playing the piano for two and a half hours a day, five days a week, for six months, I would be better at playing the piano.

In the earlier example of becoming a professional pianist, I made the assumption that I would need to practice five or more hours a day. Let's average it at seven hours. Using that as a benchmark, purely for the sake of conveying a point, that would mean I would need to chalk up another four and a half hours to get to a professional level of concentration.

This means I need to identify other nonnegotiable recurring events in my average day into which I can integrate the practice of concentration.

Every day I spend on average around ninety minutes on work-related phone calls and virtual meetings. These are nonnegotiable recurring events, and perfect opportunities to integrate the practice of concentration. When I am on a call, I hold my awareness on the person I am speaking with. I don't do anything else while I am in conversation with them. I'm not checking emails, scrolling through social media feeds, or washing dishes. The person on the other line has my undivided attention.

Doing this allows me to clock another ninety minutes of concentration practice. Now my daily average is four hours!

You can also amass more concentration practice time with the briefer nonnegotiable recurring events of the day. Brushing my teeth gives me the opportunity to solely focus on my teeth. Though it may only take a couple of minutes, doing it twice a day gives me four minutes of practicing concentration. Taking a shower is another great opportunity to focus on cleaning myself. Eating. We all do this, but we don't necessarily focus on savoring and masticating the food we are consuming. Men can use the repetitive daily call to urinate as an opportunity to focus. Getting it in the bowl, not on the floor, is a goal that has apparently failed to be conveyed to some. The men's restroom is proof that many men struggle with concentration—and aim.

It doesn't take much effort to identify the many nonnegotiable recurring events in your day before you are able to clock six to eight hours of practice a day. At this rate, after six months, you'll be quite well on your way to being a very focused person.

It was Gurudeva who gave me the profound insight of leveraging all of my day's experiences to fulfill my goals. He taught me not to classify one as more important than another, but to view each of them as an experience I chose to have as part of my life. How I act and react in each of these experiences determines so much of how my mind is shaped and my life unfolds. He taught me that they all support one another. Doing a task well, though it may appear menial, helps me build the qualities I need to do the other tasks well. They are all interrelated. They make up my day. My perspective on them and how I execute them all plays a massive role in shaping me.

This wise guidance from my guru was life-transforming for me. Every act became a stepping-stone toward leading a rewarding life. Some may consider this exhausting, but it really isn't. It's about pattern building. Habit creation with the intent of designing a lifestyle that supports achieving or fulfilling one's goals and purpose. Each day you do things because you want to or need to. It's a given. It's so important for you to realize that you have the choice of how you do each of these things. If you change how you approach them, you change your life.

Devote yourself to giving your undivided attention to each of your engagements, regardless of their gravitas, from the moment you rise to when you retire at night, and take this practice into your sleep. For when we sleep, we are awake in another world, and our ability to focus will determine what we reap from our time there. It is, after all, where we spend almost a third of our earthly life.

There are many layers to this insight that Gurudeva shared, and if you were to contemplate it deeply, you would begin to unravel and understand the profound wisdom of it. It leads to living in the eternity of the moment, being present in all our experiences and being consciously aware of awareness every given moment of the day.

Other Opportunities

As you seek to identify "nonnegotiable recurring events in your average day," you can look beyond your home. If you spend most of your weekday at an office, then look for some of these opportunities there.

For example, every day at work you meet with your team for fifteen minutes. This is a nonnegotiable recurring event in your average workday. What a great opportunity to integrate the practice of concentration into it, as you are guaranteed of this event occurring five days a week. Give that meeting your undivided attention. Every time someone speaks in that meeting, keep your awareness on them. If it drifts away, use your willpower to bring it back to that person and use your powers of concentration to hold it on them.

The journey to and from the office would also be a nonnegotiable recurring event in your average workday. Some people drive to work. What a great opportunity to give the road your undivided attention. The CDC states, "In the U.S. in 2018, over 2,800 people were killed and an estimated 400,000 were injured in crashes involving a distracted driver." The National Safety Council (a nonprofit public-service organization promoting health and safety in the United States) reports that cell phone use while driving leads to 1.6 million crashes each year. That is a strong enough case for being focused while driving.

Have you ever had the experience of driving somewhere and arriving there without having any recollection of how you got there? Imagine traveling in a metal box, potentially doing speeds of sixty miles per hour or more, and not concentrating . . . a little scary, don't you think? After I conducted a workshop in Germany, an entrepreneur in the group emailed me, "I used to talk on the phone all the time when I drove. Now I get in the car, place my phone in the glove compartment, and focus on driving. It became even more important to me when I realized my son was in the car with me. I would look in the rearview mirror, see him strapped into his car seat, and think to myself, 'His life is in my hands. If I am distracted while driving and he gets hurt or worse, it's all on me. He has no choice in the matter.' I needed no more convincing as to why I should focus while I drive."

The more focused you are at driving, the better your chance of avoiding an accident. If you drive, use driving as an opportunity to practice concentration.

Here's another opportunity. If you spend a good deal of your time on computers, use this time to practice concentration. If you are a programmer, for example, coding a sophisticated purchasing option on a shopping cart, then say to yourself, "I'm going to work on this for the next hour, and during this time I will not allow my awareness to wander off to anything else." Then turn off your notifications, and if your awareness drifts away, driving you to pick up your phone, gently and lovingly bring it back to coding. Now you are using this hour to develop your powers of concentration.

All of us have countless opportunities to practice concentration each day. The goal is to clock as many hours as possible of concentration practice in these nonnegotiable recurring opportunities throughout the day. The more hours in each day you practice concentration, the better you become at concentration. By approaching it this way, you are not adding any additional tasks to your life, but rather leveraging the tasks you are already doing daily by doing them differently—as opportunities to practice concentration.

Establishing Concentration Rituals

R ituals are all around us. The earth ritually circumambulates the sun, as the moon does the earth. Animals embrace rituals, and so do humans, though most may not be conscious of the rituals they perform daily. But rituals have long been the lifeline of the wise, thoughtfully constructed and consciously integrated into their lives for the fulfillment of specific purposes.

The decade spent living as a Hindu monastic wedded me to the concept of rituals. Its power to transform is immeasurable. And what better way to bring the practice of concentration into one's life than to create daily rituals?

Now that I've shared with you that the best way to integrate the practice of concentration into your life is to integrate it into the non-negotiable recurring events in your average day, let's look at the best way to do so.

To begin, I would like you to write down five nonnegotiable recurring events in an average day that you can leverage as opportunities to practice concentration. In the previous lesson I gave you a few examples. You are welcome to use some of them or come up with your own. The important factor is that they need to be nonnegotiable and recurring in your average day.

List these opportunities from one to five in the order you would like to implement them. Select the first opportunity, and integrate it into your life for one month. Put the other four on hold.

Let's say the first opportunity that you selected to begin with is giving your spouse your undivided attention in all your conversations together. Throughout the day, whenever you speak with your spouse, give your spouse your undivided attention. Keep your awareness on your spouse. If it drifts away, use your willpower to bring it back. Then use your powers of concentration that you are developing to hold awareness on your spouse. Be relentless with this practice.

This is the only time in the day when I want you to make a conscious effort to focus. And I'll share with you why.

Imagine I went to the gym every other day and bench-pressed 20 pounds. After three weeks of this, should I increase the weight to 22 pounds or 100 pounds? I'm no gym expert, but I'm going to assume 22 pounds is the better option. We want to build our muscles in incremental steps.

The mind is no different. You can look at the mind as a muscle that you want to develop. As with bench-pressing, take an incremental-step approach. If you try to integrate the practice of concentration into your whole day, you will most likely not be successful. Repeated failure to do so will only lead to discouragement and potentially the abandonment of the entire practice.

If after a month—or more, if needed—of giving my spouse my undivided attention whenever I speak with her, I find myself doing this really well, then I can add another opportunity to my daily routine. I look at my list and I take the second item and integrate that into my average day, similar to bench-pressing, where I add more weight and lift this for a period of time.

If the second opportunity is giving my daughter my undivided attention, then I have two opportunities to practice concentration throughout the day: whenever I speak with my spouse and whenever I speak with my daughter. This now forms my daily concentration practice routine, and the only times during the day where I make a conscious effort to focus. I place the other three opportunities on hold. I work on these two opportunities until I get to a place where I can give both my spouse and my daughter my undivided attention really well.

Now, it may take me a few months before I get to a place where I feel I am doing really well at giving both my spouse and my daughter my undivided attention. Say it takes me five months, and at this point it is time to add more weight to my bench-pressing exercise, which means it is time to add my third opportunity to my daily ritual.

I carry on in this manner until all five opportunities are being practiced throughout the day. At this point you will find yourself beginning to consciously focus during other opportunities in the day.

Know that as you add more opportunities each day, you are also increasing the amount of time you are investing in practicing concentration. Before long you may find yourself practicing concentration five or six or more hours a day and well on your way to being a professional concentrator. Eventually, you'll find that it does not take much effort to concentrate at all, because you've built a pattern in your subconscious, a habit, of keeping awareness on one thing at a time.

The key thing I want you to take away from this is that to become good at anything, the best approach is to do so incrementally. Any monkey can change for a day or a month, but to sustain change month after month, year after year—that is the holy grail of self-development. When we take an incremental approach to developing a skill or quality, we take an approach that allows us to sustain that change.

So many people want to get from zero to one hundred right away. They forget that there are ninety-nine numbers in between that they need to pass through. There is no quick fix. There is no hack. If running is not part of your daily exercise routine, don't expect to successfully complete a marathon tomorrow. We must build up to what it is we want to get to.

It's important for you to keep in mind that if you are forty years old and you've never learned how to concentrate and practice concentration, you can't expect to read about it once and walk away a focused human being, having made no greater effort than reading a book. You have forty years of programming to reshape, and that takes time and effort. New patterns need to be built. Constructing a beautiful building takes time, as does constructing a beautiful mind. It's going to take weeks, months, or even years to make significant changes. But as Gurudeva would often say, "The rewards are far greater than the efforts put into it."

Be patient and compassionate with yourself on this journey. You will stumble, fall, and bruise yourself many times. Lovingly lift yourself up and keep going. Review the lesson "The Power of Small." When you focus on one opportunity, you are taking small steps. Small steps are doable. Small steps are achievable. Small goals create no pressure. Do not underestimate the irrefutable power of small.

Tracking Progress

You don't improve anything that you don't track.

~RAGY THOMAS, FOUNDER AND CEO OF SPRINKLR,
DEAR FRIEND, AND MENTOR

In the opportunities I described here, I repeatedly said, "Give my undivided attention really well." Let's define "really well." How do I know if I am doing something really well, and how do I know if I am improving at what I am doing? The best and most honest way to know is to track my progress. Though this is nothing new and something that has been part of many people's lives for centuries, the concept was first introduced to me by my guru. When I was a monk in his monastery being trained by him, he made me track how well I was doing my *sadhana* (spiritual practices). It was a simple but highly effective self-evaluation process.

Every night when I retired to my humble abode, a ten-by-ten-foot austere concrete structure next to a stream under a banyan tree, I spent a few minutes evaluating all of my rituals of the day. I had a sheet of paper with thirty-one columns (one for each day of the month) and a row for each of my rituals. On this sheet, lit only by a small oil lamp on the floor, I graded how well I had performed each of my rituals. Upon completion of my evaluation, I folded the sheet and tucked it in between a couple of books of scripture that sat at the foot of my futon mattress on the floor. I would repeat this process every night.

At the end of the month I would place that sheet on my guru's desk in his office. One day when I went to do so I found him at his desk, so I handed the sheet to him personally. I expected him to look at it, but he took it from me, opened his drawer, and placed it in a folder. Many of the things I learned from him were nonverbal. Often, with his incredible ability to focus, he would send me a clear intuitive message. As is the nature of an intuitive message, it is always succinct and clear, and it comes across in a flash though it would take many words to detail it. This message was "You are doing this for you, not for me."

I realized at that moment it didn't really matter to him what I wrote on that sheet. The whole reason for this exercise was for me to track whether I was making progress with my practices. Since it was a self-evaluation, I could have lied to myself and given myself the best scores. But this would not have served me well. Truly, the only person who benefited from this exercise was me. It behooved me to rate my performance of each ritual in the most honest way possible. This would then allow me to see if I was making progress.

Since I had just graduated from engineering school, my mind, which was trained in approaching things in a goal-oriented and structured way, outlining steps and defining processes, wholeheartedly embraced this approach to spiritual unfoldment. It was one of the many things that drew me to my guru. He was practical, methodical. This was what I had always sought in a spiritual teacher—someone who taught from personal experience but could also outline a step-by-step, practical path to a clearly defined goal.

One of his fundamental teachings to his monks was to "lean on your own spine." He would say, "Don't lean on me, because when I am no longer here, you will fall over." It's easy to become so dependent on those who mentor us, who lead and guide us, that they become a crutch as opposed to a catalyst. Many guides abuse this privilege. It's a great business model, I should say, as it keeps students coming back for more. A great recurring revenue stream. Who does not want that? But I prefer the approach my guru took: helping people define the goal and the path that leads to it, and then empowering them with the tools and practices to help them get there. His approach was truly selfless, and it made me realize that he genuinely cared for my unfoldment.

But how do we know if we are making progress? Signposts! My guru would help me recognize signposts of progress. These signposts of progress imbued me with confidence that I was making progress as a result of my own self-effort. If I am driving from San Francisco to San Diego and I see a signpost that says "250 miles to San Diego," then I know I am heading in the right direction. If two hours later I see a signpost that says "150 miles to San Diego," then I know I am making progress.

I can evaluate how well I do, and the data from my self-evaluation can tell me if I am making progress, but the ultimate display of progress is the impact that my change in behavior has on my life.

If I am diligent with my concentration rituals each day, I will notice that the number of times my awareness drifts away when I am speaking with my spouse decreases over time. At the very onset of my practice I may notice my awareness drifting away five times in a ten-minute conversation. A month later, after diligently working at bringing my awareness back every time it drifts away, I notice that my awareness has not drifted away even once in a ten-minute conversation. This is a clear sign of progress.

This has consequences. The person I am with feels my complete presence, which in turn results in them feeling valued, cared for, and loved.

The better my ability to focus, the more profound my interactions with the people I am with. I can be present because I can focus. I can listen better because I can focus better. Each interaction, even if they are brief, is rewarding because I am able to be present in each of the moments that make up that experience. A five-minute interaction with my daughter allows me to experience all three hundred seconds of that experience without wasting a single second of it. The outcome is that I feel I am living a truly rewarding life. And my daughter knows that when her father is with her, he is completely present. What better way of saying "I love you" to someone?

When my team or clients speak with me, I can be completely focused, and hence completely present in every interaction. I can hear what they are saying. I am observant of things because concentration leads to observation. I notice the subtle unsaid things. I can support them in ways that they may not have expressed the need for. These are among the benefits of a focused mind. We will explore more of these benefits in subsequent chapters.

Keeping Score

In this lesson you will find a page that gives you a table you can use to track how well you performed each of your concentration rituals. For the sake of brevity, I've outlined only fourteen columns, to allow you to track for two weeks. There are five rows in which you can list all five of your opportunities.

In the top row, write down the first opportunity when you would like to consciously practice being focused. And in the subsequent rows below that you can list the other opportunities, though I encourage you to begin them only as I have prescribed.

Each day you can give yourself a score of 0, 1, 2, or 3. I define these numbers as:

3: I performed this ritual extremely well

2: I performed this ritual reasonably well

1: I did not put much effort into this ritual

0: I did not perform this ritual

N/A: I could not perform this ritual today due to unavoidable circumstances

At the end of the month, tally up your score. In a 31-day month you can get a maximum score of 93 points. Based on this you can calculate your percentage score for that month. Six months after you begin, you will be able to chart it out and see if you are making progress or not, based on your self-evaluation. But keep in mind, the biggest demonstration of your progress is a change in your behavior.

I have also digitized the process in my Dandapani app, which is available in the App Store and Play Store. I have a feature called "Rituals" that will allow you to track the progress of your daily rituals. Each day you are prompted to enter your self-evaluation score, and the app keeps track and charts your results. The Rituals are focused on helping you navigate awareness in the mind and develop concentration and willpower.

Opportunities to Practice Concentration	Day														Total
	1	2	3	4	5	6	7	8	9	10	11	12	13	14	

Chapter 7

WILLPOWER—LIFE'S GREATEST FORCE

LESSON 7.1

Defining and Understanding Willpower

Will is the fuel which carries awareness through all areas of the mind,
that spirit, that spiritual quality, which makes all inner goals a reality.

~GURUDEVA

In the previous chapters I've referred to using willpower to bring
awareness back every time it drifts away. I've also mentioned that
the two qualities needed to control where awareness goes in the mind
are concentration and willpower. In order to use willpower, we need
to understand what willpower is. In this chapter we dive into the study
of life's greatest force.

My guru once said to me, "The greatest thing you can develop in
life is willpower. With willpower you can accomplish anything that
you want."

I'd heard of willpower growing up. I thought I had some understanding of it, but it wasn't until I met my guru that I really came to
gain a deeper understanding of willpower. Besides finally understanding what it means, one of the biggest insights I gained from him was
that you can actually develop your willpower.

What a novel concept to my mind! Never had this idea even been
intimated to me my entire life until the day he said that to me. Like

concentration, no one teaches us what willpower is, or how we can go about cultivating it and using it to our benefit. Most people go through life never developing one of the greatest assets they have—an asset capable of monumentally changing the direction of their life.

All of us are born with varying levels of willpower. Some people have tremendous amounts of it and appear to superficial observers to almost effortlessly plow through life with the sheer power of it. Then there are those who have not discovered or cultivated the latent power of their soul, and have surrendered in silent acquiescence to life's capricious whims.

It's easier to observe how much inherent willpower there is in a person when they are a child than when they are an adult. If you are a parent with a few children, you may have observed that they have varying levels of willpower. How each one responds to life's experiences can often be a telltale sign of how much willpower they have. For example, a child wants to buy a toy, so he asks his mother, "Mom, can I have fifty dollars to buy this toy?"

His mother replies, "Sure you can. You just need to work and earn it. And I can give you a few things to work on over the next few months to earn that money." Disheartened to hear this, he responds with, "Really? I'll just wait for my birthday and get it then," despite knowing that his birthday is eight months away.

His sister is keen to get a toy worth the same amount of money and received the same response from their mother. She, however, responded with, "I'm going to pick lemons from our tree, make lemonade, and sell it every weekend. And I'm going to do the work you have for me, Mom. I will make the money I need in a month or two. I'm certain of it!"

Observing both children, you can tell the latter has more willpower. There is a great determination in the daughter, a calling forth of all her inner energies that she directs toward a single point of focus to accomplish her goal. That is willpower.

Deciphering Willpower

My guru defines willpower as the "channeling of all energies toward one given point for a given length of time."

To explain to a child what willpower is, which I have done, I describe it as a mental muscle. This is *far from an accurate description* of what willpower is, but it permits an uncomplicated and elementary visualization of it and how it functions.

If I could draw biceps on either side of my mind, then that would be my mental muscle, my willpower. Willpower, my mental muscle, is what I use to bring awareness back every time it drifts away. I use those biceps to grab hold of that ball of light as it drifts away, and I draw it back to what it was focused on. Viewing willpower as a mental muscle helps us to understand how willpower is used to direct awareness within the mind. Governing and focusing awareness in the mind is the raison d'être of this book.

If willpower is a mental muscle, the biceps of the mind, then I would go about developing it the same way I would develop my biceps. I would use my willpower to develop my willpower, just as I would use my biceps to lift weights to develop bigger, stronger biceps.

Because most people don't realize that they can actually develop more willpower, they end up only working with the willpower that they are born with and inadvertently developing very little more of it throughout the course of their lives. Sadly, not much is accomplished in life when so much more could have been. On the other hand, those who have been trained to develop willpower and work to do so throughout their life end up accomplishing a great many things.

Like a muscle, the more you use your willpower, the more you develop it. The more willpower you develop, the more willpower is available for you to use. Use your will to develop your will. My guru would say, "Strengthen the will by using the will."

Here's another insight my guru shared with me about willpower.

The willpower that you build up always remains with you. It never, ever goes away. It never needs to be replenished and is always available for you to draw upon, in this life, or the next.

Individuals who exhibit high levels of willpower have been nurturing this force for many lifetimes. They enter this incarnation channeling this ever-growing wave of energy, and with the force of a tsunami are able even to pivot the course of humanity. This has been demonstrated time and time again. Such willpower is never cultivated over one life.

The Negative Side of Willpower

Willpower is a double-edged sword, best cultivated alongside one's nature. Without the influence of a refined, conscientious mind and nature, the force of one's will can be channeled toward negative traits and impact one's life in a less than desirable way.

The fundamental building blocks that make up a refined mind and nature are qualities such as humility, selflessness, empathy, compassion, kindness, patience, and more. The continual cultivation of these qualities is the framework that guides awareness to higher-minded ways of thought, speech, and action. They are the guidelines that steer willpower toward creating an uplifting life.

Realize that the more willpower one develops, the stronger its hold over awareness, and hence the greater the need for a conscientious mind and nature, without which it's highly conceivable that awareness may be led astray for iniquitous use.

It's common to hear the phrase "He's so stubborn!" cast at highly focused individuals—a classic echolalia of the ignorant who mistake determination for stubbornness. This determination, the single-minded focus born of due reflection, reason, and clarity of purpose, can often be mistaken for stubbornness. They're easily confused because stubbornness is the determined action of willpower holding awareness in single-minded focus as well, but devoid of reason and governed by the instinctive nature.

Over the years I've met many people who have developed significant amounts of willpower but have not worked at cultivating a conscientious nature. How do I know they have significant amounts of willpower? I've seen them accomplish great things in their lives and overcome challenging obstacles. But not having cultivated a conscientious nature has held them back from accomplishing much more.

For example, a stubborn person may receive guidance on doing something in an alternate way that would result in a better outcome, but their unrefined nature causes them to hold awareness in an area of the mind that is devoid of reason. Lacking humility, they remain firmly obstinate even though they could experience a better outcome by embracing the wise counsel that has been shared with them—a classic example of the negative use of willpower.

If willpower and focus are the wings that awareness uses to soar through the mind, character traits are the feathers that form those wings.

The Greatest Reason to Develop Willpower

Nothing in life happens without will. Even as death beckons and life slips away, our will is the last thing to depart, desperately clinging to every sinew of life.

Though there are innumerable applications of the conscious use of willpower, there is none greater than controlling the journey of awareness in the mind. Willpower is the reins that harness and steer awareness. As willpower directs awareness, it simultaneously directs where energy is flowing and hence what is manifesting in life.

Your life is a testament of the application of your will over your awareness. To control awareness is to control your life.

I develop my willpower, my mental muscle, so that I can use it to bring my awareness back to what it was focused on every time it drifts away. This is the rudimentary application of my willpower. When awareness is brought back from its saunter through the mind, I use my powers of concentration to hold it on what it is meant to be focused on.

Once awareness is trained in the fine art of concentration, willpower takes on a different role. It relinquishes its outgrown capacity as a guardian and assumes its new mantle as a steward of awareness.

The more familiar one is with one's willpower, the more sovereignty one has over it. The hand of a master painter is no stranger to him, and obliges his desires with the reverence of a loyal servant. And so it is with willpower and the mystic. The mystic wields his will with the finesse and precision of a master painter.

His mastery over his will is his mastery over his awareness. His destination is the ineffable depths of the mind, the refined realms of the superconscious, to experience the very essence of his being. On the journey there, he must gracefully navigate awareness through the mind with his indomitable will, eluding the myriad of fascinating and tantalizing areas of the mind waiting to ambush and ensnare awareness in endless distraction. As distracting as the outer world may seem, the world within is infinitely more distracting.

And upon awareness's arrival in the refined realms of the superconscious, the precision with which the mystic uses his will and powers of concentration allows him to not be startled by the profound experiences of the superconscious mind. Should he, even for a moment, release his viselike grip over his awareness, it would be unsettled by its experience, causing it to be drawn out to the conscious mind. Here in the hallowed halls of the superconscious, held so poised, awareness experiences the grandest realms of our being—accessible to all, sought by few, and experienced only by those with an indomitable will, unwavering focus, and an unquenchable desire to know oneself.

Three Ways to Develop Willpower

The understanding of what willpower is, the ways to develop it, and the know-how of its conscious application to manifest goals in life should be taught to every human being. The latent power of the mind, focus, and will are heavenly gifts; though accessible to all, they have remained veiled to many.

Gurudeva taught me three simple but highly effective methods to develop willpower. They are:

1. Finish what you start;
2. Finish it well, beyond your expectations, no matter how long it takes;
3. Do a little bit more than you think you can.

All three of these methods require effort, and that exercising of your effort is the exercising of your will. Remember, you strengthen the will by using the will. Let's explore each of these methods individually, so we can understand them better and see how they help us to develop willpower.

Method 1: Finish What You Start

To experience a sense of exultation at the end of a project that is greater than that which we experienced at its onset requires the conscious administration of willpower. It can only be experienced if we finish what we begin. The energy born of a new idea is a breath of fresh air to the mind. The exhilaration of it propels the effort until that uncontrolled energy, also known as excitement, loses its vigor.

The path to a triumphant end is an inverted bell curve, for after the euphoria that accompanies the beginning of a project, the labored journey to the finish line is an endeavor of seemingly diminishing returns. As energy, inspiration, and excitement dissipate, the will needs to rise to the occasion to carry the idea from vision to manifestation.

Willpower is always needed to bring anything to completion.

In the majority of conversations, most topics are never brought to a natural conclusion before another commences. A conversation can lose its way and drift aimlessly, like a balloon in the sky. Though it may appear inconsequential to bring each topic to closure, most don't realize that a pattern is being crafted in the subconscious mind, which feeds the notion that the failure to complete things, even things as seemingly small and insignificant as a conversational topic, has little to no detrimental effects on one's life or mind.

This pattern of not completing things then begins to seep into every area of life. Initially, the mundane tasks that we need to complete for our mere existence, such as doing the dishes and the laundry and tidying up our home, are scoffed at as a waste of time. This way of thinking eventually makes its way into other aspects of life that have more significant consequences. This then shapes one's nature to enjoy the euphoria of beginning things and to shun the idea of completing them, causing a person to hop from one unfinished task to another. All of this tends toward dampening the will.

It takes willpower to harness awareness and guide it to the natural conclusion of things. The ability to do so empowers the subconscious with the experience that it can complete the tasks or endeavors that it begins. This is powerful. The materialization of an idea is a completion of that idea. As these experiences recur, impressions in the subconscious, small as they may be, build upon one another, and a self-belief that "I can create and manifest" comes to form as a concrete mindset. Confidence ensues and grows in strength as one endeavor after another is completed. Now life becomes an opportunity to create and manifest.

Finish what you begin, no matter how small, mundane, or insignificant you may consider a task. Every time you do so, you are developing your willpower, that mental muscle.

Method 2: Finish It Well, Beyond Your Expectations

Finishing what you begin is the first stage of completion. But there is no need to stop here. Those determined to develop their willpower will be happy to know that there are more opportunities to do so.

You can finish your project and just stop there, or you can choose to finish it well beyond your expectations. This is the second step or method to develop your willpower. The act of finishing it well beyond my expectations requires effort, and the exercising of that effort is my willpower.

Let me share with you my very first experience of being schooled in this by Gurudeva. Each day the monks would spend thirty minutes cleaning a part of the monastery that they were assigned. I was assigned the meditation room for a period of time, and I would spend my allocated time ensuring the room was clean and tidy.

One day I was done early, as the room looked clean to me. As I left the meditation room I ran into Gurudeva. "Are you done with your task?" he asked me.

I replied, "Yes."

"Could you have done it better?"

"Possibly, but everything seemed clean."

"Let's go look at the room together," he said as he strode across the courtyard. He slid open the door and stepped into the meditation room. I followed him.

There was always a palpable feeling of leaving one dimension and stepping into another when I entered this room. It was here, in the early hours of the morning, that the monks, a little over two dozen of us, gathered most days of the week to meditate together with Gurudeva. Decades of untold inner experiences born of renunciates' solitary pursuit of the Self had saturated every nook and cranny of this sacred space, creating a sanctuary that exuded an empyrean vibration not of this world.

It was a simple room with a pitched ceiling and walls wrapped in dark wood. The age of it was felt but not seen. A considerable-sized carpet covered most of the tiled floor. Large sliding glass doors lined a big part of the southeast wall, and a fireplace with a chimney, clad in lava rock, made up the rear of the room. Toward the front, a seat slightly above the ground was set up for Gurudeva. The walls on either side of it were each draped with long scrolls that detailed maps of the inner mind, scribed in Shum, a mystical language he had channeled many decades earlier to effectively train his monks in the fine art of meditation and the experience of Self-Realization. I had spent many hours meditating with Gurudeva in this room and was graced with many profound experiences and insights from him.

As we stood in the middle of this room, he said to me, "Most people only do the bare minimum, or what they can see. If you look around really closely, you will find so many more things to clean. I'm sure no one has cleaned behind that closet in a long time. The fans could be wiped and those cobwebs in the corner could be cleared.

"Always ask yourself, 'Can I do better than what I have done? And what more can I do?'"

This lesson left an indelible impression in my mind and forever shifted the way I do things. The lesson is that with a little bit of effort, by using my willpower, I can finish things well beyond my expectations. And by doing so, I am developing my willpower and completing tasks in a much better way than I would have before.

Method 3: Do a Little Bit More Than You Think You Can

You can finish a project and finish it well beyond your expectations, better than you thought you could, and stop there. Or you can summon your willpower and do a little more.

To do a little more than you think you can requires effort, and again, that effort is the exercising of your will.

I once knew an entrepreneur in Northern California who built luxury homes. When his company completed construction on a home, they would place beautiful bouquets of flowers in some of the rooms on the day they handed the keys to the owners. The flowers added a special touch to the owners' experience of stepping into their new home. Though it was not part of the agreement, the builder did it because they wanted to do a little more than they thought they could. What a great way to bring Method 3 into one's business and to develop willpower at the same time.

Clarifying the Difference between Methods 2 and 3

Over the years I've heard people share with me that they struggle to distinguish between Methods 2 and 3. To dispel any possibility of ambiguity, let me share an example that can elucidate the difference between them.

Just say I decide to paint a room in my house. Method 1 would guide me to begin the painting process and then complete it. Method 2 would urge me to finish it well beyond my expectations. Having not been trained in the art of house painting, I may turn to a few videos online that could enlighten me with a few painting tips and tricks that would allow me to create a finish in the room that is beyond my current level of expertise. This would certainly help me to finish it better than I had initially thought I could and exceed my expectations.

Method 3 encourages me to do a little *more* than I think I can. The room is now painted, and it looks more beautiful than I had initially visualized. To fulfill Method 3, I decide to head out to a local artisan store and purchase a vase that will complement the room. I also acquire two paintings to hang in the room on one of the walls that was looking quite bare. Acquiring the vase and the paintings can be viewed as doing a little bit more than I think I can.

Don't be the person who is satisfied with doing the bare minimum, who merely wants to get the job done and move on. Be the person who is exercising his or her will at every opportunity by calling upon your willpower to do a little bit more.

LESSON 7.3

Integrating Willpower into Life

As precious as a morsel of rice is to a beggar, so is a second in a day to the wise. To focus awareness in the present, as the hands of the clock fall and rise, is a testament of a person's homage to the preciousness of time.

Every moment is an opportunity. Should we be graced to see it as such, we can leverage these moments, just as we have with concentration, to develop our willpower. One should not feel burdened by this. As I have shared previously, in every moment of our day we are engaged in doing something, so why not choose wisely how we do each of those things? When each moment is used intentionally, life becomes fulfilling and rewarding.

Not unlike concentration, the development of willpower needs to be integrated into every aspect of one's life. One can't spend ten minutes a day developing willpower and be engaged the remainder of the day in acts that undermine it. Not much progress will be made this way.

Observation will lead you to see that your entire day is filled with opportunities to develop willpower. Akin to concentration, you can leverage the "nonnegotiable recurring events in your average day" as opportunities to do so. A person saves money so they can apply it to a specific purpose in the future or to have it available should they need or want it. Willpower is no different. The more willpower you develop, the more of it is available for you to call upon.

The first step is to identify the nonnegotiable recurring events in an average day. Once this is done, the next step is to apply the three methods of developing willpower to each of these events.

Ask yourself these questions: "What is one of the nonnegotiable recurring events in my average day? And how can I insert the three methods of developing willpower into it?"

Gurudeva identified sleep as one such event and taught me, at the onset of my monastic life, to use sleep as an opportunity to develop my willpower. Upon rising in the morning, we were guided to make our bed. The act of making the bed in the morning was completing the process of sleep.

More than two decades later, I continue this act of making my bed. The process of sleep begins when I make the decision to retire for the night. I floss and brush my teeth, then climb into bed and look forward to a long night of facial massages as my toddler kneads my face with her feet. I wake up most days in a tangled spaghetti of sheets and blankets deftly constructed throughout the night by a swirling toddler, an impromptu solo performance that would impress any whirling dervish.

Gone are the days when it took me half a minute in the morning to straighten the mostly unruffled solitary sheet and pillow on the futon mattress in my humble monastic dwelling. Family life has added a few more layers of effort and fabric. I disentangle the mess and begin the process of making the bed: straightening the sheets, fluffing the pillows in accordance with the tutelage I received from my wife, and deciphering which pillow goes where and in what order. Yes, there is more than one on the bed.

Making the bed fulfills Method 1 of finishing what I begin. Methods 2 and 3 instruct me to finish it well beyond my expectations and do a little more than I think I can. I make sure all the sheets are neatly tucked in and the comforter is smoothed out. Then I summon my creativity and fold one corner of the comforter at an angle like they do in some hotels, and I arrange the pillows in a creative way.

In the end I have a bed that looks neat, tidy, and welcoming, and creates an uplifting feeling in the bedroom. When a piece of furniture that takes up substantial square footage of a room looks immaculate, it has a significant impact on the room's vibration. It uplifts the space, which then naturally directs awareness to higher-minded areas. More important, I've started my day by developing my willpower.

There have been days where I had a lot going on in my life, or when I overslept, and I felt the urge to skip making the bed and move on to the more pressing demands of the day. The temptation was strong, but I've always resisted. Regardless of what obstacles came up, all of which were in my mind, I would force myself to make the bed and not break the continuity of this ritual. Making the bed is not a difficult task. It's the consistency that trips people up.

Why Make the Bed?

Of all the things I share in my in-person workshops and keynotes, making the bed resonates with people the most. I'm assuming that's because it's an easy practice to integrate into one's life. At the end of the day we all sleep, and at the beginning of the day a significant number of us wake up. As the first task in front of us each morning, making the bed is a low-hanging fruit, an act of will that can be accomplished without too much effort.

Some among the bed-making enthusiasts have shared photos of their made bed on social media and tagged me. I've had a few email me photos of their bed, and others come up to me and enthusiastically share with me how they have not only adopted this practice but have been unwavering in the execution of it daily.

It's not uncommon for me to hear a person proudly say, "Dandapani, I've been making my bed every single day since I heard you speak about it."

I rejoice in their success and respond, "Congratulations! What a great accomplishment. Truly. You should be proud of yourself for your consistency!"

Then I earnestly inquire, "Tell me, please, based on what you've heard me say, why do you make your bed in the morning?"

The answer has *almost* always been, "Well, it gives me a sense of accomplishment first thing in the morning." Another common answer is, "I'm starting my day with a win."

These responses are not incorrect, but they completely miss the mark of what I have shared regarding why one should make the bed each morning. Yes, it does give you a sense of accomplishment, and you do start the day with a win, but that is not the intent for making the bed that I have articulated.

You make the bed in the morning for the purpose of developing willpower. It is an opportunity to integrate the three methods of developing willpower into a nonnegotiable recurring event in an average day. We develop willpower so that we can use our mental muscle to harness and direct awareness within our mind. As we direct awareness within the mind, we guide the flow of our energy. And whatever it is that our energy flows to begins to manifest in our life. That is why we make the bed in the morning. It serves a much greater purpose, one that has to do with how our life unfolds.

That is the *sankalpa*, the Sanskrit language term for purpose and intent. Clarity of intent is paramount. Purpose should and must drive everything. Having clarity about why you make the bed in the morning is highly important. To simply develop willpower is not enough. We need to understand why we are doing so and, ultimately, what we will use that willpower for.

From now on, when you make the bed in the morning, tell yourself that you are engaged in a ritual that is focused on developing your willpower. Reinforce in your mind that the willpower you are developing is what you need to use to control where your awareness goes in your mind, hence where your energy is flowing, which then determines what is manifesting in your life. Carve this sequence into your subconscious mind with the power of repetition and the clarity of intent.

A person can make their bed, but it may not look much better than when it was unmade. Or a person can put some thought and effort into it and make their bed look beautiful. Observing a person's life, their surroundings, and the manner in which they complete tasks (or don't) unveils much of who they are, how they function, and how much willpower they have.

The ritual of making your bed in the morning has another significant benefit. Upon waking and making your bed, you are giving a clear directive to your mind that you are in control of where your awareness goes and what it should engage in, thus setting a clear precedent for the day. Should you surrender the reins of awareness to your environment, you may instead, for example, find yourself engaging in an endless buffet of rabbit holes to go down that your phone has rustled up over the course of the night and is now serving you on the platter of its screen. Develop your will so that you can control where awareness goes, as opposed to allowing your outer or inner environment to control it. Only when you can control where your awareness goes are you controlling where your energy is flowing, and thus controlling what is manifesting in your life.

By making the bed upon arising, you are also exercising your will

THE POWER OF UNWAVERING FOCUS • DANDAPANI

over your mind, body, and emotions, asserting to them that you are in charge of your awareness and what it should engage in. They (your mind, body, and emotions) are being trained that they do not have control over your awareness and that they are here to serve you, not the other way around. So don't let them dictate where your awareness goes, for you are their master. Establish your dominance over them by making your bed.

Establishing Willpower Rituals

T he events that occur each day, especially the nonnegotiable ones, are perfect opportunities to integrate the practice of developing willpower. These events are ones we have accepted as a natural part of our life, so why not leverage them as opportunities to make our life better?

In the previous lesson we looked at one example, making the bed. I'd like to share a few more examples that you can leverage as opportunities to develop willpower.

Eating, like sleeping, is nonnegotiable. Meals are a wonderful opportunity to integrate the three methods of developing willpower, because we all have meals every day. Every morning I have breakfast. If I have time to make and eat breakfast, then I certainly have time to clean up my breakfast dishes. It's important to resist and not succumb to the seemingly insurmountable list of tasks lying ahead in the day and say, "I really have to get going, so I'll just do the dishes later."

Once I am done consuming my bowl of fruit, I wash the bowl and leave it on the drying rack to dry. I return a couple of hours later (I work from home), when Mother Nature has helped me with the task of drying the bowl, and I put my dish away. Now I've completed the process of having breakfast. I've finished what I've started.

You may decide instead that you are going to wash the dish, dry it right away with a cloth, and place it back in the cupboard to complete the task immediately. Or you may define this process as complete after you put the dish in your dishwasher and wipe the counter clean of any food scraps. It's important for you to know that you must define for yourself what "finish what you start" looks like. Once you have defined this, then stick to it. Your ability to stick to your process is your willpower in action.

If you do not define "finish what you start," you can end up spending the whole morning cleaning the kitchen. Similarly, define to yourself what "doing a little more than I think I can" and "doing it better than I think I can" mean to you with regard to each task. If I did not do that, I could spend an hour or two making the bed in the morning. I could wash the sheets, iron them, dry the pillows in the sun, and God knows what else in the pursuit of developing my willpower. This would not be practical and reasonable. Always use wisdom in applying all of these principles and tools. Never abandon reason.

A lot of people have at least one meal at home. Within the creation of this meal are many opportunities to apply the three methods of developing willpower—from preparation to cooking to cleaning up before and after eating the meal. If you're committed to developing your willpower, leverage this opportunity that occurs daily. Examine it closely and you will find many opportunities to apply the three methods. In fact, every time you eat or drink is an opportunity to be conscious of the process of preparation, consuming, and finishing, and leveraging it to develop your willpower and your practice of concentration.

Many offices have eating spaces or a space to prepare a beverage.

After you've used the space, apply the three methods of developing willpower. Clean the counters. Wash the coffee mug, dry it, and put it away. Bring the practice of developing willpower into your workplace.

Gurudeva would counsel the monks to "leave a room better than you found it." When we left a room, we made every effort to make it look a little nicer than when we came in. I began to realize from the consistency of applying this guideline that even the smallest act of doing so left an appreciable difference.

My family and I go barefoot at home, and that prompts us to remove our footwear before entering the house. As we return home, we finish the act of going out, and part of this process is taking off our footwear and placing it in its appropriate place. Doing more and doing better is aligning the footwear neatly—a simple act that even my toddler has become skillful at.

It's easier to take off one's coat and throw it on the couch than to hang it on a hanger in the closet, and to leave dirty clothes lying on the bedroom floor as opposed to in the laundry basket. The day is filled with endless opportunities to develop willpower should we choose to look at it that way. Once clarity of purpose for doing so is firmly cognized by the conscious and subconscious mind, these opportunities are willingly embraced, rather than looked at as a chore or burden.

These opportunities eventually turn into habits. At this point, no effort needs to be exerted in the execution of them. They simply become how you do things.

You complete thoughts on a topic in a conversation. You always wash your dishes and put them away. You take your footwear off and place it neatly. Your coat is hung in the closet. When you step out from a table, you slide the chair back in. The way you live your life is a reflection of your mindset—a mindset that is shaped to develop willpower and the ability to focus. These rituals become part of the rhythm of your life, an effortless flow of your life force through a structured subconscious designed to fulfill a very specific purpose.

Developing Willpower

I would like you to write down five nonnegotiable recurring events in an average day that you can leverage as opportunities to develop willpower. In this and the previous lesson I have given a few examples that you may use as these opportunities, or you may come up with your own. As with concentration practice, it is important that they be nonnegotiable and recurring in your average day.

List these opportunities from one to five in the order you would like to implement them and select the first opportunity. Take the first opportunity and integrate it into your life for one month. Put the other four on hold.

If the first opportunity that you have chosen is making your bed upon rising in the morning, then set out to do exactly that each day. Apply the three methods of developing will as you make the bed. If after a month you find that you have not been performing this ritual consistently and well, continue to do it until you reach a place where you find yourself executing it really well.

At the end of this lesson, you will find the same self-evaluation table that was in the concentration chapter. You can use the same instructions to track and evaluate your practice of developing willpower. For the sake of brevity and simplicity I will not repeat those instructions here. A digital version of this exists in the Dandapani app under the section called "Rituals."

When you are satisfied that you are making the bed really well, then add the second opportunity to your daily ritual. Perhaps the second opportunity is to begin the ritual of washing your dishes after you've had breakfast. Focus on doing so every morning, and again, when you get to a place where you find yourself executing both rituals really well in the morning, then it's time to add a third opportunity to your daily ritual.

Remember what I shared about bench-pressing and adding weights in an incremental manner? We want to adopt this philosophy in our development of willpower as well. It's paramount that you be patient with yourself as you work to develop this quality. Haste and impatience will assure failure.

Though a number of these tasks may appear mundane and unimportant, I don't view them in the same light. I view everything I do throughout the day as an act I have made the conscious decision to engage in; hence each deserves my undivided attention and care. These seemingly small acts are a significant part of my life. Significant because they recur every day, and the unbroken consistency of this has extraordinary power to shape my life.

Knowing that with a developed will I can control where my awareness goes in my mind is enough to convince me to dedicate my day to cultivating this power. With willpower I can direct my awareness to the more refined areas of my mind, the superconscious, and experience higher states of consciousness—states that exist within all of us at this very moment, patiently awaiting the presence of our awareness. Ultimately, for me, developing willpower is not only about manifesting the life I want, but, more important, for experiencing higher states of consciousness and, ultimately, Self-Realization.

Opportunities to Practice Willpower	Day														Total
	1	2	3	4	5	6	7	8	9	10	11	12	13	14	

The Source of Willpower

A vegetable farmer has a twenty-acre piece of land on which he grows a variety of vegetables. The life of his crops is greatly dependent on the amount of water they receive. Being an experienced farmer, he has set up a thoughtfully designed irrigation system that draws water from the deep well on his property to ensure all his vegetables are fully watered. A year later he acquires an additional four acres of land and converts that parcel to a vegetable farm as well. Knowing where his source of water is, his well, he knows exactly where to go on his property to draw more water for his new farm.

It's a public holiday in the middle of the week, and you're lounging on the couch, enjoying your day off and immersed in a novel. As you turn another page of this gripping thriller, your subconscious shatters your focus, reminding you that you had made a plan to go to the gym in the morning.

You let out a huge sigh as you recall that mental commitment you made to yourself in a moment of despair after last night's dinner. "I did, didn't I?" you mutter to yourself.

To fulfill that plan, you need to first bring your awareness to attention. You find your awareness completely anchored in the book and the suspense of what will happen next as the plot unfolds. The extremely feeble attempt you make to separate awareness from that which it is aware of is entirely futile. At this moment, you have little to no desire to leave this comfy web you've woven for yourself. In fact, you are dreading the thought of changing into your gym clothes and driving over to the gym for a workout.

At this point you realize that the only way you are going to the gym is if you summon the willpower that you have been cultivating for years. Do you, like the farmer with his well, know where to go to draw upon that willpower? Do you know the source of your willpower?

Over the decades, as I strive to be the better version of myself, there have been and continue to be many mental and emotional chasms that I have to bridge, and personality traits to humbly acknowledge, own, and adjust. I recall one day, as a young monastic, feeling mentally defeated as I battled a deep-rooted subconscious pattern that I needed to adjust.

Feeling vanquished by my own instinctive nature, I went looking for my guru. I found him seated on a chair in his room. The light coming in from the window was filtered by a screen, filling the room with a subdued, cold light. I prostrated before him in humble and loving obeisance, as was tradition, then sat cross-legged in front of him. His presence enveloped me with hope. I could see he sensed my defeat.

No words had been exchanged. Finally, he broke the silence and said, "The answer to your question is willpower." There was a long pause as he allowed those words to sink into me. Then he said, "You need to go to the source of willpower and draw upon your will. That source is within you."

I listened with undivided attention, which he always had from me, and then asked, "Where within me is the source of willpower?"

He laughed and replied, "I'm not telling you. You have to discover this for yourself." And that closed the book on that topic with him.

If I were to lay everything out in great detail in this book, I would rob you of the joy of seeking, discovering, experiencing, and realizing a great many things for yourself. The experiential learning that you will have if you discover it for yourself is vastly different than if I told it to you. Once you can identify the source of willpower, you can always return to it and call upon it for anything that you may need in life.

The quest for discovering the source of willpower is an endeavor worth embarking on. Because the farmer knows the exact location of the well, he can repeatedly return to it and draw from it the amount of water he needs for his farm to flourish. Your discovery of the source of willpower will empower you with a resource beyond your comprehension. I wish you well in this quest.

LESSON 7.6

Doing the Deep Work

One of my goals with this book, as I shared early on, is not to inundate you with practices to the point that you can't keep track of them, let alone perform them. But for those of you who would like to dive deeper into developing willpower, here are two long-term practices that you can adopt.

My counsel is that you embark on them after you are able to sustain the practices of developing willpower in the five opportunities you identified in an average day.

Long-Term Exercise 1

I would like you to identify five projects in recent years that you began but have yet to complete. Perhaps you started these projects with a lot of excitement and inspiration, but partway through the project, for one reason or another, you decided to stop working on them, and so they were never completed.

*It is not developing your willpower by having a lot of half-finished jobs
and by starting out with a bang on a project then fizzling out.*

~GURUDEVA

Let me clarify this exercise further by elaborating on it. Some of you may be able to identify five projects that need to be completed that you have begun in the last twelve months but not finished. Others, who have been better at completing what they began, may have to dial back the years and perhaps identify those five projects over a longer period of time.

Not all projects can be completed right away. For example, my wife and I began our project of creating a spiritual sanctuary and botanical gardens in Nosara, Costa Rica, in 2013. Siva Ashram, the name of this sanctuary, is a work in progress, and the gardens, especially, will take years to complete, not due to lack of willpower but rather to the time it takes for nature to flourish.

The projects you list can be large or small, it doesn't matter. Write them down and identify which of them you wish to tackle first. Define what finishing would look like to you and how you would apply Methods 2 and 3 to take them to the next level. Similar to the approach I have defined for developing focus and willpower in previous lessons, start with one of these projects and focus on completing it before you move on to the next one. Before you begin on your first project, set a completion date for it. Then use your will to complete the project by the newly assigned deadline.

As you tackle each project, strive to recall why you abandoned working on it. See if you can clearly identify the reason, and make a note of this. There's often a lesson to learn here.

Upon completing a project, take some time to congratulate yourself and celebrate your win by having consciously exercised your will to accomplish a task. Know that the act of doing this will create a positive impression in your subconscious, an impression that you know how to use your will to begin and finish endeavors. As you complete one project after another, this impression gets reinforced, and you are on your way to manifesting a great many things in your life.

Once you've completed these five projects, you may want to consider looking back on your life and making a list of all the projects you have started and not finished. When you have made a list of these projects, make a firm and final decision on which of these you want to bring to completion. For all the ones you want to complete, apply the three methods of developing willpower and complete them. For the ones you choose not to complete, you can come to terms with renouncing them, knowing that you've used your wisdom to guide your decision that these projects are no longer worth investing your energy and time in.

Long-Term Exercise 2

Along the same lines as the first long-term exercise, I would like you to look back over the last twelve months and identify five occasions where you told someone you would do something but have not done it.

For example, you said to a friend a few months ago, "I'm going to buy you my favorite book and send it to you as a gift," but you have yet to do so.

Identify each of these occasions and what it was that you said you would do. Write it down in detail. As you write down and review these assurances you've made to others, identify whether you will or will not fulfill them. Perhaps wisdom tells you that you should not fulfill some of them now. Then you should listen to this voice of reason.

For the ones you have identified as assurances that you will go about fulfilling, go ahead and do so as part of finishing what you started. If applicable, apply Methods 2 and 3 as well. Assign dates by which you will complete them.

Identify why it was that you never ended up fulfilling what you said you would do. Is it because you have a tendency to overcommit? Or do you say things with the understanding that not everything you say you need to act on? Again, there is a lesson to learn here, and one that, if understood, could positively shape the development of your willpower.

Once you've completed fulfilling the five assurances you listed, you may want to consider looking further back in your life and identifying any major promises you've made and not fulfilled. Identify which of these you want to fulfill and which you do not. Then proceed with fulfilling the ones you've recommitted to.

Going forward, be very conscious of what you say to someone. Every time you tell someone you are going to do something, use your willpower to do so. Keep in mind that this has nothing to do with proving yourself to others. It has to do with strengthening your will. If every time you say you are going to do something, you don't, then you are only dampening your will, and creating patterns within the subconscious that do not support the development of your willpower. However, if you always do what you say, then you create patterns that strengthen your will.

You should adopt this attitude not only toward others but to yourself as well. If you tell yourself you're going to do something, then you should go ahead and do it to the best of your ability and a little more. Setting a time frame for when you will get it done can encourage the timely completion of it, lest you procrastinate.

Work hard, strive to accomplish,
strengthen the will by using the will.
~GURUDEVA

Chapter 8

COGITATIONS ON
CONCENTRATION

LESSON 8.1

Technology and Concentration

It was the obligatory bathroom break at one of my half-day workshops. Well, obligatory for everyone except me. My bladder had renounced the idea of ever seeing the inside of a restroom during these breaks. I'm always approached during these intermissions by one or more people who are eager to ask or share something with me. Today was no different. When the break was announced, a lady seated halfway down the hall emphatically jumped up from her seat and made a beeline for the stage. She parted the opposing flow of crowds bound for the restroom with the force of her determination and arrived at the stage before I could even take a sip of water.

She looked at me, unable any longer to contain the thoughts that had been brewing in her mind, and burst out, "I love everything you've said about focus. We truly must teach people, especially children, how to focus." I craned back in slow motion as she spoke, in sync with the force of her words. Barely were those words out of her mouth before she lifted the hand that was holding her smartphone, held it to my face, and said with utter disgust, "These things are ruining our lives! They are causing us to be so distracted." For something that she held in such contempt and blamed unequivocally as the source of ruin of many lives, she clutched it like a mother would a child.

I've heard many people blame technology, specifically smartphones, as the cause of distraction. It's an opinion that I do not share. Smartphones are not ruining our lives. What is ruining people's lives is their inability to exercise discipline around the use of their smartphones.

Objectively, smartphones are amazing devices equipped with a great number of invaluable capabilities, including the magical feature of being able to almost instantaneously connect you visually with anyone anywhere in the world. This device, which is held more than the average child, can also give you access to vast amounts of information available on the internet, solve complex problems, and unleash one's creative juices. Its front-facing camera—the ego's personal "mirror, mirror on the wall"—can effortlessly evoke frustrating and ennuied acts of repeatedly taking and deleting photos of oneself. Its sleek aerodynamic design could probably work well as a self-defense weapon, a nonreturning boomerang to be chucked at an approaching assailant. I love my smartphone for this and many other reasons. It is an indispensable tool, and like any tool that has changed the course of history—such as a knife or a vehicle—it can be destructive if not used wisely.

The World Health Organization (WHO) states that almost 1.3 million people die each year as a result of road traffic crashes. Can we then justly conclude that vehicles are bad? That would not be a wise conclusion. A better conclusion would be that the untrained use of vehicles has damaging consequences, such as injuries and death.

Similarly, to say that technology causes you to be distracted is misdirected. Technology has great potential to distract you, and some of it is intentionally designed to keep you engaged, but ultimately it is you who have control over your awareness. You always have the decision-making power to choose whether you wish technology to have control over your awareness or whether you prefer to have complete dominance over your own awareness.

The advent of technology in our life, and its uninhibited, exponential growth unaccompanied by the imperative study of its impact on its users and the education of its users in its proper use, should be considered one of humankind's gravest mistakes.

Technology is a tool, and it is a tool that we need to exert governance over.

There are aspects of technology that are inherently distracting and ultimately train your awareness to be distracted. The news on television is a perfect example. When you turn on the TV, you see the anchor sharing news of major events from around the world. You are paying attention, so your awareness is trained on her. She says, "Today in Afghanistan, a car blew up, thirty people died, and fifteen were injured." As she concludes her sentence, a video appears to the right of her showing scenes from that car bomb. She continues sharing more details of that devastating incident, and as she does so, the video continues to play. Now your awareness is shifting back and forth between her and the video.

In this scenario, what is your awareness being trained to do? It's being trained to be distracted as it jumps back and forth between the newscaster and the video. An external force, in this case the news, is determining where your awareness goes.

As if that were not enough, a banner is scrolling across the bottom third of the screen listing headlines of breaking news. Needless to say, it often highlights the world's most despairing news: "255 dead as hurricane devastates Bangladesh." As that makes its way off-screen, the next one slides in, reading "12 dead in mall shooting in Green Bay, Wisconsin." And so the calamities of life on earth are shared with unflagging ardor, as only a news channel can.

Awareness is now pinballing between the news anchor, the video playing to her right, and the breaking news on the banner. The master class on distraction is well on its way.

Believe it or not, there are actually even more things taking place on the screen. Below the scrolling breaking-news headlines, announcements from the stock market are being served up. Now your poor awareness has four things to bounce between. But seriously, why stop there? On the bottom-right corner of the screen, an icon of the sun fades in along with information to let you know that it is "28 degrees Celsius and sunny in Rio de Janeiro." Temperatures and weather forecast updates from various cities around the world are shared for the entire duration of the news.

Watching the news for twenty minutes would be no different than sending awareness to the distraction gym for a thorough workout. In that duration, awareness bounced between all five information points on the screen, which were perpetually changing and vying for your attention. In this case, you can rightly say that technology is distracting. In the church of the media and on the altar of the flat-screen, many have sacrificed their peace of mind.

How do I handle this, you ask? I simply do not watch the news on television. If I need the latest news, I pick a specific news source online and drill down to the section on their website or app to read the latest information on a particular topic.

Some aspects of the internet can be distracting as well if you have not cultivated sufficient powers of concentration. YouTube, the black hole for awareness, has been designed to keep you in its clutches. When you're done watching a video, it suggests an additional one, along with a slew of enticing thumbnails that form a column to the right. One of these thumbnails is always an outlier—the trapdoor to the black hole. "Five-Headed Snake in Indonesia." Is there such a thing? Click! And so begins awareness's journey into the universe of distraction.

The smartphone, the pocket black hole for awareness, can be se-

verely distracting for those who struggle to consciously navigate awareness in the mind. It calls to you like a distressed calf, and you answer
with the unconditional devotion of a loving mother. If you fail to control awareness, then awareness can begin a seemingly endless journey,
bouncing between social media apps, text messages, emails, phone calls,
browsing the internet, and whatever else your smartphone is offering.

The manufacture of increasingly cunning ways to distract, in a
world where capturing one's attention is a paramount goal, has led to
sophisticated ways to feed this disease.

If you allow this to happen throughout the day, you're allowing
your smartphone to train you in the art of distraction. You become
good at what you practice. Your smartphone will never stop begging
for your attention. If you live in a state of reaction, which is a state of
uncontrolled awareness, then you will respond to every notification
from your phone. You have to make the choice on how you interact
with your technology. Don't blame technology for being distracting.
The truth of it is that most people allow themselves to be distracted.

On the contrary, if you have sound mastery over awareness in the
mind, you could pick up your smartphone, spend a few minutes scrolling through your Instagram feed only, as part of taking a short break,
then put it down and return to what you are doing. Would this be
considered being distracted? Absolutely not. It's not a distraction because you made a conscious choice to take a break and use the few
minutes of that break time to be on Instagram only. When you felt
you'd had a sufficient break, you brought your awareness back to what
you were doing. You refrained from engaging with other apps on your
phone. This is a demonstration of concentration in action.

If you allow technology to control where awareness goes in your
mind, then you become a slave to technology. Not only is technology
then controlling where your awareness goes, but it is also controlling
where your energy is flowing, and hence the areas of the mind that are

being developed as a consequence of energy flowing to them. These areas then become strengthened, magnetized by the perpetual depositing of energy, and gain the power to repeatedly pull awareness back to them.

If you see someone mechanically picking up their phone repeatedly throughout the hour and checking their Facebook account, for example, you now know what is happening. They've repeatedly allowed their awareness to go to that area of the mind, as a result paving a deep mental groove to it and creating a highly magnetized area of the mind that now exhibits a tremendous pull over their awareness.

Technology is distracting only if you allow it to be so. Technology is here to stay, have no doubt about it, and is an ever-growing part of our lives. There is no escape. You're on the bus headed to a technology-immersed future whether you like it or not. This makes a deeply compelling case for why you should—in fact, must—work to develop mastery over awareness in your mind, or be ruled by those who develop technology.

Technology is here to serve you, not for you to serve it. Be clear on this.

Leveraging Technology

So far, I haven't painted technology in a favorable way with regard to concentration. This does not have to be the case. I'm a big proponent of technology, and I believe technology can be used to help us develop focus and willpower without even the need to download a single piece of software or app.

In previous chapters, I shared the extremely important point of integrating our practices into the nonnegotiable recurring events of the day. Many of us spend a significant amount of time engaging with technology, such as our smartphones. Since this is a daily recurring event, it's a great opportunity to leverage this time to practice developing our willpower, concentration, and other qualities I've touched on. Here are a few practices involving a smartphone, simple as they may seem, that you may consider:

1. *Abstinence*—Refraining from unnecessarily picking up your phone. A great practice to exercise your willpower. Use the willpower you develop throughout the day and apply it here. And when you apply it here, you are developing more willpower. Every time your awareness drifts away from what you are doing and goes to your phone on the table, and the urge to pick up the phone rises within you, use your willpower to gently and lovingly bring awareness back to what you were engaged in.

2. *Purpose*—Conscious interactions as opposed to mindless ones. Let each interaction be driven by purpose. Prior to picking up your phone, decide exactly what you will be engaging in. By doing so you are training yourself to be intentional. This will help you to develop further clarity in other parts of your life and ultimately in life itself.

3. *Focus*—With intention comes focus. Pick an app that you want to engage in and focus just on that. Refrain from being a digital monkey that jumps from one app to another, or you will only be training your awareness in the art of distraction. Think Navy SEALs (which I know nothing about): you go in, get the job done, and you leave. You're not there to mingle and make friends. Pick up the phone, do what you need to, and put it down.

4. *Time*—Define the duration. Set a time and use your willpower to stick to it. For example, I periodically take five-minute social media breaks during the day. Instagram is the only social media app I regularly engage with, and during this time I scroll through my feed of carefully curated

accounts that I follow. When that time is done, I put my phone down. It requires willpower to shift awareness from whatever it is engaged in on the screen to something or someone else that is not your phone.

5. *Managing energy*—If you're on social media, be conscious of what you engage in or view. If you allow algorithms to dictate your experience—in other words, dictate where your awareness goes—then you are allowing it to dictate where your energy flows to. What algorithms serve up to you can give you energy or take energy away from you. It can also emotionally upset you, robbing you of your peace of mind and shaking up awareness unnecessarily. Choose what content you allow awareness to see and engage in.

Ultimately, technology should be used wisely and with purpose. If this approach is taken, technology can help you lead a rewarding life.

LESSON 8.2

The Wheels of the Mind

The Wheels of the Mind describes how the conscious mind and the subconscious mind work with each other to reinforce patterns within the mind. Let's begin our study of this with distraction.

When awareness wanders aimlessly in the conscious mind, a mirroring pattern is created in the subconscious. As you may recall from one of the early lessons in the book, the subconscious mind records what is happening in the conscious mind. As we allow awareness to be distracted from what it is meant to be focused on and be off on yet another saunter in the mind, we reinforce this distracted pattern in the subconscious. Repeat this process over and over again, and we strengthen the pattern in the subconscious.

What is this pattern that we are creating? It's a pattern that says to awareness, "Whenever you are made to focus on one thing, feel free to wander off as you please at any time."

Eventually this distracted pattern is strong enough to be influential over awareness on its own. This is when the real problem begins.

I knew a man who planted an *Elaeocarpus ganitrus* tree, the tree that produces the beads that Hindu monks and priests wear, close to his home. He loved the tree and cared for it like it was his child. He fed it, nurtured it, and eventually it got really big. The buttress roots of the tree made their way to the house and started to affect the structure of his home. Now he has a beast on his hands that is impossible to manage. His daily life is very much disrupted by this massive tree.

The well-fed and nurtured distracted pattern within the subconscious is not different from *E. ganitrus*. Once big and strong enough, it starts to exert its influence on the journey of awareness within the mind. When your willpower does not have a sufficient grasp over awareness, then this pattern takes over. It pries awareness away from your grasp and sends it gallivanting in the mind again, because this is what the pattern is and does.

It all began with the erratic movement of awareness in the conscious mind, which then created a mirroring pattern in the subconscious mind. The pattern that is created in the subconscious is in turn now affecting awareness in the conscious mind. As awareness is driven hither and thither in the conscious mind by this pattern, this very act reinforces the pattern in the subconscious.

Thus begins an extremely vicious cycle, a cycle I call the Wheel of Distraction. You can see why patterns can become so strong and difficult to break. People who practice distraction throughout the day are spinning that wheel of distraction. A pattern is created, then devotedly reinforced until it becomes strong enough to take over. Its takeover begins an unending repetitive reinforcing cycle.

If I went to the refrigerator and opened it to see if there was something in there I could munch on, that would not create a pattern in my mind. But if I started doing that five times a day, every day, week after week, then that would very quickly create a strong pattern in my mind.

Now, when I am sitting at my desk working, this ever-strengthening pattern would drive my awareness to open the refrigerator, causing me to get up and head over to the refrigerator again. The act of getting up and heading to the refrigerator reinforces the pattern, and thus a vicious cycle begins.

One of the reasons why people struggle to concentrate is because the patterns of distraction in their subconscious mind are so strong and are perpetually getting stronger, as they are reinforced by the pattern itself and by the repetition of distractive behavior.

Knowing all this, I hope you are starting to see why you should be very careful of what you repeat, consciously or unconsciously. The patterns that are created in the subconscious as a result of this can be challenging to overcome.

You must also be very careful what you allow your conscious mind to experience, meaning where you allow your awareness to travel in your mind throughout the day, because all experiences, whether remembered or not, get registered in the subconscious mind. And if any of these experiences are consistently repeated, they start forming patterns in the subconscious, which will in turn have an effect on awareness in the conscious mind.

Repetitively listening to music that makes you sad takes awareness to the sad area of the mind, creating a pattern of sadness that then has the magnetic power to pull awareness back to it, thus creating a cycle—a wheel of sadness. The contrary is true. If every morning you begin your day with meditation, positive affirmations, or reading scripture that extols higher states of mind, you create patterns in the subconscious mind that eventually are strong enough to independently draw awareness to uplifting areas of the mind. Throughout the day you will find awareness being drawn to higher states of consciousness. As it goes there, it reinforces the patterns that were created. The Wheel of Upliftment is now in motion.

The Wheel of Concentration

The Wheel of Distraction occurs when awareness wanders unharnessed in the conscious mind, thus creating a mirroring pattern of distraction in the subconscious, which then subsequently governs awareness in a distracted way in the conscious mind.

The Wheel of Concentration works in exactly the same way. If awareness is in a state of concentration in the conscious mind, it creates a mirroring pattern of concentration in the subconscious, which subsequently governs awareness in a concentrated way in the conscious mind.

I'll unfold this a bit more. As you hold awareness in concentration while navigating through activities in the conscious mind, patterns of focus are created in the subconscious. Remember, the subconscious registers what is going on in the conscious mind. These patterns of focus that are created in the subconscious will in turn govern awareness in the conscious mind in a concentrated way, causing awareness to be focused while it is in the conscious mind.

Awareness being concentrated in the conscious mind re-impresses the subconscious with further patterns of focus. Thus a cycle begins. But this time, instead of a vicious cycle of distraction, a positive cycle of focus is in place. As a result, whenever you are not in charge of your awareness in your conscious mind, your subconscious will take hold of awareness and navigate it in a focused way, guided by the deeply ingrained patterns of concentration that were created by the Wheel of Concentration.

A simple analogy to illustrate this concept is to look at awareness and the mind the same way we look at a plane. I'm no pilot, but I'm going to make an assumption that at any given point in time, either the pilot is manually flying the plane or the plane is on autopilot.

In this analogy, the plane is your awareness. If you are in control of your awareness while it is in the conscious mind, then you are concentrating—you are the pilot who is flying the plane manually. If you are not in control of your awareness, then either your environment or your subconscious is controlling your awareness. For the purpose of explaining this point, we will use the subconscious as the governing force and not your environment. This would then be equivalent to when the plane is on autopilot.

So if you are not in charge of your awareness, then your subconscious is governing where your awareness is going. If the patterns that have been created in your subconscious are focused, your subconscious will govern your awareness in a concentrated way. If the patterns that have been created in your subconscious are distracted, then your subconscious will govern your awareness in a distracted way. The autopilot can only, I assume, govern the plane in the way that it has been programmed to.

Simply put, the Wheel of Distraction and the Wheel of Concentration work in exactly the same way. The only difference is that one is making patterns of distraction and the other patterns of focus.

If you have spent time developing your powers of concentration, then know that you have created patterns of focus in your subconscious mind. These patterns will serve you positively during the day. You will find that your awareness is not wandering all over the place even when you are not consciously governing it, because the patterns in your subconscious are of a focused nature.

Even in a relaxed state, awareness is not racing all over the mind. It is stationary in one place. If we were to look at the analogy of awareness as a dog, then in such a scenario the dog is trained to stay where it is. You are taking a walk in a park with your dog, and after walking for a while you decide to sit down on a park bench. Your dog sits next to you and does not run off all over the park. This is how awareness is when you have practiced concentration and become really good at it. The focused patterns within the subconscious hold awareness in concentration in the conscious mind.

THE POWER OF UNWAVERING FOCUS • DANDAPANI

When this starts to happen, concentration becomes effortless because it has become a habit. Concentration is the default setting for your awareness. Awareness is in a state of concentration all the time, and therefore it's very difficult for it to become distracted. Eventually, you will find yourself in a state of concentration throughout the day— you are present in every experience. This is a beautiful and blessed mind to have.

Ruminations on Focus

Here are a few areas worth shedding some light on in our study of the mind and focus.

Wisdom

Over the years that my guru trained me, there was one rule that he made sure I understood and that I was always cognizant of. He would admonish that "Wisdom is the only rigid rule," and that this tenet should be adopted in every aspect of life. Similarly, always use wisdom to discern when and how to apply the tools and teachings within this book in your life.

He defined wisdom as the timely application of knowledge. Timing is everything. Knowledge itself does not do much for a person unless it can be applied in a timely and appropriate way that results in positive outcomes. Only then can it have an impact.

Many assume that the acquisition of knowledge per se means that one is learning and growing. It absolutely does not mean that. It only means you have gathered more information. The application of that knowledge in a timely way is what demonstrates how well a person has grasped that knowledge.

For example, in the chapter on concentration, I suggest the practice of doing one thing at a time. This does not mean that if you are driving your car you cannot be engaged in a conversation with a passenger. If one were to adopt the tenet of "Wisdom is the only rigid rule," then you would use wisdom to decide whether you should be engaged with someone in a conversation or not. Wisdom would guide you not to be engaged in a conversation when you are trying to make a challenging turn at a busy intersection. However, if you are driving on a fairly vacant road for a long stretch, then engaging in a light conversation would be acceptable. Wisdom would also take it a step further and apply a general rule for all driving circumstances: one should not be in a conversation that is serious or emotional while driving. That would have the power to deeply engage awareness and take it away from focusing on the road.

Ultimately, wisdom is the only rigid rule. Let wisdom guide you in how you apply all of the teachings in this book in your life.

Setting Awareness Free

If we are practicing doing one thing at a time, does that mean that we never allow awareness to wander off aimlessly? There are times when I may go lie down on the carpet in my living room and tell myself that for the next fifteen minutes I'm going to just daydream about designing the gardens at our spiritual sanctuary in Costa Rica. I will lie there and let my awareness drift to various areas of my mind within the realm of gardens.

There are other times when I will just lie down and allow my awareness to drift away for a fixed period of time and observe where it goes in my mind. This is always fascinating, as it quite often highlights what is in the forefront of my mind and also what is unresolved in my subconscious. But these periods when I unleash awareness and allow it to roam in my mind are always for a fixed duration. Simply setting a timer for this mental odyssey suffices to ensure that it does not go on endlessly. Remember, we do not want to train awareness to wander aimlessly in the mind, lest it become a dominant pattern.

Then there are other times where I may set aside a period of time, say ten minutes, to browse around on social media or surf the web, and let awareness be taken on a journey the same way I would if I was watching a movie. But if I find awareness being taken to an area of the mind that I don't want to go to while surfing the web, then I'll use my willpower to grab hold of awareness and bring it back to an area of the mind I want to be in. I'm very protective of where my awareness goes, and learning to pivot awareness is a practice worth cultivating.

The goal ultimately is to be in charge of where awareness goes in the mind. But in a controlled environment it is acceptable to let awareness loose. If you took your dog to a dog park, you would feel comfortable unleashing the dog, knowing it was in a controlled space. You wouldn't do that in an area that is not fenced in, where it might run onto a busy road. Likewise, use your wisdom to decide when to let your awareness off the leash of your willpower.

When I am hanging out and chatting with my most trusted friends, I will let my awareness off the leash, so to speak. I do this knowing that my awareness will never be guided to a place that I don't want it to go to. However, in conversations with strangers, I am much more observant of where my awareness is being taken, and I am always ready to rein awareness back should it be taken to an unwholesome area of the mind.

Love, Discipline, Focus, and Happiness

Love gives birth to the discipline of concentration. What do I mean by this?

When you love something, you naturally want to spend more time with it. This applies to a person you love as well. To get the most out of that time with the person or thing you love, it behooves you to be concentrated.

A person who loves playing the guitar wants to spend as much time as she can in a day doing so. In order to do so, her love for playing the guitar drives her to discipline her life. The better her ability to focus and the more willpower she can develop, the more she can use these qualities to discipline her life so as to make more time for playing the guitar each day.

Once she has successfully made time to play the guitar, her ability to be completely focused in what she is doing will allow her to experience playing the guitar fully, resulting in the greatest satisfaction. Similarly, if you love someone and you want to spend as much time with them as possible, it is your ability to focus that will ultimately determine how profound that experience will be. Many people spend time with the people they love, but their inability to focus results in unfulfilling facile and shallow experiences.

You develop concentration to experience more of what you love in a deeper way. The by-product of experiencing what you love fully is the feeling of happiness.

Remember, don't pursue happiness. Rather, design a lifestyle whose by-product is happiness. Develop willpower and concentration so that you can harness awareness and be fully immersed—fully present—in the experiences that the lifestyle you designed brings you. The outcome of this is the experience of happiness.

Listening and Understanding

The ability to listen is a trait high on the endangered list of rapidly vanishing human qualities.

If you are unable to keep awareness on one thing for an extended period of time, how can you even begin the process of listening? If your awareness only has the ability to stay on one thing for seven seconds, then that is how long you are able to listen before you get distracted.

The ability to listen is an extremely helpful trait in building relationships with people. But you cannot listen if you cannot concentrate, and a lot of people are not good listeners because they are perpetually distracted. The better a person can concentrate, the better they can listen. As a result, they can gather more information, reflect on it, and, consequently, gain a better understanding of the person they are speaking with.

So many misunderstandings that arise in relationships come from the simple fact that people aren't listening to one another, which is often due to their inability to focus. When I refer to relationships here, I mean all manner of relationships.

It is so important that we strive to understand one another, because out of understanding is born empathy, out of empathy is born compassion, out of compassion is born love, and finally, out of love comes peace. We can't love something that we don't understand. Though many may disagree, understanding is the soil from which love grows forth. To summarize the sequence: concentration, listening, reflection, understanding, empathy, compassion, love, then peace.

Listening also rewards you with the capacity to gather information. I've found that my ability to focus has led me to be able to listen better and hence gather much more information—an invaluable asset as an entrepreneur. The more information I have, the greater the opportunity to make better decisions if I am able to process the information well. I gather information by listening and being observant, and I do so with my ability to concentrate. Many companies focus on gathering as much information as possible and utilizing that data to achieve massive success and vast fortunes.

When we can give our undivided attention, we can be observant, and when this happens, a world undreamt of reveals itself to us.

Offspring of Focus

Concentration has many offspring, each profoundly extraordinary, but two of its greatest children are the ability to give another person your undivided attention and the power of observation. Let's look more deeply into both of these.

Undivided Attention

It was well before dawn when my small battery-powered alarm went off. I reached over and turned it off. My body groaned, my mind felt weary, but my will was rising. I sat up on my futon mattress, performed a series of small rituals that were related to waking up, and then stepped out of my hut. I stood for a few moments under the banyan tree that umbrellaed my simple concrete abode. The stars peeked in and out of the leaves that swayed in the light breeze. On a clear night devoid of a moon, the Hawaiian sky was always a blanket of stars.

There was a light crispness in the air. I made my way from my hut, walking past a grove of fruit trees and then along a bumpy road to the main monastery building to shower and dress for the day. When this was done, I typically headed back to my hut to perform my morning spiritual practices before we monks gathered as a group for our morning rituals.

As I was heading back to my hut, I noticed that the light in my guru's office was on. I decided to go see him. I stepped into his office, the Mahogany Room, and he greeted me in the way that he always did. I prostrated before him, then stood up and made my way to a chair across the desk from him. At times there were other monastics present, and at other times it was just the two of us.

Today it was just us. These times with him were truly precious to me. We would sit in silence or engage in conversation. Either way, I received his undivided attention. It was unconditional. His ability to focus, his mastery over awareness in the mind, was bar none. His undivided attention was a silent expression of his love for me that rang louder and clearer than any words could ever intimate. In his presence, time seemed to slow down and stretch out. In an absolute state of unwavering focus, the countless moments within each moment were experienced.

His astounding powers of concentration granted him the ability to be completely present, telling me without words that I mattered to him and that he cared about me. That he valued what I had to say. It was always an incredibly empowering experience. I will fall short, every time, of putting into words the experience of being in his complete presence. There were many, many mornings spent this way with him.

Two decades later, having left monastic life, I find myself on a picnic blanket with my daughter at Siva Ashram, our spiritual sanctuary and botanical gardens in Costa Rica. Sunlight filtering onto us through the light, bright green, doubly pinnate leaves of a royal poinciana tree as we enjoy a croissant and some juice. She's three years old but has had my undivided attention in every engagement from the day she was born. How, after countless experiences of receiving my guru's undivided attention, could I not give that same experience to her? I know it changed my life in so many ways, and I was irrefutably convinced it would change hers as well.

I've made it a point in my life to give the people I am with my undivided attention—from my spouse and family to employees, friends, and more. Giving someone my undivided attention is one of the highest forms of love and respect that I can express to them.

When I give you my undivided attention, I am telling you that of all the people and things in this world that I can give my finite time and energy to, I have made the conscious choice to give you my most precious resources. I am saying that I care about you and that you matter to me, and that what you have to say is of significance to me.

When I give you my undivided attention I am also telling you that I value *your* finite time and energy. I am acknowledging that I am conscious that you made the choice as well to give me two of your most precious resources. The undivided attention that you get from me is partly my gratitude for this gift of precious time and energy that you have given me.

When someone is speaking to you, give them your undivided attention. How do you do this? You do this by keeping your awareness on them. If your awareness, that glowing ball of light, drifts away, then gently and lovingly bring it back to them. If it drifts away again, bring it back to them again. Keep doing this until your awareness is trained to stay on one thing without moving. This is how you practice concentration. This is how you learn to give someone your undivided attention.

Giving someone your undivided attention is truly one of the highest forms of love and respect that you can express to them.

Zero Tolerance for Distraction

Around two millennia ago, the South Indian weaver sage Tiruvalluvar eloquently encapsulated the impermanence of all things in this aphorism: "Though it seems a harmless gauge of time, to those that fathom it, a day is a saw steadily cutting down the tree of life."

When a person can fully own the fact that their life is finite and that all life has a clear, definitive end to it, then adopting a zero-tolerance policy for distraction becomes an obvious decision. Time is a boon gifted to all of us, but how we choose to use it depends solely on us.

Establishing a zero-tolerance policy for distraction is an act of reverence for the precious time that has been bestowed on us. It is also a demonstration of our love for who and what matters in our life, for when we surrender a minute of our life to acts of distraction, we have consequently deprived all that we love, including ourselves, of that minute.

After deciding not to renew my monastic vows and making the decision to leave the monastery in Hawaii, I made New York City my new home. A couple of years after moving to the city, I had a meeting with someone at a café in the city that I clearly recall. After taking our seats at a table, we placed our order with the waiter and got into conversation. Every few minutes he would reach over to his phone, which was on the table, and engage with it.

This continued for a good thirty minutes, at which point I realized that I would never gain back any of the time that I was losing here watching him caress his phone, an act I had absolutely no interest in watching.

So I said his name out loud in a firm tone to bring his awareness to attention. Then I looked at him and said, "One of two things needs to happen right now. Either you put the phone away and no longer look at it or we end the meeting and I'll leave. You constantly looking at your phone while we are in a meeting together is an absolute waste of time and energy for me, and quite disrespectful. I'll let you decide how you want to proceed."

I could see from the reaction on his face that he was caught off guard. He quickly collected himself and humbly said, "You're right. I'm sorry for being so distracted. This meeting is important to me, and I'll put my phone away and work at being completely present."

It was that event that caused me to come up with a zero-tolerance policy for distraction. Adopting this policy means having the courage to call out distractive behavior. This can and should be done in a kind but firm way. After all, what excuse do I have not to be kind? None at all. I have much work to do in fully integrating this policy into my life, and it is something I am working hard at doing, for with each passing year my threshold for distraction is getting less and less.

Most of the people, if not all, that I spend regular time with know that I require their undivided attention. This is not coming from a place of needing attention, but rather a clear proclamation of the fact that I value my time and energy, as I do theirs. I only have so many minutes in this life. If you ask for a portion of those minutes, then please don't squander them. Treat them with the utmost respect by giving me your undivided attention, for that saw is steadily making its way through the tree of my life.

As you start out on this path of unwavering focus, it's important that you inform the people closest to you that you are working on learning the art of concentration and that you are committing to being present in all your interactions. Furthermore, you can share with them that the reason you are doing this is because giving them your undivided attention is one way you have chosen to express to them how much you love and respect them.

You will need to explain to them what being present means and how to go about doing that. You can share with them a few examples, one of which could be that in every interaction you would prefer for them to put their phone away so that you can give each other undivided attention.

The Power of Observation

*Observation is the first sign of the awakening
of the superconscious mind.*

~GURUDEVA

Observation is a by-product of prolonged states of concentration. The more you concentrate, the more you develop the power of observation. If I go to the gym and consistently lift weights, I will naturally develop muscle. It is a natural by-product of lifting weights. Similarly, the more you develop your ability to concentrate, the more observant you become.

So what is observation? One of the definitions of observation found in Merriam-Webster's online dictionary is "the act of careful watching and listening: the activity of paying close attention to someone or something in order to get information." My guru would often refer to observation as the "mountaintop perspective." When you are on top of the mountain, you can be observant of everything down below.

Here is a simple analogy to help shed light on the mountaintop perspective. Imagine you and your friends watching a live soccer game on television at home. A player is running down the field with the ball toward the opposition's goal. A great opportunity opens up for his team if he passes the ball to a particular teammate who is perfectly positioned to score a goal. Everyone in the room yells, "Pass it to him! Pass it to him!" but he passes the ball to someone else who is not in as good a position to score. Hands clasps heads as everyone watching the game is flabbergasted by this move. "Oh, you idiot! He was completely open!" exclaims one of your friends.

Why is it that you and your friends were able to make a better decision than a professional player who gets paid millions of dollars to do this day in and day out? Well, it's a matter of perspective. Talented as the player may be, he can only see in front of him. You were viewing the game from a camera perched at the top of the stadium, giving you a mountaintop perspective of the field and all that was going on. From this vantage point, it was much easier to see what the better pass would have been.

Similarly, a satellite, hovering high above the earth's surface, maintaining a mountaintop perspective, is able to be observant of so much more of what is going on down below than you would be able to in your car. The satellite's ability to see the big picture means it can tell you what lies ahead.

Like the camera on top of the stadium and the satellite orbiting earth, as you become more observant from your increased ability to focus, more information becomes apparent to you. The more information you have, the more informed you are, and the chances of making a better decision increase. That said, the ability to make better decisions is not based on the amount of information you have, but rather on your ability to process that information wisely and apply it in a timely manner.

Being observant, you are able to see pitfalls and opportunities in your life. This does not mean you will always avoid those pitfalls and take those opportunities, but the fact that you are observant of them provides you with countless possibilities to make choices that result in better outcomes. I cannot begin to tell you how many times I have observed pitfalls in my life, and despite observing them, have stepped into these messy life experiences. These have more to do with subconscious patterns that need to be adjusted.

> *Problems are not problems. They are subconscious*
> *patterns that need to be adjusted.*
> ~GURUDEVA

The first step in making these adjustments in your subconscious is to be observant of them. You can't change something that you are not observant of. This is another reason why learning to concentrate is so important: it helps you become more observant, thus allowing you to see the patterns within you that need adjustment and begin the process of doing so.

Observation helps me to see the bigger picture, and because I can see the bigger picture, I have the possibility to make better decisions in my life. When I make better decisions, I have better outcomes. One of the by-products of that is happiness, because I am creating a lifestyle for myself that results in my feeling happy. The power of observation is truly one of the great benefits of concentration.

LESSON 8.5

Demystifying Focus

The many misconceptions surrounding focus arise because people don't understand what focus is. Their misconceptions often lead people to have a very skewed or misinformed perspective on focus, and thus to shun focus as a quality to cultivate in life. Let's address some of these misconceptions here in order to dispel them and recalibrate people's understanding of what focus actually is.

Being Focused Is Exhausting

A gentleman once remarked to me, "It takes so much energy and effort to be focused all day. It's quite exhausting!"

I replied by asking him, "How much effort and energy does it take for you to be distracted all day?"

He replied without hesitation, "None at all. In fact, I can effortlessly do it all day."

"You can practice distraction all day because you've spent years

245

developing distractive patterns within your subconscious. Because of this it requires no effort on your part to do so, and hence it is not exhausting. For the person who has been trained in the fine art of concentration, who has spent years creating patterns of focus in the subconscious through devotion to the practice of concentration, whose awareness is under the dominion of the will, being in a state of focus all day is effortless and not exhausting as well."

Anyone who has not been trained in the arts of concentration will find it exhausting to concentrate for extended periods of time. If you ask your mind to do something that it does not have deeply ingrained patterns of or has not been trained to do, then naturally it will require a lot more energy to do.

An arborist can prune trees for hours, having built the muscles needed for this task, whereas a person who is pruning a tree for the first time may find the experience quite exhausting. It is not any different with the mind. Anything that the mind is not used to doing requires a lot more effort and energy and can be deemed exhausting.

And speaking of exhaustion, it is worth pointing out that it is very exhausting for a focused person to spend time with someone who is highly distracted. To follow someone's awareness as it bounces indiscriminately within the mind is very exhausting. The focused awareness is now being asked to do something it is not used to doing, and the very act is exhausting. As awareness bounces all over the place, energy flows all over the place, leading to a significant loss of energy.

Fear of Missing Out

I had a person once say to me, as he raised his hands to either side of his face, mimicking having blinders on, "I don't want to be so focused that I miss out on other things in life."

It's common for people to think that when you are focused you have tunnel vision. It's true that awareness is locked on one thing, but as you know now, focus gives birth to observation. So contrary to popular belief that focus makes you miss out on things, it actually does not. In fact, focus makes you more observant, which means you become more conscious of everything around you.

Blocking Everything Out

It's quite common to hear athletes say, "I just block everything out and focus on the game." Let's analyze this statement. To block something means that awareness has to go to what it is blocking.

Take a defensive linebacker in American football, for example. One of his jobs is to stop the running back from getting past the defensive line. In order to "block" this person, he needs to go to him. If there were only one linebacker, then he would have to run up to each offensive player and block each of them individually. Similarly, if you say "I am going to block everything out," in the context of what we have covered in this book you are saying that your awareness, like the linebacker, is going to everything, one at a time, to block them out. Essentially that is what a person is saying when he says, "I just block everything out." That is anything but focused.

It is highly critical to train ourselves to understand how the mind works. One of the key factors in doing so is using the correct terminology and words. This can come only from having a solid understanding of how awareness and the mind work, and that is why I spent much time focusing on this in the early chapters of this book.

The athlete would be better off saying, "I'm going to be completely focused on the game." By doing so he is observant of what is going on around him, but his awareness is not engaged in what is going on around him. Awareness is completely absorbed in playing the game.

There is nothing to block out on the path to achieving unwavering focus.

Absence of Joy

If a person were to visualize someone focusing, they would, most likely, visualize a person whose eyes are slightly squinted and locked in on the subject of focus, the forehead slightly crinkled, with an absorbed and attentive look across her face. With such a visualization it is hard to imagine that that person is relaxed.

On the contrary, if the same person were asked to visualize a relaxed person, they might perhaps visualize a person running carefree on a beach, arms stretched out to the sides, embracing the wind blowing on her face and through her hair. With this visualization, it's easy to conclude that she looks free, relaxed, and joyous.

With both visualizations placed next to each other, one would want to say, "I don't want to be so focused that I can't enjoy life. I want to be relaxed and happy, not focused and serious all the time."

Again, this misunderstanding is born out of the fact that people are not clear on what focus is. A person who has been trained to focus does not walk around with a crinkled forehead, slightly squinted eyes, and an absorbed look. Focus is her natural state of mind. For her, it takes no effort to be focused. She can be relaxed and focused at the same time. And because she is focused, she gives everything and everyone in her life her undivided attention, which results in a fulfilling experience in every engagement. Contentment, joy, and happiness are only some of the feelings experienced as a result.

Mindfulness

I would be remiss if I did not admit that the word "mindfulness" invokes in me the same reaction I have when I hear fingernails scratch across a blackboard. A needless gentle reminder that I am human and there are things that irk me. The use of the word is grossly perverted, and its devil-may-care use sees more action than a turnstile at the

WINGS OF THE MIND

Times Square subway station in Manhattan. I'll rein in my feelings and direct my awareness to the purpose of bringing up this topic.

Let's define mindfulness. The *Oxford English Dictionary* defines mindfulness as "a mental state achieved by concentrating on the present moment." A careful examination of this definition would reveal that mindfulness is a by-product of concentration: a mental state that results from being focused.

Merriam-Webster's dictionary defines mindfulness as "the practice of maintaining a nonjudgmental state of heightened or complete awareness of one's thoughts, emotions, or experiences on a moment-to-moment basis." I am going to abbreviate this definition but still keep the meaning and the words used and say, "The practice of maintaining a state of complete awareness of one's experiences on a moment-to-moment basis." (Note that they use the word "awareness" differently than I do.)

Based on both these definitions, I can surmise that if I were able to concentrate, keep my awareness on one thing long enough, only then could I be conscious (mindful or observant) of what it is I am focused on.

From this we can conclude that we don't practice mindfulness. We don't practice being observant. Instead, what we do is practice concentration. Mindfulness and observation are states of mind that come as by-products of awareness being trained to be concentrated for prolonged periods of time. In other words, concentration is necessary to experience the state of mindfulness or observation.

When you hear someone say, "Practice mindfulness," technically they are making an incorrect statement. What you *can* practice is concentration, and what follows is a state of mindfulness. Concentration gives birth to the mental state of mindfulness, which without it would not be born.

If a person is distracted, which means that their awareness jumps from one thing to another in an uncontrolled way, how can they "maintain a state of complete awareness of one's experiences on a moment-to-moment basis"? They simply can't. To tell someone who is distracted that they need to practice being mindful is a nescient request.

One must first tell them to practice concentration. Once they are able to hold awareness on one thing for an extended period of time, only then can they begin to become conscious of their experience on a moment-to-moment basis. Now they can experience being mindful or observant.

Similarly, you don't practice being happy. You experience being happy. It is a state of mind. Happiness is an emotional by-product of an experience you have or awareness being in a particular area of the mind.

So instead of telling people to practice mindfulness, tell them to practice concentration. And mindfulness will be a mental state achieved by concentrating on what they are engaged in. This would be the proper use and understanding of the term "mindfulness."

Understanding Multitasking

The shorter way to do many things is to only do one thing at a time.
~WOLFGANG AMADEUS MOZART

Multitasking, like distraction, is the antithesis of focus. To understand multitasking, it's best that we define it.

Merriam-Webster's dictionary defines multitasking as the performance of multiple tasks at one time. The Oxford dictionary defines multitasking in two ways. With regard to a person, it defines it as the ability to "deal with more than one task at the same time"; with regard to a computer it defines it as the ability to "execute more than one program or task simultaneously." These are very clear definitions of multitasking.

When a person is "multitasking," what essentially is happening is that his awareness is shifting back and forth between two things. Awareness cannot be in two places at the same time.

A person who is driving and talking on the phone at the same time is having his awareness move back and forth between the conversation and driving. This is not only dangerous but is both time and energy consuming. Energy consuming because, remember, where awareness goes, energy flows.

Let me use an analogy to illustrate how multitasking is hugely energy consuming. Imagine for a moment awareness is like a car, and the gasoline that fuels the car is energy. If the car traveled back and forth between two neighboring cities repeatedly, it would consume a lot of gas in comparison to the car that is just idling in one place. It is the same with awareness. As awareness travels back and forth repeatedly between two things, it consumes a lot of energy. Awareness has to engage with Item A for a brief period, then disengage from it in order to engage with Item B. Now it is engaged with Item B for a brief moment before needing to disengage with it and reengage with Item A. When it reengages with Item A, awareness must now identify where it left off previously and then reengage itself in that particular area of the thread of conversation or activity again.

All of this is hugely energy consuming. As this process is repeated over and over again in the process of multitasking, vast amounts of energy are consumed. Productivity and efficiency plummet to much lower levels than what they could be if a concentrated state of mind were maintained.

So many people multitask, delusionally believing that they are being highly productive and getting lots done. On the contrary, they are only vastly wasting two of their most precious resources—their time and energy.

My perspective on multitasking and what it does to a person is not from scientific, physiological research. Rather, it is from an inner experience of awareness and the mind. If you are interested in reading about scientific research on multitasking, I suggest you search online, where you will find plenty of neurological and psychological studies suggesting that "multitasking" is a myth.

PART 4

A PANACEA FOR
THE MIND

Chapter 9

THE FOUR FOES

Being Present—the Remedy

T he mind, left unchecked, can suffer many maladies. Many of these ailments can be better managed and even overcome if we have a solid understanding of awareness and the mind, and can better navigate where in the mind awareness goes. In this chapter, I want to address the four foes that terrorize many minds. They are worry, fear, anxiety, and stress.

Before addressing each of them, we must first learn one crucial application of focusing awareness, which is to be present. I'll begin our study of being present with a story that an entrepreneur shared with me.

"We were whisking across the cerulean sea in a private boat to a remote island when I looked up from my phone to notice that my wife and kids were fully absorbed in enjoying the breathtaking experience I had planned for our family. It was at that moment that I realized I had spent the last fifteen minutes glued to my phone's screen," he disappointedly told me, chagrined at his inability to be present in that experience. "That experience with my family was lost forever," he lamented.

People spend much of their lives working to earn an income that will provide them with the opportunity to create experiences for themselves. These experiences can range from having a meal at a hawker stall with friends to cruising on a private yacht and everything in between. Regardless of what the experience is, one thing will determine how much you get out of that experience, and that is your ability to be present in that experience. Sadly, many painstakingly manifest unique experiences only to squander them with their distracted mind.

I can be said to be present when my awareness is fully engaged with who or what I am with, or in the experience I am having. Being present is no different from being in a state of concentration.

Like mindfulness, being present is only possible if one can concentrate. And, similarly, you don't practice being present; rather, you practice being concentrated, because when you are concentrated you are fully engaged with who you are with, and the result is that you are present in that experience.

To tell someone to be present is erroneous. Instead, it would be better and more accurate to tell someone to be focused if you wish them to be present, presuming they have been taught how to focus. How can you be present if you can't be focused? Focus precedes being present. Being present is an effect of being focused. If one has a solid grasp of the concept of awareness and the mind, and of what concentration is, then not much needs to be said about being present.

Have you had the experience of having a conversation with someone in person, and noticing that you are no longer present, they ask you, "Where are you?" The correct, cannot-be-argued-with response is, "I'm right here."

In the context of this book, a technically correct question would instead be, "Where is your awareness?" Physically, I know you are here, standing in front of me. It's clear as day. Your physical body is always in the here and now. But your awareness has long since left our presence, and as a result you are no longer present.

Now, how does one know if someone is no longer present? Can you reflect for a few minutes on this and see if you know the answer based on what you've learned in this book?

The answer is that you no longer feel their energy. Remember what my guru said: "Where awareness goes, energy flows." If a person's awareness shifts from you to something else on their mind, then that is where their energy is flowing now. If you are sensitive to energy and no longer feel their energy flowing toward you, then you know they are no longer focused on the conversation; thus they are no longer present, even if their subconscious is mechanically nodding their head in response to what you are saying.

I hope it is becoming self-evidently clear to you now why focus is such an important quality to cultivate. It is at the crux of many of the qualities we strive to cultivate in our life.

The Eternity of the Moment

A critical piece in being in the moment, or being present, is having a basic understanding of time. In a simplified view of time, we can divide time into three parts: the past, the future, and the now or present. At any given moment awareness can be in any one of these three parts of time.

If awareness loses itself in the past, you will find it rummaging through the anthology of your life's experiences, procured ever since your arrival on this planet and stored in the museum of your subconscious. Unlike most museums, the subconscious, a compulsive hoarder of memories, unless trained in the art of organized memory, is typically a shambles of experiences, habit patterns, and more.

And when you find awareness marinating in a memory of the past, you may hear yourself voice the memory: "Remember that time when we were in Prague in the middle of winter and they served us hot wine? That's the first time I ever heard of or drank hot wine!"—a verbal confirmation of where in time awareness is. Many people spend vast amounts of time indulging in the past, and in doing so, unknowingly permit the only moment that truly matters, the present, to slip by unbeknownst to them.

That said, the past can be a great educational resource, providing us with many insights and learnings that can enable us to make wiser decisions in the present, and so create a better future.

If awareness travels to the future, you may hear yourself voice what you are visioning: "I can't wait to get to Kuala Lumpur next week and gorge on its street food. The first dish I'm going to indulge in is definitely roti canai." Another verbal confirmation of where in time awareness is.

When awareness spends a great deal of time absorbed in mental fantasy and daydreaming about the future, disappointment, sadness, and depression may follow. This is because what you are conjuring up in your mind is not what you are manifesting in the physical world. Having a clear mental picture of the future is a very important step in manifesting what you want, but the work to manifest the future needs to be done in the present. That's where the future is created—in the here and now!

There is absolutely nothing wrong with allowing awareness to travel to the past or the future if it is done consciously and wisely. Over-indulgence in either can be detrimental. Some people spend much of their time expressing what they are going to do, but never get around to being in the present to do any of it. Others spend much of their time reminiscing about the past, relishing and loathing memories, unaware that life has mercilessly moved on. If you are observant, many times it will be keenly obvious to you where in time someone's awareness is by what they are saying.

Then there are those who spend the majority of their time in the present, engaged with unwavering focus on whatever it is they are doing. They are the creators. The manifesters. The leaders. The ones who know that all things are created in the here and now, in the eternity of the moment.

My guru drove the understanding of "now is the only reality" into every sinew of me. It took effort on his part to do this, and his approach varied based on the need of the layer of my mind he was attempting to impress with this axiom. Here's one experiential teaching I had from him on this.

I was wrapping up work for the day at my desk. It was past six in the evening, the designated time we had to stop our daily work.

The phone rang. I reached over and picked it up. "Dandapani," I heard Gurudeva say.

"Hi, Gurudeva."

"I want you to move to the Windbell forest," he said. At that moment, many thoughts raced through my mind.

The Windbell forest was a wooded section of the then fifty-one-acre monastery grounds. Somewhere within it, upon crossing a bridge-less stream and walking a pathless path in the forest, was a hut, a very austere hut.

It was made out of wood with a tin roof. Imagine a tube cut lengthwise to create a semi-cylindrical shape. That was its shape. Hoisted on four wooden posts about three feet off the ground, its wooden base, the floor of the hut, was about three feet wide and perhaps seven feet in length. Now picture a metal sheet nailed to the long side of it and wrapped around and attached to the other side of the half-cylinder. The entrance was an operable door with a wood frame wrapping around a wire mesh to permit airflow, and mirrored on the opposite end as a fixed panel.

I could crawl into it, sit on my rear, and have a luxurious three inches of space between my head and the curved metal sheet that made up the roof, which was held in place by long wooden rafters.

This roughly twenty-one square feet of Hawaiian real estate was now to be my new home. I had just been instructed to renounce my former massive one-hundred-square-foot bungalow.

I replied slowly, "OK. I'll move into it in the morning." Twilight was fast setting in, and this was not something I was enthused about doing in a dark forest.

Gurudeva responded, "You can do it now."

"But it's getting dark," I gently pushed back.

"You have a flashlight, don't you?"

And that was the end of that conversation. Upon hanging up, I dropped all that I was doing to relocate the few possessions I had as a monastic to my forest dwelling.

This was a great learning experience for me. For one reason or another, we procrastinate. In this case, moving to a forest dwelling made me feel uncomfortable, perhaps even slightly fearful. By getting me to move immediately, Gurudeva intentionally brought my awareness to the present moment, allowing me to face my discomfort and any possible fears. By getting me to do things now and not later, he was also teaching me one of the key ingredients of manifesting things in my life. The future is manifested in the here and now. Not later or tomorrow.

The first night, a gecko, a roommate that I was unaware of, slid off his bed, the wooden rafter above me, and fell onto my chest. I felt something light land on me, but before I could react, it frantically ran across my face. I'm sorry, but I have to ask: If a monk screams in the forest and no one hears it, did he actually scream? The months spent living in this hut brought more lessons than I could have imagined.

Though now is the only reality, we must ultimately always use our wisdom in deciding when to do things now and when not to.

Let me summarize the steps to get to living in the moment. First, know there is a clear separation between awareness and the mind. Then understand that in any moment awareness can be in the past, present, or future. For awareness to be anchored in the here and now, the present, use your willpower and powers of concentration to hold awareness on who and what it is engaged in. Doing so ensures you are living in the moment, that you are completely present.

Our ability to focus allows us to live in the moment, which then allows us to fully experience all of life's experiences. Not a moment is wasted. Life is lived to its fullest.

The Root Cause of Worry

Fear and worry are mental plagues that have survived the test of time. They have robbed people of their peace of mind, ransacked them of their energy, and made themselves unwelcome squatters in the minds of many. All valiant attempts made to evict these mental leeches typically fall short of success, and most end up reluctantly accepting them as cohabitants of their minds.

Left to their own devices, they are poisons steadfast in their resolve to permeate every part of our lives, from our mind and body to the lives of those we touch each day, with devastating consequences. They cripple the will and paralyze awareness, slowing life to a grinding halt. But we need not acquiesce to them and live as their slave in mental squalor. There is a panacea to ameliorate such a state of mind and eventually free the mind from the shackles of fear and worry.

Mastery of awareness in the mind is the cure, the time-tested elixir to end this tyranny—available to all who seek it, exclusive to none. But not all who seek it are determined to possess it; thus this cure, unfortunately, lies in the hands of a few determined souls. And these are the souls who courageously drive humanity forward.

Worry

We pulled into an empty spot in the parking lot of the Coconut Marketplace, a quaint shopping and dining village located on the eastern shore of the island of Kauai. I was accompanying Gurudeva and a senior monk on an excursion. We stepped out of the van and onto the path that took us into the center. As we walked, Gurudeva turned to me and said, "When you are in the conscious mind, you need to play by the conscious mind rules."

Worry is one of the children of the conscious mind. When awareness is in the conscious mind, the instinctive mind, you expose it to the experience of worry. If you spend much of your time in the conscious mind, it behooves you to be cognizant that the experience of worry is a possibility. The level of your mastery over awareness in the mind determines how much you subject yourself to worry.

Though many people are more intimately familiar with worry than a cat is with napping, it's best that we define worry so that we can be on the same page about it. This will also help us to see how we can use what we've learned in this book to overcome it. Merriam-Webster's dictionary defines worry as "mental distress or agitation resulting from concern usually for something impending or anticipated." The Cambridge dictionary gives a definition that is perhaps a little easier to digest: "to think about problems or unpleasant things that might happen in a way that makes you feel unhappy and frightened."

As for me, I'll define worry for you by telling you a story that my guru shared of his early life. It was 1934, the snow was falling heavily, and he was traveling home in a car with his family near Fallen Leaf

Lake in Northern California. As the snow came down thick and heavy, he began to worry.

"What if we get stuck in the snow? What if we don't make it home in time? I'll miss my favorite radio show," he worried.

Upon thinking this, he observed what was taking place in his mind. He saw his awareness leaving the present moment and traveling into the future. Upon its arrival in the future, it created a situation *in his mind* of the family car being stuck in the snow. Now that this visualization was created, his awareness returned to the present and he started to worry, to be mentally distressed and agitated, about the situation he had created in his mind.

Having observed all of this taking place in his mind, he asked himself, "We are not stuck in the snow yet, are we?" and he replied, "No." He then asked himself, "Are we still on time to get home for my show?" and he replied, "Yes."

In a great moment of realization, at the mere age of seven, he cognized that he was all right, right now. He then affirmed to himself, "I am all right, right now." He realized that in the eternity of the moment everything is OK. That worry was future based. He had seen his awareness go into the future, create a situation that had not happened, and then return to the present and worry about it. And that, in summary, is what worry is.

This experience of his has provided me with the most clarifying insights into worry. Upon first hearing it, it instantaneously dissipated many of my own worries. I am unable to look at worry the same way again. I can see it for what it is: awareness uncontrolled, conjuring up stories in the future that cause distress in the present.

If I ever observe awareness venturing into the future and beginning to create worrisome situations in my mind, I will rein it back to the present with my willpower and hold it in the present with my powers of concentration. That's the very same willpower that I have been developing over the years by finishing what I start, by doing a little more than I think I can and a little better than I think I can. The same willpower I develop each time I make the bed, or when I align my flip-flops upon taking them off, or when I wash the dishes, or in the many nonnegotiable recurring events in my average day.

The will that I have so devotedly committed to building each day can now be summoned to prevent me from having the experience of worry. This alone is well worth developing your willpower for, though it is a fragment of what you can use your will for. I hope you can see now the crucial application of willpower to maintain a worryless mind.

And once I have reined awareness back to the present from the future worry it was about to create, I will hold it in the present with my powers of concentration. These are the very same powers of concentration that I have been developing over the years by giving my spouse, daughter, and the people I engage with my undivided attention and by doing one thing at a time.

The ability to focus that I have so faithfully committed to building each day can now be summoned to hold awareness in the present, to prevent it from heading off into the future and creating uncalled-for worrisome situations.

Every time you worry, observe what is happening in your mind. Observe awareness leaving the present and venturing into the future. Observe it crafting stories, creating situations, fabricating outcomes, all distressing in nature, for you to worry about upon its return to the present moment.

What you've learned in this book so far is a systematic approach to overcoming worry. First understand that awareness and the mind are two distinctly separate things. Then know that awareness moves and the mind does not. Realize that willpower and concentration can be developed to harness and direct awareness within the mind. Now, if awareness goes into the future to create worrisome situations in your mind, use your willpower to rein it back to the present and use your powers of concentration to hold it in the present. This is the key to eliminating worry from your life.

The Future and the Past

I am not saying that we should never allow our awareness to go into the future and create negative scenarios. Doing this can be helpful at times, as it allows us to figure out solutions for potential problems that may arise.

Imagine you are a restaurateur. You're almost done with designing your latest restaurant. To make sure you've covered all the bases, you allow your awareness to go to the future and create potential problems. In one scenario, your awareness is in the future in your mind, painting a picture of a bustling restaurant on a Friday night. In this visualization you see a fire breaking out in the kitchen. You then stop your visualization and bring awareness back to the present.

Now that awareness is back in the present, you solve for this highly likely culinary mayhem. You consult experts and find the best solutions to ensure that if such an event were to occur, you have the best solutions in place. So, even though you allowed awareness to go into the future and create a problematic situation, you never allowed it to create distress in your mind. You achieved this by finding a solution to your problem. This is very different from awareness going back and forth into the future, reexperiencing the problem without actually solving it.

The past, on the other hand, is not where worry lives. You can't worry about anything that has happened in the past because it has already happened. There is absolutely nothing that you can do about it. But what you can worry about is the consequences of your past actions that may manifest in the future.

Say you stole a fancy pen from a store. A couple of days later, in conversation with a friend, you find out that the store had installed, over a month ago, a state-of-the-art security system that includes well-hidden cameras. This information disturbs you, rattling your awareness and sending it into the future, where it constructs a story of the owner reviewing the security footage and calling the police, resulting in you being arrested. Having created this story, awareness returns to the present and starts worrying about the possibility of this happening.

Not much later, awareness heads off again into the future, in your mind, to create another possible scenario, giving you an additional thing to worry about. This repeats itself. As each story is conjured up, each one distressing to some degree, awareness returns to the present and worries about it, wreaking havoc on your mind and immersing you in a world of perpetual worry.

The past leaves nothing to worry about. But the future is where worry lives and thrives.

Manifesting Our Worries

Worry is awareness going into the future, creating a problem in our mind that has not happened, then returning to the present and being distressed about that problem. Now, if awareness were to repeatedly visit that exact problem in the mind (which essentially is the act of worry), then it would be strengthening that problem each time it visits it. This is because every time awareness goes to it, that is where energy is flowing, and that problem in the mind is being strengthened.

Everything manifests on the mental plane first, before it manifests on the physical plane. In the case of a worry, it found its origins in you, allowing awareness to travel to the future in your mind and create a problem. When awareness did that, it manifested it on the mental plane. Now, if you allow awareness to repeatedly visit that problem in the form of worry, repeatedly depositing energy into it, you are strengthening this problem in your mind. The more energy that is deposited into this pattern in your mind—the worry—the stronger it becomes. As this process repeats itself consistently over time, we begin to materialize that worry on the physical plane.

Shortly after leaving the monastery, I conducted my first workshop in New York City. In this workshop I spoke about how things manifest on the mental plane first before they manifest on the physical plane. When the workshop concluded, a man came up to me and said that he did not believe we could manifest things with our mind. I asked him, "What is your occupation?"

He replied, "I trade stocks on Wall Street."

I said to him, "Would you be so kind as to conduct an experiment for me? I would like you to mentally visualize and feel that all your investments are failing and you are losing hundreds of thousands of dollars. And I would like you to do this exercise at least seven times throughout the day for a week. Would you do it?"

He looked at me, devoid of any expression, and said, "No!"

Not much more needed to be said after that. Similarly, if awareness is allowed to repeatedly go to a worry, then we have begun the process of manifesting that worry on the physical plane. Whatever it is we invest in consistently in our mind, be it positive or negative, will start to manifest in our life.

Conquering Fear

Fear is the portal to all lower emotions. It is the highest state of consciousness for the instinctive mind; therefore, it is the doorway to all lower states as well. If worry is a mental thug, fear is the godfather, the mob boss, of all lower emotions that terrorize the mind.

In close examination, one will find that fear, like worry, is a result of awareness going into the future, creating a situation in our mind that has not happened, then returning to the present and fearing it. Allow me to elaborate.

It is a pitch-dark night and you find yourself walking down a dingy, lonely, unlit street in a dodgy part of town. The sound of your boot heels hitting the road is the only thing that shatters the eerie silence. Why you are here, we are not quite sure. The weather is brisk, and you cross your hands in front of you and rub your bare arms. You begin to wonder if you are starting to feel afraid or just cold.

Your awareness walks ahead of you in your mind, about fifty paces, to an abandoned vehicle parked on the side of the road. In a flash it conjures up a scene of a disheveled-looking man leaping out at you from behind the car. Barely is that scene over than awareness races back to the present. The fabricated scene is fresh in your mind and a cold shiver runs down your spine. Fear grips you. You slow your stride and cautiously walk forward.

The fear you are experiencing now triggers a memory in your sub-conscious that is vibrating at the same frequency. Your awareness is immediately drawn to the memory of a movie you once saw where a woman was walking down a dark street and was ambushed by a gang of zombies who proceeded to maul her to pieces. The fear you experienced watching that scene is rekindled, and awareness is cata-pulted into the future again, this time imagining zombies lurking in the shadows of this scary street, waiting to pounce on you and re-create that gory scene.

Awareness, now unhinged, goes back and forth between the pres-ent and the future, conjuring up more petrifying scenes out of sheer fear, pushing you to the fringes of your sanity. You can't decide if you should run or just crumple to the ground in tears.

There are a few things to take note of in this fictitious story in-volving you.

Firstly, what plays out in the mind in fear is no different than in worry. Fear, like worry, is future based. You can't fear the past. The past has happened, and there is nothing that can be done about it—though we can fear the repercussions of our past actions that may manifest in the future. At the core of the eternity of the moment, you are pure energy that cannot be created or destroyed. Fear does not and cannot exist here. In the eternity of the moment, you are always "all right, right now." The only place fear lives is in the future.

When our willpower and powers of concentration lose their grip on awareness, we essentially throw awareness to the wolves. The lon-ger we leave awareness out in the wild, so to speak, unchecked and unharnessed from our will, the more we subjugate it to our environment and our subconscious. In the case of this story, the environment started to dictate where in the mind awareness went.

As you can see from the story, not only was the eerie street causing fear, but the subconscious can wreak havoc on the mind as well. Past experiences in the subconscious that have not been dealt with can cause awareness to repeatedly experience fear. Reliving these emotions of fear only causes them to compound upon one another, creating stronger patterns of fear in the subconscious. You could call it the Wheel of Fear. This eventually becomes the dominant force in one's mind and cripples a person from taking any action in life that is outside the safe and narrow norm. Because of this, it is really important that we be conscious of what we impress our subconscious with. I'll circle back to this shortly.

As with worry, bringing awareness back to the present is the key to overcoming fear. When awareness is back in the present, we have the opportunity to solve this problem. In the case of this story, when awareness is anchored in the here and now, in the present, it can perhaps decide to choose an alternate route, to call a friend or a car service to come pick you up, or to find other alternatives to avoid the experience of walking down that street. But if you leave awareness unharnessed and allow it to go into the future and create situations in your mind that cause you fear, you put yourself in a mental state of being absorbed in fear.

The fear state of mind has no capability to make rational decisions. In Hindu metaphysics, which I was trained in and which this book is based on, if you were to look at the mind as a multistory building where each floor is a state of mind, you would see that reason resides two floors above fear. If you are on the fear level of the mind, you would have no capacity to reason, and if you were totally immersed on the reason level of your mind, you would simply reason yourself out of fear. If you were living in a multistory apartment building and someone was living two floors above you, you would not be able to communicate with them without the assistance of some device. What they experience on that floor would also be different from what you experience on yours. Your perspectives would also differ.

Fear is not always a bad thing. We live in a physical body, and that body is tied to our instinctive mind. That is the animal nature of us, and it can sense an actual threat or danger, which then brings about a sense of fear in us. So at times, the fear we experience is a self-protective mechanism. If we heed this sign, we can use it to avoid a harmful experience. But if we allow that fear to grow and dominate our awareness, that is when things start going to hell in a handbasket.

Protecting the Mind

There are people who enjoy watching scary movies. They revel in the experience of having their awareness taken to the fear area of the mind and experiencing all levels of fear. As you know now, the consistent repetition of this experience causes a deep groove, a well-trodden path, to be built to the fear area of the mind. Vast amounts of energy are deposited here as well, causing this area to be highly magnetic and to have a significant pull over awareness. Should one find oneself on a scary street at night, prompting awareness to move to the fringes of the fear area of the mind, it would be very easy for awareness to slide into the established deep groove and be pulled by the strong magnetic force into the heart of the fear area of the mind. Awareness responds vastly differently to being on this scary street from the fear area of the mind than it would from an uplifting area of the mind.

If awareness was on the floor of reason, it would reason its way down the street. But if it was on the fear floor, it would send terror through your body and nervous system. One floor above reason is willpower, and if awareness was on this floor, it would muster courage and walk fearlessly down the street. One floor below fear is anger, and here awareness may be angry at itself for getting into such a position.

Where awareness is in the mind determines our perspective. It determines how we see things. How we respond to experiences. How we react to life. How we feel. It determines everything. Can you see now why understanding awareness and the mind is so critical?

The first step in overcoming fear is moving awareness out of the fear area of the mind with our will and powers of concentration. This then provides us with the opportunity to begin to examine what is the root cause of that fear. You can't understand fear while you are in fear.

Those who fathom the power of the mind are highly protective of it. If the fear area of the mind is nurtured, then that will be one of the default places that awareness goes to in challenging situations. Poor decisions are made here, resulting in even poorer outcomes. Therefore, you would avoid doing anything that would nurture that area of the mind, such as watching scary movies. Most kitchen sinks have a strainer to prevent food waste from going into the drainpipe and clogging it up. If we do that for our kitchen sink to protect our pipes, should we not have a strainer to prevent trash from entering our mind and clogging it up? Protect your mind at all costs. Your mind is your greatest asset. Be wisely discriminating as to what you allow into it and what you allow to breed in it.

Then there are bullies, instinctive-minded people who relish making others feel fear by repeatedly taking their awareness to the fear area of the mind. Unbeknownst to them, they are creating a well-formed path to fear in the minds of their victims. The most ignorant of these bullies, the cowards of society, do it to children, unaware that the mind of a child is deeply impressionable and that these repeated acts will create patterns that can and often do last a lifetime. These patterns of fear can dictate decision-making and alter the way that child will live their life. Bullies have essentially taken this child to the precipice of all lower emotions and left their undeveloped mind at the mercy of their base nature, sentencing them to a possible life of living in lower consciousness. This is one of the worst things that can be done to a child. One of the first steps in uplifting human consciousness is to get people out of experiencing fear in their life.

In summary, every time you find awareness going into the future and creating a situation in your mind that causes you to feel fear, use your indomitable willpower to bring awareness back to the present and use your powers of concentration to hold awareness in the here and now. By all means do not let your awareness reenact that situation repeatedly and compound the feeling of fear in you. If the fear you see in your mind has a strong possibility of manifesting itself, then find solutions to ensure that it does not happen. Seek support if needed.

Affirm to yourself, as my guru did as a child, "I am all right, right now!"

Overcoming Anxiety and Stress

We've looked at worry and fear; now let's get to know the other two cohorts that are equally skilled at plundering many people's energy and peace of mind.

Merriam-Webster's dictionary defines anxiety as "apprehensive uneasiness or nervousness usually over an impending or anticipated ill." Oxford Learner's Dictionaries defines anxiety as "the state of feeling nervous or worried that something bad is going to happen." Hmm . . . they both sound a little like being concerned about something in the future.

Let's examine "impending or anticipated ill." When awareness leaves the present, heads to the future, creates a negative outcome in the mind, then returns to the present and worries about what it has created, it is worrying about an anticipated ill. The more awareness repeats this process, creating a variety of negative outcomes, the more one feels uneasy and worries that something bad is going to happen. Repeat this process over and over and you start to live in a state of anxiety. Prolonged states of worry lead to anxiety. This is one way in which anxiety comes about.

The state of anxiety is also created when awareness is allowed to go from one unfinished thing to another in an uncontrolled way. Here's a simple example to explain this. Imagine you need to work on four different projects. You begin with Project A, and five minutes into it you allow awareness to drift away to Project B. In this brief moment that it visits Project B, you realize that you have not sent the payment that was due yesterday to the vendor. You sigh and tell yourself you will get right on it when you finish what you're doing on Project A. Awareness returns to Project A.

A few minutes go by and awareness wanders off, this time to Project C. While here, you become cognizant of the fact that you never got an approval on the budget from your finance chair on Project C. You mutter to yourself, "I really need to follow up with her on this." Annoyed, awareness heads back to Project A and desperately tries to find what it was that it was working on before it left on its saunter. Disgruntled awareness can barely stay focused on Project A before it heads off to Project D and the realization that you failed to sign the contract with the new client. "Shit!" you exclaim, praying the client is not too annoyed.

As awareness highlights in your mind one incomplete task after another, you start to feel the burden of what you have to do. You question whether you will get it all done in the time frame that you've been given. A feeling of worry, nervousness, and unease about this uncertain outcome starts to set in. Anxiety has established its presence. The solution is to keep awareness on one project at a time. If it drifts away, bring it back. If you have an idea about Project B while working on Project A, write down that insight and return to working on Project A until you consciously choose to move awareness to another project.

Repeatedly thinking about something that needs to get done does not get it done. Repeatedly thinking about something that needs to get done causes anxiety. As awareness regurgitates this cycle of high-lighting incomplete tasks, it compounds the feeling of anxiety. Pro-longed states of anxiety lead to stress.

The Mental Health Foundation in the United Kingdom defines stress as "the feeling of being overwhelmed or unable to cope with men-tal or emotional pressure." The Britannica dictionary defines it as "some-thing that causes strong feelings of worry or anxiety." Your level of stress is an indicator of how little control you have over awareness.

Understanding which behavior of awareness causes anxiety is criti-cal in overcoming anxiety and stress.

I focus so much on understanding things because once you un-derstand how something works, you can control it. Most people can't control their anxiety because they don't understand the mechanics of awareness and the mind, and the behavioral patterns that awareness takes on that cause anxiety. Understanding the mechanics of how anx-iety is created allows you to identify when it is taking place, and then to do what is needed to prevent it.

Awareness going from one unfinished thing to another in an uncontrolled way causes anxiety. But it's not only unfinished things. Allowing awareness to jump from one thought to another in an un-controlled way can also cause anxiety.

A young woman may sit and think to herself, "What if I never meet the person I am supposed to marry? Then I'll always be alone." A few moments later she says to herself, "Maybe it's because I am not pretty enough." A half hour goes by and she says, "I think I'm just ten pounds overweight, and that is why guys don't find me attractive." This line of thinking continues day in and day out.

Revisiting one of the definitions of anxiety, "the state of feeling nervous or worried that something bad is going to happen," we can conclude that in this case, the "something bad" this young woman feels worried about is that she will always be alone. The thought of this causes her anxiety. But the key thing to comprehend, from the perspective of awareness and the mind, is what action led to this. It was the repetitive process of allowing awareness to jump from one thought to another in an uncontrolled way that led to her feeling anxious.

A teenager may post something on Instagram and refresh his feed every minute to see how many people liked his post. If he is not getting the numbers he feels he should, and if he has not much control over his awareness, then his awareness can begin to irrationally jump around in the mind. As it does so, anxiety builds in him, finally reaching a tipping point where he concludes that it was a bad post and makes the decision to delete it from his feed. He formed the conclusion from his irrational thinking, which was a result of allowing awareness to go from one thought to another unchecked.

To examine the deeper causes of why the individuals in both of these examples think the way they do is not the purpose of this book. Each case of anxiety has its own origins. The causes are endless. *The purpose of this lesson is strictly to understand the cause of anxiety and stress relative to awareness and the mind.* Awareness unhinged is insanity personified.

A distracted mind is an anxious mind. If one cannot exert control over awareness, how can one exert control over where awareness goes in the mind? If one can't control where awareness goes in the mind, then one can't control what one is thinking. In both examples I just shared, that was clearly the case. On the contrary, if you can control awareness, then you can control where it goes in the mind and, consequently, what you are thinking. Should you find yourself in an area of the mind where you are thinking in a way that is unwholesome, you would have sufficient control over awareness to move to an alternate area of the mind. This would prevent you from repeatedly thinking things that would cause you to be worried, nervous, or uneasy.

This teaching, given to me by Gurudeva when I was in my early twenties, which I have come to understand through my own inner experience of awareness and the mind, has allowed me to no longer experience anxiety and stress. This is because I know what behavior of awareness leads to anxiety, and as soon as I notice awareness beginning to behave in that way, I correct it.

There are times when I feel pressured by the number of projects that I have going on, but I do not feel anxiety or stress. Feeling "pressured" is the realization that one has potentially more to do than one could possibly get done in the given time, but awareness is still in check. Awareness is not going from one project to another in an uncontrolled way and creating the feeling of anxiety and stress. Here's a story to further elaborate on the difference between feeling pressured and feeling stressed.

One of the best basketball players in the world is about to take a free throw. Three seconds remain on the clock in the championship-determining game of the NBA finals. An extremely focused individual, he feels pressured but is not stressed about it. *Pressured* means he feels the anticipation of his team, the fans worldwide, and everyone watching the game, but he has complete control over his awareness. He holds awareness in unwavering focus on the task at hand and does what he does best, which is get the ball in the hoop.

Stressed would mean he is losing or has lost control over awareness. As he stands at the free throw line, about to take the shot, his awareness is all over the place. It's traveling into the future, seeing himself score the winning shot and become the hero of his team and fans. As soon as that visualization is over, awareness travels to the other extreme. He sees himself missing the shot, the final whistle being blown, and the media crucifying him the next day. This and more all takes place within seconds in his mind. With so little control over awareness at this point, he throws the ball and misses.

The next time you experience anxiety, observe what is happening to awareness in your mind. What is awareness doing that is resulting in you being in a state of anxiety?

The ability to control awareness in the mind and hold it on one thing at a time in unwavering focus is the key to eliminating anxiety and stress from your life. It is the cure for worry and fear. It is the greatest panacea for the mind—the first and undeniable step in beginning to handle all mental health issues.

Once you master the ability to control your awareness and concentrate, anxiety and stress will become concepts you are familiar with, or something you observe other people experiencing, but not a part of your daily life.

Chapter 10

●

TOOLS IN ACTION

LESSON 10.1

Regrettable Reactions

I was exhausted. It had been a long, arduous day of traveling in India with the group I had taken there on my annual Spiritual Adventure. The sun was about to set, and the train we were on had just pulled into the station of the next city on our itinerary. There is no better way to see India than on a train, and the kaleidoscope of experiences we had just had was one for the memory books.

I urged my group to hastily disembark the train amid the disorderly invasion of passengers boarding the carriage, but my directives were drowned out by the cacophony of sounds from the station. We somehow finagled our luggage and ourselves off the train, spilling onto the platform only to find ourselves immersed in an otherworldly pandemonium—the apparent normality of an Indian train station. The discordant sounds, sights, and smells were an assault on our foreign senses.

I had made plans for us to stay in the beautiful and charming old city, which was a catacomb of small narrow dusty lanes and a warren of bazaars and homes. It was no place for a tourist bus large enough to fit my group of eighteen spiritual seekers, so I had planned for us to exit the station and find auto rickshaws to take us to our hotel.

We lugged our oversized tourist luggage along the platform, the only people at the station who appeared to have packed for Armageddon, smacking local travelers in the knee as we zigzagged our way in a game of human Tetris. We finally squeezed ourselves out of the station into the parking lot in what seemed nothing less than a hot, sweaty birthing experience.

A fleet of auto rickshaws were neatly lined up in the parking lot, bringing some organization to the bedlam we had just experienced. There was no need to call out to the drivers. It was a matter of seconds before they had circled us in mass numbers, like at an accident scene, offering their services. Some proactively grabbed our bags and loaded them into their vehicles.

In a few minutes of chaos, negotiations were made, and bags and befuddled travelers were loaded onto these three-wheeled metal cages. We were whisked away, weaving in and out of traffic, humans, and livestock in a way that had the profound ability to reestablish anyone's faith in God. It wasn't long before we arrived at our hotel. My weary travelers stumbled out and made their way into the hotel, while I stayed back to make sure all the bags were unloaded and the drivers paid.

When I headed over to pay the last of the rickshaw drivers, his price had doubled. I asked him why, and he responded that he had extra luggage to carry. I knew for a fact that this was not true and that he was simply hustling me for more money, and I shared my grievance with him. He stepped out of his vehicle, stood firmly in his gray tank top as sweat weaved its way down his well-rounded hairy arms, and insisted I pay him double.

I snapped. The last threads of willpower lost their grip on my awareness. My ball of light catapulted itself into the angry area of the mind, and before I even knew what was happening, I retorted, "I'm not paying you one fucking rupee more!"

That statement was enough to catapult his awareness into the same area of the mind I was in. In a flash, he was overcome with rage and shouted at me, "You pay now. Full price. Don't cheat me!" garnishing me with particles of his saliva. Disgusting!

He was probably trying to see if he could get some extra cash from me and potentially call it an early day. Who knows. I was upset because of the principle of the thing. We had agreed on a price, and now he was gouging me. It was April in India, the height of summer. It was hot, humid, and dusty, and we were both obviously exhausted and mentally frayed. The conditions were perfect for both of us to have uncontrolled reactions—two powder kegs waiting to explode.

My wife, a hardened New Yorker, who had witnessed what was going on from a distance, stepped in and defused the situation gracefully. In all honesty, I have very little recollection of how she did it or what she said. All I remember is that the driver got paid some money, and he and I headed off in opposite directions.

Later that night when I retired to my hotel room and finally had a moment to myself, I felt a wave of disappointment overcome me. I sat on the edge of the bed, my arms resting on my thighs, fingers intertwined and my body leaning over my legs. Staring at the only thing in the room that was slightly cold, the hard marble floor, I thought to myself, "I lost it. I lost control of my awareness." At that moment I recalled hearing my guru once define anger to me as a state of temporary insanity.

"Well, that is the damn truth," I thought to myself.

In that area of the mind called anger that I had visited earlier, there was no reason. There was no reflection on what was going on. There was no moment of pause. Just an uncontrolled reaction that was purely instinctive.

As I sat there with my thoughts, it felt like decades of self-enforced personal discipline of controlling awareness in the mind had all amounted to nothing. I'm not one who is new to failure. Failure was more a friend than a distant concept. I regretted how I had responded to the rickshaw driver. I was more disappointed by my inability to control my awareness than by what I had said to him, as I'm sure that was not his first verbal battle with a tourist.

In the years I lived in New York City, I never got angry about anything or at anyone. I had a viselike grip over my awareness, despite all of what the city threw at me. It was the same anywhere else in the world that I had traveled. But India was the last stronghold. Somehow, on every trip here I managed to lose control of my awareness and have an uncontrolled reaction.

It became clear to me that India was now my training ground. I concluded that I must return every year and put myself to the test again. The goal would be to leave India without losing control of my awareness even once. And so it began: my Indian challenge. Every year, I would travel to India and consciously work at not losing control of my awareness. Three years later, on my third visit since I began my challenge, I left India without having once lost control over my awareness. I felt a small sense of accomplishment. But I knew one victory was not enough. I must now repeat this same success on upcoming visits. I made it a point to visit India each year so I could test myself. How I visited was crucial. A five-star vacation was not going to test me. But hauling a group across India on an intense Spiritual Adventure itinerary designed to help them with their growth would tire me and leave me vulnerable to losing it. I had to push myself.

I'm proud to say I have not had the experience of losing control of my awareness again on my subsequent visits to India. That said, I'm always vigilant on each visit to my greatest adversary, the land I love the most. It is here, in this land of extremes, that I've experienced the depths of frustration and the realms of divinity.

In the early years of my life, including the early years of my monastic life, I cannot tell you how many times I regretted not being able to control my reaction to a situation or experience: getting upset by what someone said or did, saying something I wish I had not said. It was the aftermath of the reaction that was difficult to live with: what I felt or how others may have felt as a result of my uncontrolled reaction. That was uncomfortable and unpleasant, and something I desperately wanted to change. It was the understanding of awareness and the mind that paved the way to better managing my reactions and responses in life.

One Merriam-Webster definition of "reaction" is "a response to some treatment, situation, or stimulus." With this in mind, let us define reaction using the understanding of awareness and the mind. When I experience a situation or am treated a certain way, and I am unable to control where my awareness goes in my mind as a result, I create an uncontrolled response to that situation or treatment. Thus, I have a reaction.

Imagine yourself walking around a fair holding a helium balloon tied to a ribbon. You suddenly spot a clown comically juggling knives while balancing on the side of a barrel. This makes you laugh, and in that instant you realize you've released your grip on the ribbon. The balloon begins to float away, but you swiftly clench your fist and rein the balloon back.

Reactions are no different. Say you are going about your day and you have an experience that dislodges your awareness from your grasp and sends it on its way toward the angry area of the mind. You are observant of what just took place, and as swiftly as you reached out to catch the balloon that was floating away, you reach out and grab hold of awareness and bring it back. Had you not done so, awareness would have gone to the angry area of the mind and caused you to have a reaction. The reaction could be mental: you express some angry thoughts internally. It could be verbal: you yell in outrage. Or it could even be physical: you may react violently.

THE POWER OF UNWAVERING FOCUS • DANDAPANI

A reaction is awareness being driven to an area of the mind by an external or internal source and causing an uncontrolled response.

An external source would be your environment (the people and things around you). An example of an internal source is awareness reacting to an unresolved emotional experience in the subconscious. As you recall a traumatic childhood experience, your awareness is driven to the sad area of the mind, causing an uncontrolled reaction: you begin to cry.

Though I've given examples of negative reactions, reactions can be both positive and negative, and there may be times when our positive reactions become regrettable as well. A senior member of a company is celebrating a recent success at the company's annual party, and in the excitement of it all he loses control of his awareness. He excitedly divulges information on the company that he should not be sharing with the entire team. This is a regrettable reaction as well. A word from the wise: replace excitement with enthusiasm. Excitement is uncontrolled energy (awareness); enthusiasm is channeled energy (awareness).

Ultimately, our ability to control awareness in the mind determines how much control we have over our reactions and how we respond to life's experiences. The better I can control my awareness, the better I can control my reactions, and the more say I have over my state of mind.

Control of Speech

It may benefit us all to set up a traffic light on the highway that connects our mind and our mouth, guiding us as to when to speak freely, when to reflect before we speak, and when to simply hold our tongue. Control of speech is deeply intertwined with managing our reactions.

One's inability to control speech is a telltale sign of many things. Among them are a cluttered, thus a confused, subconscious; lack of clarity; and the inability to sufficiently control awareness in the mind, to name a few. When a person opens their mouth, they create a window for all to see into their mind. You can learn so much about someone from what they say versus what they do not say.

Many people struggle to control their speech, often resulting in complicated or emotionally charged outcomes, causing them to regret what they have said and wish they could take back their words. One reason for our uncontrolled speech is our inability to control our reactions, which is an outcome of our inability to control where our awareness goes in our mind.

For example, a person comes up to me at an event I am speaking at and says that the shawl I am wearing is really ugly. His emotionally charged words have the potential power to move my awareness to an upset area of the mind—should I allow it to happen. My ability to control my awareness allows me, at that moment, to choose where I wish to move my awareness. Upon hearing his words, if I choose to move my awareness, with my willpower and powers of concentration, to an uplifted area of the mind, then I will have an uplifted response. If I allow *the power of the emotion in his words* to direct my awareness to an angry area of the mind, then I will have a response that is not uplifting.

The most common reason for uncontrolled speech is people's reaction to what is happening to them or around them. If you can control awareness, you can choose where in your mind to move awareness so that you can give the most appropriate response, or simply not respond at all. People's reactions and inability to control their speech is a public revelation of what is in their mind.

It is important not to confuse control of speech with the disabling of free speech. I would define "control of speech" as the ability to wisely choose what is said—and when. The combination of wisely chosen words and their timely delivery is of the essence. When you can control your speech, you can still speak freely; the only difference is that you are always in control of what you say and when you say it. Thereby you massively influence the outcome of your speech and what unfolds in your life.

Here's something for you to ponder—I won't go into it deeply. If you do not have much control over your awareness, when someone says something to you and the emotion in his words is angry, or vibrating at the frequency of anger, then his words will take your awareness to the same area of the mind those words came from. His emotional words charge your awareness with the same emotion (energy can be transferred), dragging it to the same vibratory space of the mind. In the same way, a love song charged with sentimental emotional energy can take you to the same area of the mind as the singer; when you listen to it, you feel the emotions that the singer wants you to feel.

Emotion has massive power over awareness. Emotion embedded in words has the power to move awareness to the area of the mind that vibrates at the frequency of that emotion. To not react to the words, your willpower must be greater than the power of the emotions coming at you.

The words I said to the Indian rickshaw driver were highly charged with my angry emotions. The emotion in my words transferred energy to his awareness, causing it to vibrate at the frequency of my emotion, anger. His awareness then functioned in the angry area of the mind and reacted accordingly.

How do you know you're making progress in controlling your speech? When what you say results in more uplifting outcomes than complicated emotional outcomes, this is one sure sign. And progress in this practice of speech control is a sign of progress in the practice of controlling awareness in the mind.

LESSON 10.2

Mental Arguments

So much time and energy are wasted, and peace of mind sacrificed, by the vast number of mental arguments people indulge in. Mental arguments—mostly issues with others that we keep trying to hash out in our own minds—are a massive distraction as well.

This lesson is not about how to resolve mental arguments. Rather, it is about how learning to control awareness in the mind can help free you from being plagued by incessant mental arguments.

Often the cause of a mental argument is a misunderstanding you have with someone. When this issue is not resolved, it sits in your subconscious, and every time awareness interacts with it, you run through the argument again. The more emotion this unresolved experience contains, the stronger its power to draw your awareness to it.

Each time awareness gets pulled to it, it causes you to relive the whole or parts of the experience again, going all through the emotions, which in turn causes you to react to them again.

As you react, you quite often will enter into a mental argument, having a full-on back-and-forth verbal mudsling with the person you are upset with. You say something to them in your head and see them react to what you said. Now you've upset this person again, but this time in your head. He replies with more verbal abuse toward you—in your head. You are shocked by what you just said to yourself on his behalf. The back-and-forth continues as the situation escalates in your head.

With each passing second you get more and more worked up by this mental argument. Five minutes later, you are furious at this person for being such a jerk. Your nervous system is a mess. In a massive huff, you yank your awareness away from that unresolved emotional experience and go back to what you were doing before you got into this mental argument.

Not ten minutes have gone by and your awareness is pulled back to this war zone in your head. Another verbal tirade ensues, and your poor mind, body, and nervous system are put through another spin cycle of your emotions. This excruciating mental experience is repeated throughout the day, to the point that some can lie in bed at night unable to go to sleep as the mental battle continues.

It is important to realize that in this entire mental argument process, you—let me emphasize *you*—are the one who is speaking on behalf of both parties in your head, resulting in a heated argument that is your own doing.

Unresolved emotional experiences in the subconscious mind are land mines awaiting the presence of your awareness. The key to overcoming them is to resolve the issue. That may be easier said than done, depending on the intensity of the experience and the emotions attached to it. As I shared in a previous lesson, there are a few ways to resolve such issues, including seeking therapy.

But another thing can help with mental arguments, and that is learning to control awareness in the mind. When you control awareness, you can choose when you wish to address an unresolved emotional experience. Let me give you an example. A colleague at work says something to you at a meeting that upsets you. You return to your desk upset but immediately dive into your email inbox to work.

A few minutes go by and your awareness is pulled to this experience you just had in the meeting that upset you. As awareness enmeshes itself in this experience, you start reliving it, going through the emotions again and reacting to them.

Now, if you have sufficient control over your awareness, you can grab hold of awareness as it leaves your email inbox and makes its way to this unresolved emotional experience in your subconscious mind, and you can bring awareness back to what it was doing or move it to an alternative area of the mind.

The ability to do this tells us a few things:

1. That we have a clear understanding that awareness and the mind are two distinctly separate things.
2. That problems reside in the subconscious, which is an area of the mind, and we have the choice whether to go to that area of the mind or not.
3. We can also conclude that if we have sufficient willpower, we can redirect awareness to any area of the mind that we want to go to, and use the powers of concentration that we have developed to hold awareness in the area of the mind that we want to be in.

Knowing this, and having the ability to execute on all of the above, leads to tremendous freedom and peace of mind.

A lot of people, reading this, will think that I am advocating ignoring the problem or pretending it does not exist. That is not what I am suggesting at all. The problem clearly exists, and the first step to re-solving it is to acknowledge its existence. What I am suggesting here allows you to choose when to move awareness to that area of the mind where the problem resides, address the issue, and resolve it.

This is a powerful choice that, sadly, most people do not have, but can have if they develop a sound understanding of awareness and the mind, and sufficient control over their awareness.

When we have this choice we can say, "I know I have this unre-solved issue in my subconscious, but I am not going to let my aware-ness go to it now. I have a break from work at 2:00 p.m., and at that time I will find a quiet space to sit, move my awareness to this issue, and address it. In the meantime, I will use my willpower to firmly hold my awareness in the area of the mind I choose to be in."

This is very different from allowing awareness to be repeatedly pulled to the problem throughout the day. That is mentally and emo-tionally exhausting, and a massive waste of energy and time. The im-pact of such a repeated experience on your mind, body, and nervous system is so detrimental, not to mention the impact it has on all the people around you and on the performance of your tasks.

Imagine the peace of mind you would have if you could control your awareness and choose exactly when you wish to deal with an is-sue. Call it having a meeting with your unresolved issue, and meet-ings work better if the time and location are predetermined.

Set an appointment, a predetermined time and location, to have a meeting with your unresolved issue. Until that time comes, use your willpower and powers of concentration to hold awareness on who or what it is engaged in. Every time you feel awareness being pulled to the emotionally charged unresolved issue in your subconscious, gently and lovingly bring it back to what you were engaged in. Tell yourself, "It's not time yet for me to engage with my unresolved issue."

As with any appointment, there is no need for you to go to the location every ten minutes prior to the meeting to check whether the person you're meeting is there. You simply would not do that. Similarly, when you've set an appointment with your unresolved issue, there is no need for awareness to go visit it multiple times before your meeting time. Doing so would only upset you.

Setting an appointment to deal with your unresolved issue and exercising your ability to control awareness in the mind are key to helping you avoid mental arguments. When the time for your appointment comes, go to the location that you have chosen, move awareness to the unresolved issue in your subconscious, and begin the process of resolving the issue.

So many people are mentally crippled each day by mental arguments, rendered unable to perform daily tasks as awareness repeatedly gets pulled to unresolved emotional experiences. This is no way to live. To have the choice of when to deal with our problems, we need to learn about awareness and the mind, and develop our willpower and powers of concentration so that we can learn to control awareness in the mind.

Here's something else to keep in mind about mental arguments. Remember the quote by my guru, "Where awareness goes, energy flows"? Let's bring that into the context of mental arguments. Every time you allow your awareness to go to the unresolved emotional experience in your subconscious mind, you are allowing energy to flow to it. If energy is flowing to it, you know now that you are strengthening that unresolved emotional experience. The pattern that is in your subconscious that is housing those unresolved emotions is being fueled with more emotion every time your awareness goes to it, making it stronger and stronger.

In addition, you are quite likely changing the narrative of the experience by having countless emotionally disturbed monologues in your head. This only creates greater confusion in your mind surrounding this experience and makes it even more difficult to come to a resolution.

The better your ability to control awareness in the mind, the more you empower yourself to choose when to engage with an unresolved issue in your mind. The better you are at this, the significantly fewer mental arguments you will experience.

LESSON 10.3

A Game Changer

Throughout this book I have conveyed the teachings in a way that is applicable to anyone who is serious about living a focused life. This lesson shares how these teachings can be used in the world of sports to help improve performance and mitigate mental health challenges. We do not need to restrict these teachings to the most advanced athletes. Any individual, child or adult, engaging in sporting activities can learn and leverage them to better their performance and to have a healthier mind.

It's half-time at one of the most crucial league matches in the English Premier League, perhaps the most watched and followed soccer league in the world. A team is gathered in the locker room for the half-time break. They are two goals down and they desperately need to get a draw or a win if they are to make a final run for the title. Just before the team departs the locker room for the second half, the coach imparts one final message to them: "Guys, we really need to focus when we go out there." A natural and sensible request.

Though the exhortation to focus is heard over and over again in the world of sports, it is seldom, if ever, accompanied by instructions on how to do it. As I covered in an earlier chapter, telling someone to focus is very different from training them to do so. In sports or in business, urging and expecting your team to focus when you have never taught them how is an act that has not been thought through. Most, if not all, of those who give these instructions are completely oblivious to the fact that they are asking someone to do something that they probably have never been trained to do and may not be good at.

Hundreds of millions of dollars are invested in sports teams around the world. It is a multibillion-dollar industry. Players on the best teams are given the best coaching and training facilities, and access to the best resources for improving performance. But most of these players have probably never been taught how their mind works, how to focus, and how to handle the stress of elite competition. I can say from personal experience of working with athletes at the highest level that the mental health training they are given is nowhere remotely close to the level of physical training they receive, and well below what is needed at their level of excellence.

It's the semifinal of the soccer World Cup and a player steps up to take a decisive penalty kick. If he scores, they win. He has practiced taking penalty kicks thousands of times. There is no question that on a subconscious level he has a well-created pattern on how to execute this successfully. He places the ball on the penalty spot and takes a few steps back in preparation for the kick. Eighty thousand people in the stadium are watching him and millions more around the world are glued to the screen, focused on this game that is being televised live. Breaths are being held. Nails are being bitten. All eyes are glued to this man. This player has to lean on his training now.

A lot of the battle, if not all of it, is in his mind. Can he control his awareness? Has he let his awareness go into the future, ten seconds from now, and visualize how he is celebrating his winning penalty kick? Or has he let his awareness go into the future and think that if he misses, he will have disappointed his entire team and country? His awareness drifts to the fear area of the mind, and he questions whether he should stick to the plan of where to place the ball or do something different. All of this is taking place in a few seconds, though it seems like eternity to him. The referee blows the whistle indicating for him to take the kick. He steps forward . . . and the rest is history.

A player's ability or inability to control his awareness in such a high-pressure situation is one of the biggest factors in success or failure. There's a beautiful quote from an anonymous US Navy SEAL: "Under pressure, you don't rise to the occasion, you sink to the level of your training." This not only applies to athletes, but to everyone. If you've never been trained in how to control your awareness in the mind, how would you expect to do so in the most demanding situations, when that is the one thing you need the most?

The player can't control his awareness if he doesn't know how the mind works. And if he has never been taught how to focus and hold awareness in unwavering focus on just one thing, how can he be completely absorbed in just taking the penalty? Imagine the same soccer player taking that penalty in the World Cup semifinal, but this time imagine him as someone who has been trained on how to control awareness in the mind. The narrative would be very different.

He steps up to take a decisive penalty in what probably is the most important game of his life. The intensity is palpable. He has to lean on his training now. Awareness is held in a viselike grip by his willpower and powers of concentration on the task at hand, anchored in the present. He does not allow his awareness to drift off to the future or the past to imagine successes not yet attained or relive failures previously experienced. He calmly steps forward and kicks the ball, hammering it into the back of the net. As he watches that happen, he lets his awareness off the reins of his willpower and the adrenaline of it all drives his awareness to the excited area of the mind. He and millions of his fans celebrate the goal in jubilant joy!

Contrary to what is often heard—as I shared previously—his state of focus is not a blocking out of all that is around him. Rather, it is a complete absorption of his awareness in what it is engaged in. This state of total absorption brings nothing else to his consciousness. Understanding the mind and learning to focus awareness can significantly impact the level of an individual's or a team's performance. *It would not matter if no athlete or team were ever told to focus. But if you're telling your team to focus, then you should train them in how to do so.* And this book is a manual for doing so.

But it's not all about increased performance. High-performance athletes are challenged in many other ways. For example, learning to control reactions on and off the field is another critical need that so many of them are faced with. Their ability to control awareness determines their ability to manage reactions to slurs from opposition players, verbal and even racial attacks from fans, highly critical words from the media, and social media onslaughts. If an athlete can control her awareness, she can control her reactions, and hence control the subsequent fallout that undoubtedly will influence every part of her life and her game.

So many athletes step onto the field or court mentally tormented by the world around them. So few of them are ever given the training and tools needed to effectively manage their state of mind. The frequent, extreme emotional ups and downs can have a devastating impact on their mind and nervous system that last beyond their career. Mental health challenges for high-performance athletes are real. The exhilaration and the glory of the game do a good job of masking them, but, rest assured, they are present. These are a few of many challenges that the teachings and tools within this book can significantly mitigate and eliminate.

At the Heart of Commerce

R avi works for a Fortune 500 company. He's an executive in their senior leadership team and plays a significant role in the company. He's great at what he does, and that's why he holds the position that he does. But no one has ever taught him how the mind works. He has no understanding of awareness and the mind, or that one can control where awareness goes in the mind. Neither has anyone ever taught him how to focus. Over the years, as the demand for his time and attention has increased, he has found himself becoming more and more distracted.

Today, Ravi struggles to keep his awareness on one thing at a time, though he is unable to articulate that this is what he experiences throughout the day. The need for his attention, coming in from all directions, has caused him to grant sovereignty over his awareness to his environment. He often says he is "all over the place," which means, in our terms, that his awareness is all over the place. This explains why he is always exhausted: because his energy is flowing all over the place. The more he practices distraction, the better he becomes at it. And at this point in his life he's an expert at it.

When he gets home, he is unable to hold his awareness on any of his children or his spouse for longer than a few seconds. As a result, they don't feel his energy coming toward them; thus, they feel disconnected from him. They love him, so they tolerate this, and soon it becomes a norm in the household. He, too, feels disconnected from them, and it saddens him, but he does not know what the solution is. He lies in bed struggling to fall asleep every night, as he is unable to detach awareness from the work area of the mind. He eventually falls asleep from exhaustion, and when he wakes up, the intense magnetic force from the work area of his mind, where he has deposited most of his energy, pulls awareness to it before he can even consider anything else. He picks up his phone and immerses himself in it while lying in bed.

As awareness jumps from one email to another, one text to another, and across a slew of other messages and prompts on his phone, anxiety builds. It doesn't take long to get to this state. He has paved a path to this area of the mind a long time ago, the preferred purlieu of his awareness.

Ravi is frayed in every sense of the word, though he will barely admit it to himself, much less let it be known to his colleagues or peers. There are times when he wishes he could ditch it all and take his family to go live somewhere where he can experience peace. This, unbeknownst to him, is a false notion, for wherever he goes, the state of mind that he has so devotedly cultivated for years will accompany him. It's not a companion you can abandon at will. There is no peace for Ravi, not even by the beach, in the midst of a tranquil forest, or in the serene foothills of a mountain. Fleeting moments of peace, perhaps, but that's about it—captured in a selfie and shared on a timeline to reassure oneself and others that all is good in life.

Back at work, his uncontrolled awareness is consistently fueling his anxiety. He leads a team of around 200 people. He feels greatly responsible for their performance and the goals that have been defined for them. His awareness makes frequent trips into the future in his mind, often conjuring outcomes that fall short of the set goals, and occasionally envisioning epic failures. Worry sets in, and fear of failure lurks on the fringes of his mind, so close he can smell it. This is all so corrosive to his nervous system, which is a wreck from the daily battering that awareness is put through, and his body harbors more impressive knots than a sequoia tree.

The human mind and body are phenomenally resilient at enduring consistent lambasting, and many are not shy about subjecting them to it. Often feeling thwarted by life, Ravi knows he can't throw in the towel. After all, he has his kids' private schooling to cofund, college tuition to save up for, a healthy mortgage to pay off, a lifestyle to sustain that he and his family have grown accustomed to, and more. Ravi's life is not an uncommon story. So many endure varying degrees of similar tribulations.

Companies and entrepreneurs must realize that a thousand shoreless oceans can never quench the thirst of desire. The pursuit of endless growth, stemming from unbridled desire and creativity, is a race to the edge of a cliff. Desire must be harnessed and wisely directed, and not fulfilled at the expense of the mental and physical health of the people that manifest that desire. At the heart of commerce are people, and we must genuinely care for them. Failure to do so is a slow but certain road to extinction. Vast amounts of statistics show that the degradation of mental health in the workplace is a serious concern globally.

Should this realization dawn upon a company, then the question becomes: Where do we begin the process of creating a thriving and joyous life for our members? What is the solution for Ravi and others like him who are on the brink of mental and physical exhaustion? My answer is, and always will be, the understanding of awareness and the mind, and the learning and developing of focus and willpower. Needless to say, there are deeper issues to solve at a company level, but on an individual level, the most impactful gift you can give your team is the gift of understanding their greatest asset, their mind, and learning how to leverage this asset to create a truly rewarding life.

For the entrepreneurs who care about the lives of their team, about their mental health, the quality of their life, their need to feel they are leading a rewarding life: to these entrepreneurs I say, train them in how the mind works. Empower them with the simple understanding of awareness and the mind as I've outlined it in this book. Teach them, through your own example, the art of learning and developing willpower and focus, and their wise application to overcome worry, fear, anxiety, and stress. Share with them the ability of these teachings to help them have more profound experiences with the people they love and be fully immersed in the experiences they've worked so hard to finance for themselves and their family. It's the simplest, most cost-effective investment that has life-changing results.

What a gift to give your team—the understanding of how to use and leverage their greatest asset. This gift that my guru gave me almost three decades ago is still with me today, even though I am no longer a monk in his monastery. It has only grown through my consistent application of it and continues to reward me in ways I cannot begin to fathom. With my understanding of awareness and the mind, and my ability to focus, I can be present with my family and friends. I can enjoy each moment of my life with them and the experiences I've created for myself. Though I experience challenges in life, I have the tools and the know-how to apply them to better handle those challenges. With the ability to focus and reflect on myself, I have been better able to know myself and what I want in life. I've found purpose. I've defined priorities. I can focus my energy toward them. I can use my will to persevere and never give up. I can manifest my goals. Each day is full. Not a moment is wasted—how can it be if I am present in each of them and I know what to do with each of those moments? Would you not want to give this gift to the people who have dedicated so much of their lives to the creation, sustenance, and success of your company?

Yes, you can teach them other skills. You can teach them to communicate better. Breathe better. Adopt a better diet. Exercise their bodies. Practice better mental health habits. But have you realized that what they need to learn any of these skills well is their mind? It is at the heart of it all. It is the center of their lives. If they don't understand how their mind works and they have not been trained in harnessing and focusing it, how do you expect them to use it to thoroughly learn and absorb all the skills you wish them to acquire?

It's hard to learn something new when you don't understand the very tool you are using to learn that thing. All the books in the world would mean nothing if a person could not read. The first irrefutable step is teaching a person how to read so that he can read books. Similarly, we must begin with the mind.

If you do give them this greatest of gifts, commit to the process. Ensure that they truly grasp the teachings and understand how to apply them in their lives to create effective and sustained change. Only then is the gift a demonstration of your genuine care for your team.

LESSON 10.5

Focus in Business

O f all the employee trainings that companies around the world spend millions of dollars on, the most important one they could possibly invest in would be teaching their teams the understanding of awareness and the mind, and the art of focus. As I have shared before, *if your team can focus, they have the skill to pay attention and learn all the other skills you want them to learn.* If they are distracted, it is going to be hard for them to listen and learn no matter what someone is trying to teach them. If you can't focus, how can you concentrate long enough to even listen to what is being said to you? Don't put the cart before the horse.

In this lesson I won't dive into how to concentrate in the workplace, because this book already gives you the essential training you need in how to concentrate. This training is applicable everywhere. If you are asking, "What are some of the best ways we can practice concentration in the workplace?" then you've failed to grasp what I have shared in the previous chapters, and I suggest rereading the book. You don't need to be trained in a special way to concentrate at work. You just need to learn how to concentrate. Once you know how to do so, you can apply it anywhere.

The purpose of this lesson is to make the case to companies for why they should consider understanding the mind and learning how to focus a fundamental part of their employee training.

A founder of a multimillion-dollar company is ending her meeting with her leadership team. They are about to make their biggest pitch ever to what could potentially be their largest client. Should they get this client onboard, it would be a game changer for the company, and the founder and her team know this. As she is about to dismiss her leadership team from the meeting, she stands up, leans forward, places her hands on the beautiful oak desk that graces the meeting room where the most trusted members of her team are gathered, and says, "We truly need to focus over the next two days leading up to the pitch. Make sure your teams are completely focused on this." A natural and reasonable request.

I've brought this up a few times now, but I'll bring it up again with regard to businesses. Like sports coaches, so many leaders within companies tell their teams to focus but never teach them how. As a business owner, you would never approach a member of your HR staff and ask them to start programming and developing the next version of your mobile app, would you? You wouldn't do it because you know they do not have the training to do such a thing. They've been trained in HR, and that is why they are working in that department. Why, then, do so many leaders not see the resemblance between asking an HR person to write code and asking a person who has never been trained in the art of focus to concentrate?

In the corporate world, where productivity and efficiency are so prized and pursued, most companies fail to do the fundamental thing that can have the greatest impact—learning and practicing the art of concentration. I'd like to believe that they don't teach their teams how to focus because they are simply unaware of the cost of distraction and the fact that focus is a skill that must be learned and practiced. Most assume that we can "just focus," and that by telling someone to do so, it magically happens. It does not. But it's not just learning to focus that is important. It's learning to develop willpower as well, and the prerequisite to both, which is learning about awareness and the mind.

You are only distracted if you have not been trained in how to focus or if you do not know what to focus on. I think most companies are quite clear about what they want their teams to focus on. The missing piece is actually training them to focus.

Fatigue and Distraction

If someone had to drive a car from New York City to San Francisco and on to Dallas, then to Chicago, and from there to Miami, it would consume a tremendous amount of gas. If the car idled in place, it would consume nowhere near as much gas. For the sake of this analogy, think of awareness as the car and energy as the gas that is powering awareness's journey through the mind. If awareness has to go to five different areas of the mind, it consumes a lot more energy than it would if it stayed in one area.

A focused awareness consumes far less energy than a distracted awareness.

A distracted mind consumes tremendous amounts of energy. As energy levels plummet, so do productivity levels. The internet is inundated with data and statistics on the impact of fatigue on safety, productivity, efficiency, and more. There are many reasons for fatigue, but distraction is rarely recognized as one of them. But you can see now that when awareness is uncontrolled in the mind, energy is all over the place, being consumed unnecessarily in places where it does not need to be. And as energy levels drop, outcomes suffer.

Concentration Breeds Efficiency

One morning while engaged in a project, I came across a work-related issue that I needed my guru's insights on. So I walked over to his office, and when I got there, I saw that his office door was open and he was seated at his desk, working on his laptop. I knocked on the doorframe and asked, "Gurudeva, may I speak with you?"

He replied, "Come in and have a seat. I will be with you in just a minute."

He finished what he was doing on his laptop, lowered the display so that it was almost closed to indicate he was done with it, then turned to me and gave me his undivided attention. He asked, "How can I help you?"

I asked my question and he replied. I asked for clarification of his answer, and he clarified it. I thanked him for his help, got up, and left. That conversation lasted maybe two minutes at most. It was highly efficient because he had trained his monks in the art of concentration. Our awareness always stayed on topic; therefore, no time or energy was wasted by awareness going elsewhere. I can't even begin to describe how efficient meetings become when everyone present knows how to concentrate.

How many work-related conversations go on and on because people are not focused enough to stay on topic or to really listen to what the other person is saying?

When people can't focus, the clarity of communication and the transfer of information plummet. How many times have you been in conversation with someone while they are busy typing away on their laptop or their phone? They are nodding their heads in response to what you are saying to indicate they are listening to you, but you know now, from what I've shared on multitasking in this book, what their awareness is doing. As much as that person may think they are listening, they are not.

So much time and energy are wasted like this, not to mention the financial cost, which would be hard to calculate accurately. Large amounts and critical pieces of information are missed, opportunities and pitfalls overlooked, because people do not know how to focus.

What can we do about this? We've covered this in earlier chapters. If you notice a project team member becoming distracted, bring their awareness to attention, then redirect their awareness to the topic at hand. Don't be afraid to tell the person you're speaking with that you would like their undivided attention. Share with them what a big difference this will make in what needs to be done.

Concentration breeds efficiency and productivity. Period.

Distracted Meetings

The inability to stay on topic in a meeting is so costly. I've sat in on my fair share of meetings, and it is always fascinating for me to watch where people's awareness goes during these gatherings. It starts off in one direction, and as with a dog in the park, the slightest rustling in a bush is enough to dispatch awareness in a completely different direction.

Here's an experience I had once. An owner of a company that wanted to hire me to conduct a retreat for their senior management team invited me over to her office to discuss the details. I sat down with her and a few members of the senior team, and we began our meeting. At one point the topic of dates came up. I was asked if the end of February would work for me.

I responded, "I'm sorry, it won't. I'll be in Sydney, Australia, at that time."

A senior member of the team reacted to my response by saying enthusiastically, "Oh, I love Sydney. It's one of my favorite cities in the world. I love sitting at one of the outdoor restaurants in Darling Harbour, enjoying a nice glass of Australian wine . . . looking at the opera house. It's so gorgeous there. What are you going to be in Sydney for?"

I realized at this point I had a choice. I could indulge in a chat about Australia with her, or I could shift her awareness back to the topic. If I had not been observant of her awareness straying away from the topic, I would have naturally indulged in a conversation about Sydney.

I chose to shift her awareness back to the topic, and so I replied, "Yes, it is gorgeous there. I'm going there to give a talk. Does the second week of March work for all of you?" I'm not saying we should not indulge in friendly off-topic conversations. What's critical to discern is the timing for doing so. Timing is everything.

The meeting went on in a similar fashion for its entire length. Topics were brought up but never fully closed, meaning no conclusions were reached—not from a lack of information, but from the inability to stay on a topic and see it through to its end. This meant the same topic would need to be brought up again at a later time, everyone would have to be reengaged somehow, and a conclusion would need to be reached that would have been so much easier to get to while everyone was gathered in person at this meeting.

When awareness strays from a topic, and thus from an area of the mind, we lose the possibility of gaining further insights from that area of the mind. If I picked up a thousand-page book, held it in my hands, and fanned through the pages in five seconds, I would gather no information. But if I opened the book and focused on one page, I could read its contents and absorb its information. If awareness is allowed to move so quickly from one area of the mind to another, you will never be in one place long enough to gather the information that is there.

It takes concentrated effort to delve into a topic during a meeting, and that effort is lost every time awareness is distracted. The momentum is lost. Now, to bring everyone's awareness back to that same location in the mind where you all were before awareness was distracted requires a lot more energy and effort, and may not be so easily achieved. The group got to that point by following a cohesive train of thought, which is now derailed.

The more we allow people to stray off topic during meetings, the more we train them in the art of distraction. This training, then, is carried through into the rest of the workday, and carried home as well. Training our team to stay on topic is training them in the fine art of concentration. Every time their awareness drifts away, gently and lovingly bring it back. You can acknowledge what they said and then shift their awareness back to the topic, like I did in my response to the Sydney enthusiast's comments.

In that meeting, every time I noticed someone getting distracted and I saw their awareness drifting away to another topic, I gently and lovingly brought their awareness back to the conversation at hand. How did I do this? By staying concentrated. Only by being focused could I observe that they were getting distracted. As they did so, I would say, for example, "I'm sorry to interrupt, but I'd like to stay on the topic we were discussing, as it's an important one to decide on."

You can be organized with all the strategies and tools that make for a successful meeting, but unless those attending can focus, the chances of that meeting being efficient and productive are very slim. My purpose here is not to tell you how to run great meetings, but to share with you how significantly the ability to focus can impact the outcome of meetings. People spend considerable time in work-related meetings, and the time spent could be reduced and the outcomes improved if everyone was taught how to concentrate.

Interruptions

I once advised a fashion company, and their lead designer shared an experience with me. She was at her desk designing a jacket for the fall collection of the brand when a colleague came in and asked her, "Do you know where they moved the photocopy paper?"

At this interruption, her awareness left the design area of her mind where she was so focused, channeling her intuitive creativity, and shifted to her colleague as she spun around in her chair. She said it took her a couple of seconds to readjust to an external state of mind and then respond.

"They moved it to that cupboard over there."

"Thanks," her colleague replied, and left.

She turned back to her sketch and realized that her awareness was no longer in that area of the mind where her creativity had been flourishing. She admitted how frustrated this made her feel as she struggled to get back to the same place. This experience, I imagine, is so costly to the company. How many times do you think these types of interruptions happen in companies around the world?

This happens more than most companies can imagine. Interruptions can come in the form of physical interactions or as digital distractions such as text messages, calls, chat rooms, or direct messaging, to list a few. Every time awareness is distracted, it needs to disengage with what it was immersed in and then engage with the new thing that is calling for its attention. Once it's done there, awareness needs to trace its way back, if it even can, to the area of the mind it was in before it got distracted. This constant engagement and disengagement is greatly time and energy consuming. Priceless continuity is broken. The potential for greater insights, solutions, and creativity is lost.

Interruptions are a form of distraction. Most companies attempt to deal with this by blocking out distractions in various ways. Building quiet rooms, silent areas, and the like is helpful, but this is a patch, not a cure. The cure is to teach people how to focus. If they know how to focus and can do it well, companies won't have to figure out how to shield them from distractions so much. Part of this book was written every weekday morning for a few months at the New York City Bagel and Coffee House in Astoria. I would buy a cup of coffee and sit at a table and write. It was never quiet here. The excellent coffee and bagels drew in a constant stream of people. But the noise, music, and crowds did not bother me. My awareness was locked in on what I was doing. All this is to say that we can put time, energy, and finances into devising ways to protect our employees from distraction—or we can simply teach them how to focus.

Interruptions also happen because often one person has no idea what another person is doing. Growing up in Australia and loving to spend time on the beach, I observed how the public was informed of the status of the sea by the simple use of flags. Red flags meant no swimming, and yellow flags indicated "Caution required. Potential hazards"—simple signs that sent a clear message. Without going too deeply into this, I have, over the years, encouraged many companies to adopt a mutually agreed-upon system of signs that each individual could use to silently convey to their colleagues their level of concentration. For example: "High" = please do not interrupt; "Moderate" = urgent matters only; and so on.

By training our teams not to get into the habit of interrupting one another, we are indirectly helping them to practice concentrating for longer periods of time, thus improving their ability to focus.

Adopting a Focus Policy

For companies that wish to adopt the teachings in this book, the first step is getting the owner or the leaders to buy in. Focus in a company works only if it is top-down. The leaders of a company have to believe in it, and then adopt it into their lives and be an example to everyone else. That is the first step. The second step is making the case to the team. The leaders need to get *them* to buy in. This is critical for success.

Once that is accomplished, then I highly recommend implementing the teachings in small groups. For example, if the ten people who make up the marketing team wish to embark on this endeavor, here's what they can do.

1. Begin reading this book at the same time.
2. Review each chapter as a group and make note of the most important points that stood out to each of you. Share these points among the group and discuss how they can apply to what the group does on a daily basis.
3. Commit to using the correct terminology in all communications with one another.
4. Identify the nonnegotiable recurring events in an average workday that each person can use to develop their willpower and powers of concentration. Group events, such as meetings, are perfect opportunities. Hold one another accountable with kindness and gentleness.
5. Self-evaluate and keep track of progress. Always remember "The Power of Small." Celebrate milestones and wins.
6. Gently and lovingly support one another in your efforts to govern awareness in the mind. Exercise patience and compassion.
7. Support one another by helping to bring the practice into their lives outside of work. The practice of focus needs to be integrated into all of life.

Benefits of a Focused Mind

Let's not forget: when you teach your team how to focus using the specific principles in this book, you are not only teaching them to concentrate, but you are also teaching them:

- How to control where their awareness goes in their mind, which in turn is . . .
- How to control where their energy flows, and thus what is manifesting in their lives (including their work projects);
- To apply the three principles of developing willpower in everything they do;
- To be present in all engagements;
- To manage and overcome worry, fear, anxiety, and stress by harnessing awareness;
- How to manage reactions and responses.

My goal here is to make the case to companies for adopting the principles in this book as part of their training curriculum. Not only will they be contributing to better workplace performance, but they also will be empowering their teams with the teachings and tools for better mental health, and subsequently the ability to live more rewarding lives. This benefit does not stop here. Every individual whose life is positively transformed will have the experiential know-how to then empower their loved ones with these teachings and tools to help them live rewarding lives as well.

Recall the story I shared earlier in the book about how Gurudeva lifted the center of the tissue, and as he did so he said, "You are energetically connected to all those that are in your life. As you uplift yourself, you uplift all of them as well." By empowering and uplifting the people that make your company what it is with the fundamental understanding of the mind, focus, and willpower, you are making the conscious choice to positively influence all who matter to them. You are now helping them to create a life of which at least one by-product is happiness.

CONCLUSION

Twenty-seven years ago, my guru shared with me the profound insight into the understanding of the inner workings of the mind. These time-tested teachings have been passed down for more than two millennia through monks of the spiritual lineage that he and I belong to.

The ones who have realized the depths of these teachings—the simplicity of them, the practicality of them, the ability of them to bring profound states of realization if they are understood and applied in one's life—those are the ones whose lives are never the same again. I am one of those people. I am one of those whose life has been transformed and so deeply impacted by these teachings. How could I not share this with you?

This book has been a labor of love. I wrote it for you so that you, too, can experience these teachings that have changed my life and that of many others. These teachings, as profound as they may be, are completely useless if they are not understood and consistently and correctly applied in your life. The burden of responsibility is on you and you alone. You can walk the path of words where you talk about what you have read and learned, or you can walk the path of personal experience where you apply these teachings in your life and experience the transformation they bring about. The choice is yours.

"So, where to from here?" you may ask. Strive to understand the teachings. Read them again and again. Let them permeate every cell of your being. Bring them into every aspect of your life. And, most important, practice, practice, practice! You learn to master awareness in the mind because you love what that brings to your life.

As you proceed to implement these teachings in your life, be understanding, patient, and compassionate with yourself. Remind yourself that you are a work in progress, a building under construction. There are some parts that are messy, but that is OK as long as you are working on them slowly but surely.

You've been blessed with the greatest gift of all—life itself. The contents of this book can help you live a truly amazing life. The understanding of awareness and the mind, and the ability to steward and focus awareness, is one of the greatest gifts you can give yourself. It is the untold panacea for many of the mind's ailments. It is the essential ingredient for manifesting your life's goals and living a purposeful life. Joy, happiness, and contentment are among the outcomes experienced as a result of this, but the greatest of outcomes that can come from it is to "know thyself."

I'll leave you with one of my favorite quotes from Gurudeva: "Proceed with confidence!"

ACKNOWLEDGMENTS

Gratitude and appreciation are the key virtues for a better life.
They are the spell that is cast to dissolve hatred, hurt, and sadness,
the medicine which heals subjective states of mind, restoring
self-respect, confidence, and security.

~GURUDEVA

Nothing is ever produced by just one person. It always is a collective effort, and it takes a village to write a book. This book was made possible by all the people who believe in me and supported me in the process.

Gurudeva, Yogaswami, and the gurus of this lineage: Thank you for the unconditional love, wisdom, and guidance you bestowed upon my family and me over the last five generations.

Alice Martell, my literary agent: This all started with your belief in my work at the very onset of this endeavor. Thank you for making it happen.

Adrian Zackheim, my publisher: Thank you for believing in this work and for your audacious support of my choices. You have been profoundly encouraging.

The team at Portfolio and Penguin Random House: Thank you for all that you do—seen and unseen. Your efforts made this book and its mission to uplift and change many lives possible. Please know that I greatly appreciate all of you. Special thanks to Annie Gottlieb.

James Landis, Michael Lützenkirchen, Robert van der Putten, and Ragy Thomas: I'm deeply honored by your support and for believing in Gurudeva's and my work.

Sadhaka Haranandinatha and Sadhaka Tejadevanatha: Thank you for being my monastic brothers and for your love and belief in me that has spanned lifetimes.

My amazing team (Marilyn, Yeimi, David, Icho, Alex, and Georgii): Thank you for not missing a beat while I was absorbed in the creation of this book. I am so grateful for each of you.

My mother, for her unbridled love and support. You got me here and to where I am going with your love.

My daughter, Meenakshi: Thank you for your love, for the deep joy you bring me every day, for coming when I called, and for inspiring the section "The Veiled Truth" with your questions and understanding of awareness and the mind.

My wife and best friend, Tatiana: Thank you for your incredible love and patience and for always being my number-one supporter. This book would not have been possible without your continuous support and encouragement. I am truly blessed to have you in my life.

INDEX

Italicized page numbers indicate material in tables.

awareness (*cont.*)
  and deep paths created in the mind,
    110–14
  definition of, 68–69
  detaching/separating from, 130–36
  drifting/wandering of, 77, 87, 123,
    129, 232–33, 312–14
  and emotion's power, 89–90, 292
  energy's relationship with, 98–102,
    107, 108
  environment's control of, 90–93,
    137–38
  and fear, 272–73, 274–75
  fundamental principles of, 126
  goal/purpose of learning about,
    117–20
  of happiness, 69–70, 75, 80
  of itself (awareness), 135–36
  jumping uncontrolled between
    thoughts, 279–80
  and mansion analogy of the mind,
    74–77
  mastery of, 108, 114, 117, 138, 264–65
    (*see also* concentration; control of
    awareness)
  and meditation, 112–13
  and memory retrieval from
    subconscious, 124–25
  mind as related to, 71, 77, 126, 262
  movement of, through mind, 69, 71,
    77, 95, 121–26, 137, 153
  observational states of, 130–31
  in past, future, or present, 259–60,
    262–63, 268–69
  plane analogy for, 228–29
  and reactions, 290
  of sadness, 70
  as the self, 70–72, 77, 79, 96, 126
  stewardship of, 137–39, 188
  and strengthening of areas in the
    mind, 103
  term, 85
  as a traveler, 78–81
  and unfinished tasks, 278–79
  and unresolved emotional issues,
    106–7

  untrained/unrestrained, 94–97
  willpower over, 187–88, 199, 205

bed, daily practice of making the,
    196–200
beginner, adopting attitude of, 67
blocking everything out, 247, 302
Bolt, Usain, 163–64
breath, regulation of, 107
bullies, 275–76
buy-in from others, 20–21

cell phones. *See* phones, mobile
centering with breathing, 107
Centers for Disease Control and
    Prevention (CDC), 147–48, 168
children
  bringing awareness to attention in,
    128–29
  and bullies, 275–76
  corporal punishment of, 147
  and costs of distraction, 160
  expectations for focus, 147
  willpower in, 184
choice
  of how to interact with technology, 221
  of how to respond, 9–10
  of living a focused life, 8
  to steward awareness, 139
  of where to place awareness, 75–76
clarity
  and control of speech, 291
  and feelings of overwhelm, 51
  in purpose and intent, 198–99
coaches of sports teams, 146–47, 299
Colorado River, 54
commitments, exercise for
    uncompleted, 212–13
communication, efficiency of,
    311–12
concentration
  and ADHD diagnoses, 147–51
  definition of, 152–55
  and efficiency, 311–12
  as effortless habit, 230
  importance of developing, 145

as future based, 266
manifesting, 269–70
mastery of awareness as cure for,
    264–65
prolonged states of, 278
reined in with concentration and
    willpower, 267–68

and uncertain outcomes, 278
in the workplace, 306

yoga teachers, 52
YouTube, 136, 220

zero-tolerance for distraction, 239–41